CROCK·POT®
◆ THE ORIGINAL SLOW COOKER ◆

ULTIMATE
SLOW COOKER RECIPES

Publications International, Ltd.

Pictured on the front cover: Classic Slow-Cooked Pot Roast *(page 131)*.

Pictured on the back cover *(top to bottom):* Juicy Reuben Sliders *(page 52),* Sweet Potato and Black Bean Chipotle Chili *(page 122)* and Mexican Carnitas *(page 250)*.

Microwave Cooking: Microwave ovens vary in wattage. Use the cooking times as guidelines and check for doneness before adding more time.

Table of Contents

Slow Cooking Tips

Slow Cooker Sizes

Smaller **CROCK-POT®** slow cookers—such as 1- to 3½-quart models—are the perfect size for cooking for singles, a couple or empty-nesters (and also for serving dips).

While medium-size **CROCK-POT®** slow cookers (those holding somewhere between 3 quarts and 5 quarts) will easily cook enough food at a time to feed a small family, they're also convenient for holiday side dishes or appetizers.

Large **CROCK-POT®** slow cookers are great for large family dinners, holiday entertaining and potluck suppers. A 6- to 7-quart model is ideal if you like to make meals in advance, or have dinner tonight and store leftovers for another day.

Types of Slow Cookers

Current **CROCK-POT®** slow cookers come equipped with many different features and benefits, from auto cook programs to stovetop-safe stoneware to timed programming. Visit **www.crock-pot.com** to find the **CROCK-POT®** slow cooker that best suits your needs.

How you plan to use a **CROCK-POT®** slow cooker may affect the model you choose to purchase. For everyday cooking, choose a size large enough to serve your family. If you plan to use the **CROCK-POT®** slow cooker primarily for entertaining, choose one of the larger sizes. Basic **CROCK-POT®** slow cookers can hold as little as 16 ounces or as much as 7 quarts. The smallest sizes are great for keeping dips warm on a buffet, while the larger sizes can more readily fit large quantities of food and larger roasts.

Cooking, Stirring and Food Safety

CROCK-POT® slow cookers are safe to leave unattended. The outer heating base may get hot as it cooks, but it should not pose a fire hazard. The heating element in the heating base functions at a low wattage and is safe for your countertops.

Your **CROCK-POT®** slow cooker should be filled about one-half to three-fourths full for most recipes unless otherwise instructed. Lean meats such as chicken or pork tenderloin will cook faster than meats with more connective tissue and fat such as beef chuck or pork shoulder. Bone-in meats will take longer than boneless cuts. Typical **CROCK-POT**® slow cooker dishes take approximately 7 to 8 hours to reach the simmer point on LOW and about 3 to 4 hours on HIGH. Once the vegetables and meat start to simmer and braise, their flavors will fully blend and meat will become fall-off-the-bone tender.

According to the USDA, all bacteria are killed at a temperature of 165°F. It's important to follow the recommended cooking times and not to open the lid often, especially early in the cooking process when heat is building up inside the unit. If you need to open the lid to check on your food or are adding additional ingredients, remember to allow additional cooking time if necessary to ensure food is cooked through and tender.

Large **CROCK-POT**® slow cookers, the 6- to 7-quart sizes, may benefit with a quick stir halfway through cook time to help distribute heat and promote even cooking. It's usually unnecessary to stir at all, as even ½ cup liquid will help to distribute heat and the stoneware is the perfect medium for holding food at an even temperature throughout the cooking process.

Oven-Safe

All **CROCK-POT**® slow cooker removable stoneware inserts may (without their lids) be used safely in ovens at up to 400°F. Also, all **CROCK-POT**® slow cookers are microwavable without their lids. If you own another brand of slow cooker, please refer to your owner's manual for specific stoneware cooking medium tolerances.

Frozen Food

Frozen food or partially frozen food can be successfully cooked in a **CROCK-POT**® slow cooker; however, it will require longer cooking time than the same recipe made with fresh food. It's almost always preferable to thaw frozen food prior to placing it in the **CROCK-POT**® slow cooker. Using an instant-read thermometer is recommended to ensure meat is fully cooked through.

Spicy Sausage Bolognese Sauce, *page 140*

Pasta and Rice

If you're converting a recipe that calls for uncooked pasta, cook the pasta on the stovetop just until slightly tender before adding to the **CROCK-POT**® slow cooker. If you are converting a recipe that calls for cooked rice, stir in raw rice with other ingredients; add ¼ cup extra liquid per ¼ cup of raw rice.

Beans

Beans must be softened completely before combining with sugar and/or acidic foods. Sugar and acid have a hardening effect on beans and will prevent softening. Fully cooked canned beans may be used as a substitute for dried beans.

Balsamic-Honey Glazed Root Vegetables, *page 262*

Vegetables

Root vegetables often cook more slowly than meat. Cut vegetables accordingly to cook at the same rate as meat—large versus small, or lean versus marbled—and place near the sides or bottom of the stoneware to facilitate cooking.

Herbs

Fresh herbs add flavor and color when added at the end of the cooking cycle; if added at the beginning, many fresh herbs' flavor will dissipate over long cook times. Ground and/ or dried herbs and spices work well in slow cooking and may be added at the beginning, and for dishes with shorter cook times, hearty fresh herbs such as rosemary and thyme hold up well. The flavor power of all herbs and spices can vary greatly depending on their particular strength and shelf life. Use chili powders and garlic powder sparingly, as these can sometimes intensify over the long cook times. Always taste the finished dish and correct seasonings including salt and pepper.

Liquids

It is not necessary to use more than ½ to 1 cup liquid in most instances since juices in meats and vegetables are retained more in slow cooking than in conventional cooking. Excess liquid can be cooked down and concentrated after slow cooking on the stovetop or by removing meat and vegetables from the stoneware, stirring in one of the following thickeners, and setting the slow cooker to HIGH. Cook on HIGH for approximately 15 minutes or until juices are thickened.

Flour: All-purpose flour is often used to thicken soups or stews. Stir cold water into the flour in a small bowl until smooth. With the **CROCK-POT®** slow cooker on HIGH, whisk the flour mixture into the liquid in the **CROCK-POT®** slow cooker. Cover; cook on HIGH 15 minutes or until the mixture is thickened.

Cornstarch: Cornstarch gives sauces a clear, shiny appearance; it's used most often for sweet dessert sauces and stir-fry sauces. Stir cold water into the cornstarch in a small bowl until the cornstarch dissolves. Quickly stir this mixture into the liquid in the **CROCK-POT®** slow cooker; the sauce will thicken as soon as the liquid boils. Cornstarch breaks down with too much heat, so never add it at the beginning of the slow cooking process, and turn off the heat as soon as the sauce thickens.

Arrowroot: Arrowroot (or arrowroot flour) comes from the root of a tropical plant that is dried and ground to a powder; it produces a thick, clear sauce. Those who are allergic to wheat often use it in place of flour. Place arrowroot in a small bowl or cup and stir in cold water until the mixture is smooth. Quickly stir this mixture into the liquid in the **CROCK-POT®** slow cooker. Arrowroot thickens below the boiling point, so it even works well in a **CROCK-POT®** slow cooker on LOW. Too much stirring can break down an arrowroot mixture.

Tapioca: Tapioca is a starchy substance extracted from the root of the cassava plant. Its greatest advantage is that it withstands long cooking, making it an ideal choice for slow cooking. Add it at the beginning of cooking and you'll get a clear, thickened sauce in the finished dish. Dishes using tapioca as a thickener are best cooked on the LOW setting; tapioca may become stringy when boiled for a long time.

Milk

Milk, cream and sour cream break down during extended cooking. When possible, add them during the last 15 to 30 minutes of cooking, until just heated through. Condensed soups may be substituted for milk and can cook for extended times.

Simple Salmon with Fresh Salsa, *page 194*

Fish

Fish is delicate and should be stirred in gently during the last 15 to 30 minutes of cooking time. Cover and cook just until cooked through and serve immediately.

Baked Goods

If you wish to prepare bread, cakes or pudding cakes in a **CROCK-POT®** slow cooker, you may want to purchase a covered, vented metal cake pan accessory for your **CROCK-POT®** slow cooker. You can also use any straight-sided soufflé dish or deep cake pan that will fit into the stoneware of your unit. Baked goods can be prepared directly in the stoneware; however, they can be a little difficult to remove from the insert, so follow the recipe directions carefully.

# Breakfast and Brunch

Hawaiian Fruit Compote

MAKES 6 TO 8 SERVINGS

3 cups coarsely chopped fresh pineapple
3 grapefruits, peeled and sectioned
1 can (21 ounces) cherry pie filling
2 cups chopped fresh peaches
2 to 3 limes, peeled and sectioned

1 mango, peeled and chopped
2 bananas, sliced
1 tablespoon lemon juice
Prepared waffles (optional)
Slivered almonds
Sprigs fresh mint (optional)

Combine pineapple, grapefruits, pie filling, peaches, limes, mango, bananas and lemon juice in **CROCK-POT**® slow cooker; toss to blend. Cover; cook on LOW 4 to 5 hours or on HIGH 2 to 3 hours. Top waffles with compote. Sprinkle with almonds. Garnish with mint.

Serving Suggestions

Try warm, fruity compote in place of maple syrup on your favorite morning foods. This sauce is also delicious served over baked ham.

Orange Cranberry Nut Bread

MAKES 10 SERVINGS

2 cups all-purpose flour	2 teaspoons orange peel
½ cup chopped pecans	⅔ cup boiling water
1 teaspoon baking powder	¾ cup sugar
½ teaspoon baking soda	2 tablespoons shortening
¼ teaspoon salt	1 egg, lightly beaten
1 cup dried cranberries	1 teaspoon vanilla

1 Coat inside of 3-quart **CROCK-POT**® slow cooker with nonstick cooking spray. Combine flour, pecans, baking powder, baking soda and salt in medium bowl.

2 Combine cranberries and orange peel in separate medium bowl; stir in boiling water. Add sugar, shortening, egg and vanilla; stir just until blended. Add flour mixture; stir just until blended.

3 Pour batter into **CROCK-POT**® slow cooker. Cover; cook on HIGH 1¼ to 1½ hours or until edges begin to brown and toothpick inserted into center comes out clean.

4 Remove stoneware from **CROCK-POT**® slow cooker. Cool on wire rack 10 minutes. Remove bread from insert; cool completely on rack.

Tip

This recipe works best in round **CROCK-POT**® slow cookers.

Pear Crunch

MAKES 4 SERVINGS

1 can (8 ounces) crushed pineapple in juice, undrained

¼ cup pineapple or apple juice

3 tablespoons dried cranberries

1½ teaspoons quick-cooking tapioca

¼ teaspoon vanilla

2 pears, cored and halved

¼ cup granola with almonds

Sprigs fresh mint (optional)

1 Combine pineapple, pineapple juice, cranberries, tapioca and vanilla in **CROCK-POT®** slow cooker; stir to blend. Top with pears, cut sides down.

2 Cover; cook on LOW 3½ to 4 hours. Arrange pear halves on serving plates. Spoon pineapple mixture over pear halves. Sprinkle with granola. Garnish with mint.

Bacon and Cheese Brunch Potatoes

MAKES 6 SERVINGS

3 medium russet potatoes (about 2 pounds), peeled and cut into 1-inch cubes

1 cup chopped onion

½ teaspoon seasoned salt

4 slices bacon, crisp-cooked and crumbled

1 cup (4 ounces) shredded sharp Cheddar cheese

1 tablespoon water

1 Coat inside of **CROCK-POT®** slow cooker with nonstick cooking spray. Place half of potatoes in **CROCK-POT®** slow cooker. Sprinkle half of onion and seasoned salt over potatoes; top with half of bacon and cheese. Repeat layers. Sprinkle water over top.

2 Cover; cook on LOW 6 hours or on HIGH 3½ hours or until potatoes and onion are tender. Stir gently to mix; serve warm.

Hash Brown and Spinach Breakfast Casserole

MAKES 6 TO 8 SERVINGS

4 cups frozen southern-style diced hash browns

3 tablespoons butter

1 large onion, chopped

2 cups (8 ounces) sliced mushrooms

3 cloves garlic, minced

1 package (10 ounces) frozen chopped spinach, thawed and squeezed dry

8 eggs

1 cup milk

1 teaspoon salt

¼ teaspoon black pepper

1½ cups (6 ounces) shredded sharp Cheddar cheese, divided

Tomato wedges (optional)

Sprigs fresh basil (optional)

1 Coat inside of **CROCK-POT**® slow cooker with nonstick cooking spray. Place hash browns in **CROCK-POT**® slow cooker.

2 Melt butter in large skillet over medium-high heat. Add onion, mushrooms and garlic; cook 4 to 5 minutes or until onion is just starting to brown, stirring occasionally. Add spinach; cook 2 minutes or until mushrooms are tender. Stir spinach mixture into **CROCK-POT**® slow cooker with hash browns until combined.

3 Combine eggs, milk, salt and pepper in large bowl; mix well. Pour over hash brown mixture in **CROCK-POT**® slow cooker. Top with 1 cup cheese. Cover; cook on LOW 4 to 4½ hours or on HIGH 1½ to 2 hours or until eggs are set. Top with remaining ½ cup cheese. Cut into wedges to serve.

Chocolate-Stuffed Slow Cooker French Toast

MAKES 6 SERVINGS

1 tablespoon butter, softened
6 slices (¾-inch-thick) day-old challah*
½ cup semisweet chocolate chips
6 eggs
3 cups half-and-half
⅔ cup granulated sugar

1 teaspoon vanilla
¼ teaspoon salt
Powdered sugar
Fresh fruit (optional)

Challah is usually braided. If you use brioche or another rich egg bread, slice bread to fit baking dish.

1 Grease 2½-quart baking dish that fits inside of **CROCK-POT®** slow cooker with butter. Arrange 2 bread slices in bottom of dish. Sprinkle with ¼ cup chocolate chips. Add 2 bread slices. Sprinkle with remaining ¼ cup chocolate chips. Top with remaining 2 bread slices.

2 Beat eggs in large bowl. Stir in half-and-half, granulated sugar, vanilla and salt. Pour egg mixture over bread layers. Press bread into liquid. Set aside 10 minutes or until liquid is absorbed. Cover dish with buttered foil, buttered side down.

3 Pour 1 inch hot water into **CROCK-POT®** slow cooker. Add baking dish. Cover; cook on HIGH 3 hours or until toothpick inserted into center comes out clean. Remove dish and let stand 10 minutes. Sprinkle with powdered sugar. Serve with fruit, if desired.

Tip

Any oven-safe casserole or baking dish is safe to use in your **CROCK-POT®** slow cooker. Place directly inside the stoneware and follow the recipe directions.

Apple-Cinnamon Breakfast Risotto

MAKES 6 SERVINGS

¼ cup (½ stick) butter

4 medium Granny Smith apples (about 1½ pounds), peeled, cored and diced into ½-inch cubes

1½ teaspoons ground cinnamon

¼ teaspoon ground allspice

¼ teaspoon salt

1½ cups uncooked Arborio rice

½ cup packed dark brown sugar

4 cups unfiltered apple juice, at room temperature*

1 teaspoon vanilla

Optional toppings: dried cranberries, sliced almonds and/or milk

If unfiltered apple juice is unavailable, use any apple juice.

1 Coat inside of **CROCK-POT**® slow cooker with nonstick cooking spray. Melt butter in large skillet over medium-high heat. Add apples, cinnamon, allspice and salt; cook and stir 3 to 5 minutes or until apples begin to release juices. Remove to **CROCK-POT**® slow cooker.

2 Add rice; stir to coat. Sprinkle brown sugar evenly over top. Add apple juice and vanilla. Cover; cook on HIGH 1½ to 2 hours or until all liquid is absorbed. Ladle risotto into bowls; top as desired.

Tip

Keep the lid on! The **CROCK-POT**® slow cooker can take as long as 30 minutes to regain heat lost when the cover is removed.

Whole-Grain Banana Bread

MAKES 1 LOAF

¼ cup plus 2 tablespoons wheat germ, divided

1 cup sugar

⅔ cup butter, softened

2 eggs

1 cup mashed bananas (2 to 3 bananas)

1 teaspoon vanilla

1 cup all-purpose flour

1 cup whole wheat pastry flour

1 teaspoon baking soda

½ teaspoon salt

½ cup chopped walnuts or pecans (optional)

Butter and orange wedges (optional)

1 Coat inside of 1-quart soufflé dish that fits inside of **CROCK-POT®** slow cooker with nonstick cooking spray. Sprinkle dish with 2 tablespoons wheat germ.

2 Beat sugar and butter in large bowl with electric mixer until fluffy. Add eggs, one at a time; beat until blended. Add bananas and vanilla; beat until smooth.

3 Gradually stir in flours, remaining ¼ cup wheat germ, baking soda and salt. Stir in walnuts, if desired. Pour batter into prepared dish; place in **CROCK-POT®** slow cooker. Cover; cook on LOW 4 to 6 hours or on HIGH 2 to 3 hours or until edges begin to brown and toothpick inserted into center comes out clean.

4 Remove dish from **CROCK-POT®** slow cooker. Cool on wire rack 10 minutes. Remove bread from dish; cool completely on wire rack. Serve with butter and orange wedges, if desired.

Breakfast Bake

MAKES 6 TO 8 SERVINGS

3 to 4 cups diced crusty bread
(¾- to 1-inch dice)

½ pound bacon, cut into ½-inch dice

2 cups sliced mushrooms

2 cups torn fresh spinach

8 eggs

½ cup milk

1 cup (4 ounces) shredded Cheddar or
Monterey Jack cheese

¾ cup roasted red peppers, drained and
chopped

Salt and black pepper

Fresh fruit (optional)

Sprigs fresh mint (optional)

1 Coat inside of **CROCK-POT**® slow cooker with nonstick cooking spray. Add bread.

2 Heat large skillet over medium heat. Add bacon; cook and stir until crisp. Remove to **CROCK-POT**® slow cooker using slotted spoon. Discard all but 1 tablespoon drippings. Add mushrooms and spinach to skillet; cook and stir 1 to 2 minutes or until spinach is wilted. Remove to **CROCK-POT**® slow cooker; toss to combine.

3 Beat eggs and milk in medium bowl. Stir in cheese and red peppers. Season with salt and black pepper. Pour into **CROCK-POT**® slow cooker. Cover; cook on LOW 3 to 3½ hours or on HIGH 2 to 2½ hours or until eggs are firm but still moist. Serve with fruit. Garnish with mint.

Mucho Mocha Cocoa

MAKES 9 SERVINGS

1 cup chocolate syrup	1 teaspoon ground cinnamon
⅓ cup instant coffee granules	4 cups milk
2 tablespoons sugar	4 cups half-and-half

Combine chocolate syrup, coffee granules, sugar, cinnamon, milk and half-and-half in **CROCK-POT®** slow cooker; stir until well blended. Cover; cook on LOW 3 hours. Serve warm in mugs.

Breakfast Quinoa

MAKES 6 SERVINGS

1½ cups uncooked quinoa	1½ teaspoons ground cinnamon
3 cups water	¾ cup golden raisins
3 tablespoons packed brown sugar	Fresh raspberries and banana slices
2 tablespoons maple syrup	

1 Place quinoa in fine-mesh strainer; rinse well under cold running water. Remove to **CROCK-POT®** slow cooker.

2 Stir 3 cups water, brown sugar, maple syrup and cinnamon into **CROCK-POT®** slow cooker. Cover; cook on LOW 5 hours or on HIGH 2½ hours or until quinoa is tender and water is absorbed.

3 Add raisins during last 10 to 15 minutes of cooking time. Top quinoa with raspberries and bananas.

French Toast Bread Pudding

MAKES 6 TO 8 SERVINGS

2 tablespoons packed dark brown sugar

2½ teaspoons ground cinnamon

1 loaf (24 ounces) Texas toast-style bread*

2 cups whipping cream, plus additional for topping

2 cups half-and-half

1¼ cups granulated sugar

4 egg yolks

2 teaspoons vanilla

¼ teaspoon salt

¼ teaspoon ground nutmeg

*If unavailable, cut day-old 24-ounce loaf of white sandwich bread into 1-inch-thick slices.

1 Coat inside of **CROCK-POT**® slow cooker with nonstick cooking spray. Combine brown sugar and cinnamon in small bowl; stir to blend. Reserve 1 tablespoon; set aside.

2 Cut bread slices in half diagonally. Arrange bread slices in single layer in bottom of **CROCK-POT**® slow cooker. Sprinkle rounded tablespoon of cinnamon mixture over bread. Repeat layering with remaining bread and cinnamon mixture.

3 Whisk 2 cups cream, half-and-half, granulated sugar, egg yolks, vanilla, salt and nutmeg in large bowl. Pour cream mixture over bread; press bread down lightly. Sprinkle reserved cinnamon mixture on top. Cover; cook on LOW 3 to 4 hours or on HIGH 1½ to 2 hours or until toothpick inserted into center comes out clean.

4 Turn off heat; uncover. Let pudding rest 10 minutes before spooning into bowls. Serve with additional whipped cream, if desired.

Wake-Up Potato and Sausage Breakfast Casserole

MAKES 8 SERVINGS

1 pound smoked sausage, diced

1 cup chopped onion

1 cup chopped red bell pepper

1 package (20 ounces) refrigerated southwest-style hash browns*

10 eggs

1 cup milk

1 cup (4 ounces) shredded Monterey Jack

Fresh fruit (optional)

You may substitute O'Brien potatoes and add ½ teaspoon chile pepper.

1 Coat inside of **CROCK-POT**® slow cooker with nonstick cooking spray. Heat large skillet over medium-high heat. Add sausage and onion; cook and stir until sausage is browned. Drain fat. Stir in bell pepper.

2 Place one third of potatoes in **CROCK-POT**® slow cooker. Top with half of sausage mixture. Repeat layers. Spread remaining one third of potatoes evenly on top.

3 Whisk eggs and milk in medium bowl. Pour evenly over potatoes. Cover; cook on LOW 6 to 7 hours.

4 Turn off heat. Run a rubber spatula around edge of casserole, lifting bottom slightly. Invert onto large plate. Place large serving plate on top; invert again. Sprinkle with cheese and let stand until cheese is melted. To serve, cut into wedges.

Breakfast Berry Bread Pudding

MAKES 10 TO 12 SERVINGS

6 cups bread, preferably dense peasant-style or sourdough, cut into ¾- to 1-inch cubes	1½ teaspoons ground cinnamon
1 cup raisins	1 teaspoon vanilla
½ cup slivered almonds, toasted*	3 cups sliced fresh strawberries
6 eggs, beaten	2 cups fresh blueberries
1¾ cups milk	Sprigs fresh mint (optional)
1½ cups packed light brown sugar	

To toast almonds, spread in single layer in heavy skillet. Cook and stir over medium heat 1 to 2 minutes or until nuts are lightly browned.

1 Coat inside of **CROCK-POT**® slow cooker with nonstick cooking spray. Add bread, raisins and almonds; toss to combine.

2 Whisk eggs, milk, brown sugar, cinnamon and vanilla in separate bowl. Pour egg mixture over bread mixture; toss to blend. Cover; cook on LOW 4 to 4½ hours or on HIGH 3 hours.

3 Remove stoneware from **CROCK-POT**® slow cooker. Cool on wire rack 10 minutes. Serve pudding with berries and garnish with mint.

Ham and Cheddar Brunch Strata

MAKES 8 SERVINGS

8 ounces French bread, torn into small pieces

1¾ cups (7 ounces) shredded sharp Cheddar cheese, divided

1 cup diced ham

8 tablespoons finely chopped green onions, divided

4 eggs

1 cup half-and-half

1 tablespoon Worcestershire sauce

⅛ teaspoon ground red pepper

Fresh fruit (optional)

1 Coat inside of **CROCK-POT**® slow cooker with nonstick cooking spray. Cut waxed paper to fit bottom of stoneware; press into place. Spray paper with cooking spray. Layer bread, 1½ cups cheese, ham and 6 tablespoons green onions in **CROCK-POT**® slow cooker.

2 Whisk eggs, half-and-half, Worcestershire sauce and ground red pepper in small bowl; pour evenly into **CROCK-POT**® slow cooker. Cover; cook on LOW 3½ hours or until knife inserted into center comes out clean.

3 Turn off heat. Run a rubber spatula around edge of casserole, lifting bottom slightly. Invert onto large plate; peel off paper. Place large serving plate on top; invert again. Sprinkle evenly with remaining ¼ cup cheese and 2 tablespoons green onions; let stand until cheese is melted. To serve, cut into wedges. Serve with fruit.

Tip

When preparing ingredients for the **CROCK-POT**® slow cooker, cut into uniform pieces so everything cooks evenly.

Cherry-Orange Oatmeal

MAKES 8 SERVINGS

4 cups water
2 cups old-fashioned oats
4 tablespoons sugar
2 tablespoons unsweetened cocoa powder

2 cups fresh pitted cherries or frozen dark sweet cherries
2 cans (11 ounces *each*) mandarin orange segments in light syrup, rinsed and drained

1 Combine water, oats, sugar and cocoa in **CROCK-POT®** slow cooker; stir to blend. Cover; cook on LOW 8 hours.

2 Divide mixture evenly among eight serving bowls. Top with cherries and oranges.

Chai Tea

MAKES 8 TO 10 SERVINGS

2 quarts (8 cups) water
8 bags black tea
¾ cup sugar*
8 slices fresh ginger
5 whole cinnamon sticks, plus additional for garnish

16 whole cloves
16 whole cardamom seeds, pods removed (optional)
1 cup milk

Chai tea is typically sweet. For less-sweet tea, reduce sugar to ½ cup.

1 Combine water, tea bags, sugar, ginger, 5 cinnamon sticks, cloves and cardamom, if desired, in **CROCK-POT®** slow cooker; stir to blend. Cover; cook on HIGH 2 to 2½ hours.

2 Strain mixture; discard solids. (At this point, tea may be covered and refrigerated up to 3 days.)

3 Stir in milk just before serving. Garnish with additional cinnamon sticks.

Apple and Granola Breakfast Cobbler

MAKES 4 SERVINGS

4 Granny Smith apples, peeled, cored and sliced

½ cup packed light brown sugar

1 tablespoon lemon juice

1 teaspoon ground cinnamon

2 cups granola cereal with raisins, plus additional for garnish

2 tablespoons butter, cut into small pieces

Whipping cream, half-and-half or vanilla yogurt (optional)

1 Place apples in **CROCK-POT®** slow cooker. Sprinkle brown sugar, lemon juice and cinnamon over apples. Stir in 2 cups granola and butter.

2 Cover; cook on LOW 6 hours or on HIGH 3 hours. Serve warm with cream, if desired, and additional granola.

Overnight Bacon, Sourdough, Egg and Cheese Casserole

MAKES 6 SERVINGS

1 loaf (about 12 ounces) sourdough bread, cut into ¾-inch cubes

8 slices thick-cut bacon, chopped

1 large onion, chopped

1 medium red bell pepper, chopped

1 medium green bell pepper, chopped

2 teaspoons dried oregano

¼ cup sun-dried tomatoes packed in oil, drained and chopped

1½ cups (6 ounces) shredded sharp Cheddar cheese, divided

10 eggs

1 cup milk

1 teaspoon salt

¾ teaspoon black pepper

1 Coat inside of **CROCK-POT**® slow cooker with nonstick cooking spray. Add bread. Heat large skillet over medium heat. Add bacon; cook 7 to 9 minutes or until crisp. Remove bacon to paper towel-lined plate using slotted spoon. Pour off all but 1 tablespoon of drippings from skillet. Heat same skillet over medium heat. Add onion, bell peppers and oregano; cook 5 to 7 minutes or until onion is softened, stirring occasionally. Stir in sun-dried tomatoes; cook 1 minute. Pour over bread in **CROCK-POT**® slow cooker. Stir in bacon and 1 cup cheese.

2 Beat eggs, milk, salt and black pepper in large bowl; pour over bread mixture in **CROCK-POT**® slow cooker. Press down on bread to allow bread mixture to absorb egg mixture. Sprinkle remaining ½ cup cheese over top. Cover; cook on LOW 6 to 8 hours or on HIGH 3½ to 4 hours. Cut into squares to serve.

Raisin-Oat Quick Bread

MAKES 1 LOAF

1½ cups all-purpose flour, plus additional for dusting

⅔ cup old-fashioned oats

⅓ cup milk

4 teaspoons baking powder

1 teaspoon ground cinnamon

½ teaspoon salt

½ cup packed raisins

1 cup sugar

2 eggs, lightly beaten

½ cup (1 stick) unsalted butter, melted

1 teaspoon vanilla

1 Spray inside of ovenproof glass or ceramic loaf pan that fits inside of **CROCK-POT®** slow cooker with nonstick cooking spray; dust with flour.

2 Combine oats and milk in small bowl; let stand 10 minutes.

3 Meanwhile, combine 1½ cups flour, baking powder, cinnamon and salt in large bowl; stir in raisins. Whisk sugar, eggs, ½ cup melted butter and vanilla in medium bowl; stir in oat mixture. Pour sugar mixture into flour mixture; stir just until moistened. Pour into prepared pan. Place in **CROCK-POT®** slow cooker. Cover; cook on HIGH 2½ to 3 hours or until toothpick inserted into center comes out clean.

4 Remove pan from **CROCK-POT®** slow cooker; let cool in pan 10 minutes. Remove bread from pan; let cool on wire rack 3 minutes before slicing.

Oatmeal Crème Brûlée

MAKES 4 TO 6 SERVINGS

4 cups boiling water	½ cup granulated sugar
3 cups quick-cooking oatmeal	2 cups whipping cream
½ teaspoon salt	1 teaspoon vanilla
6 egg yolks	¼ cup packed light brown sugar

1 Coat inside of **CROCK-POT**® slow cooker with nonstick cooking spray. Pour boiling water into **CROCK-POT**® slow cooker. Stir in oatmeal and salt; cover.

2 Combine egg yolks and granulated sugar in medium bowl; mix well. Heat cream and vanilla in medium saucepan over medium heat until small bubbles begin to form at edge of pan. *Do not boil.* Remove from heat. Whisking constantly, pour ½ cup hot cream into egg yolk mixture in thin stream. Whisk egg mixture back into cream in saucepan, stirring rapidly to blend well. Spoon mixture over oatmeal in **CROCK-POT**® slow cooker. *Do not stir.*

3 Line lid with two paper towels. Cover; cook on LOW 3 to 3½ hours or until custard is set.

4 Sprinkle brown sugar over surface of custard. Line lid with two clean dry paper towels. Cover tightly; cook on LOW 10 to 15 minutes or until brown sugar is melted.

Spiced Apple Tea

MAKES 4 SERVINGS

3 bags cinnamon herbal tea
3 cups boiling water
2 cups unsweetened apple juice

6 whole cloves
1 whole cinnamon stick

1 Place tea bags in **CROCK-POT**® slow cooker. Pour boiling water over tea bags; cover and let steep 10 minutes. Remove and discard tea bags.

2 Add apple juice, cloves and cinnamon stick to **CROCK-POT**® slow cooker. Cover; cook on LOW 2 to 3 hours. Remove and discard cloves and cinnamon stick. Serve warm in mugs.

4-Fruit Oatmeal

MAKES 4 SERVINGS

4¼ cups water
1 cup steel-cut oats
⅓ cup golden raisins
⅓ cup dried cranberries
⅓ cup dried cherries

2 tablespoons honey
1 teaspoon vanilla
¼ teaspoon salt
1 cup fresh sliced strawberries

Combine water, oats, raisins, cranberries, cherries, honey, vanilla and salt in **CROCK-POT**® slow cooker; stir to blend. Cover; cook on LOW 7 to 7½ hours. Top each serving evenly with strawberries.

Hawaiian Bread French Toast

MAKES 8 TO 10 SERVINGS

6 eggs
1 cup milk
1 cup whipping cream
¼ cup sugar
2 teaspoons coconut extract
2 teaspoons vanilla
1 teaspoon ground cinnamon
1 pound sliced sweet Hawaiian rolls or bread, sliced lengthwise and cut to fit **CROCK-POT**® slow cooker

2 tablespoons unsalted butter, cut into ¼-inch pieces
½ cup flaked coconut, toasted*

To toast coconut, spread in single layer in heavy-bottomed skillet. Cook and stir over medium heat 1 to 2 minutes or until lightly browned. Remove from skillet immediately. Cool before using.

1 Coat inside of **CROCK-POT**® slow cooker with nonstick cooking spray. Whisk eggs, milk, cream, sugar, coconut extract, vanilla and cinnamon in large bowl.

2 Place bread in **CROCK-POT**® slow cooker; sprinkle butter over top. Pour egg mixture on top; press bread down to absorb egg mixture. Cover; cook on HIGH 2 hours. Sprinkle with toasted coconut.

Maple, Bacon and Raspberry Pancake

MAKES 8 SERVINGS

5 slices bacon

2 cups pancake mix

1 cup water

½ cup maple syrup, plus additional for serving

1 cup fresh raspberries, plus additional for garnish

3 tablespoons chopped pecans, toasted*

To toast pecans, spread in single layer in heavy skillet. Cook and stir over medium heat 1 to 2 minutes or until nuts are lightly browned.

1 Heat large skillet over medium heat. Add bacon; cook and stir until crisp. Remove to paper towel-lined plate using slotted spoon; crumble.

2 Brush inside of 5-quart **CROCK-POT**® slow cooker with 1 to 2 tablespoons drippings from skillet. Combine pancake mix, water and ½ cup maple syrup in large bowl; stir to blend. Pour half of batter into **CROCK-POT**® slow cooker; top with ½ cup raspberries, half of bacon and half of pecans. Pour remaining half of batter over top; sprinkle with remaining ½ cup raspberries, bacon and pecans.

3 Cover; cook on HIGH 1½ to 2 hours or until pancake has risen and is cooked through. Turn off heat. Let stand, uncovered, 10 to 15 minutes. Remove pancake from **CROCK-POT**® slow cooker; cut into eight pieces. Serve with additional maple syrup and raspberries.

Cranberry Orange Scones

MAKES 6 SERVINGS

¼ cup (½ stick) cold butter
1 cup plus 2 tablespoons self-rising flour, divided
¾ cup buttermilk
2 teaspoons granulated sugar
¼ cup dried cranberries

1½ teaspoons orange peel, divided
½ teaspoon ground cinnamon
¼ cup powdered sugar
1½ teaspoons orange juice
⅛ teaspoon salt

1 Cut one 16-inch piece of parchment paper; fold in half crosswise. Fit parchment paper into bottom and partly up sides of 1½-quart **CROCK-POT**® slow cooker. Coat parchment paper with nonstick cooking spray.

2 Grate cold butter into medium bowl. Add 1 cup flour, buttermilk and granulated sugar; stir until dry ingredients are just moistened. *Do not overmix.* Combine cranberries, 1 teaspoon orange peel and cinnamon in small bowl; toss to coat. Fold cranberry mixture into dough.

3 Sprinkle work surface with remaining 2 tablespoons flour. Place dough onto work surface; knead briefly until dough forms a ball. Press into 6-inch disc; score into six wedges. Place disc into **CROCK-POT**® slow cooker on top of parchment paper.

4 Lay a clean kitchen towel across top of **CROCK-POT**® slow cooker; cover with lid. Cover; cook on HIGH 1½ hours. Remove scones with parchment paper to wire rack. Combine powdered sugar, orange juice, remaining ½ teaspoon orange peel and salt in small bowl; whisk until blended. Drizzle over scones; serve warm or at room temperature.

Denver Egg Bowls

MAKES 4 SERVINGS

4 bell peppers, any color
10 eggs
¼ cup diced ham, plus additional
  for topping

3 green onions, chopped
1 cup (4 ounces) shredded Cheddar
  cheese

1 Cut thin slice off top of each bell pepper; reserve tops. Carefully remove and discard seeds and membranes, leaving peppers whole. Dice bell pepper tops; measure ¼ cup. Discard remaining diced bell pepper or reserve for another use.

2 Whisk eggs, ¼ cup diced bell peppers, ¼ cup ham and green onions in large measuring cup until well blended. Pour egg mixture evenly into each bell pepper; place in **CROCK-POT®** slow cooker. Fill **CROCK-POT®** slow cooker with water about three fourths up bell peppers.

3 Cover; cook on HIGH 3½ hours. Sprinkle with cheese and additional ham, if desired.

Cinnamon Latté

MAKES 6 TO 8 SERVINGS

6 cups double-strength brewed coffee*
2 cups half-and-half
1 cup sugar
1 teaspoon vanilla
3 whole cinnamon sticks, plus additional
  for garnish

Double the amount of coffee grounds normally used to brew coffee. Or substitute 8 teaspoons instant coffee dissolved in 6 cups boiling water.

1 Blend coffee, half-and-half, sugar and vanilla in **CROCK-POT®** slow cooker. Add 3 cinnamon sticks. Cover; cook on HIGH 3 hours.

2 Remove and discard cinnamon sticks. Serve latté in coffee mugs. Garnish with additional cinnamon sticks.

Overnight Breakfast Porridge

MAKES 4 SERVINGS

¾ cup steel-cut oats

¼ cup uncooked quinoa, rinsed and drained

¼ cup dried cranberries, plus additional for serving

¼ cup raisins

3 tablespoons ground flax seeds

2 tablespoons chia seeds

¼ teaspoon ground cinnamon

2½ cups almond milk, plus additional for serving

Maple syrup (optional)

¼ cup sliced almonds, toasted*

*To toast almonds, spread in single layer in heavy skillet. Cook and stir over medium heat 1 to 2 minutes or until nuts are lightly browned.

1 Combine oats, quinoa, ¼ cup cranberries, raisins, flax seeds, chia seeds and cinnamon in heat-safe bowl that fits inside of 5- or 6-quart **CROCK-POT®** slow cooker. Stir in 2½ cups almond milk.

2 Place bowl in **CROCK-POT®** slow cooker; pour enough water to come halfway up side of bowl.

3 Cover; cook on LOW 8 hours. Carefully remove bowl from **CROCK-POT®** slow cooker. Stir in additional almond milk, if desired. Top each serving with maple syrup, almonds and additional cranberries, if desired.

Mediterranean Frittata

MAKES 4 TO 6 SERVINGS

Butter, softened
3 tablespoons extra virgin olive oil
1 large onion, chopped
2 cups (8 ounces) sliced mushrooms
6 cloves garlic, sliced
1 teaspoon dried basil
1 medium red bell pepper, chopped
1 package (10 ounces) frozen chopped spinach, thawed and squeezed dry

¼ cup sliced kalamata olives
8 eggs, beaten
4 ounces feta cheese, crumbled
½ teaspoon salt
¼ teaspoon black pepper
Fresh strawberries (optional)

1 Coat inside of 5- to 6-quart **CROCK-POT**® slow cooker with butter. Heat oil in large skillet over medium-high heat. Add onion, mushrooms, garlic and basil; cook 2 to 3 minutes or until slightly softened, stirring occasionally. Add bell pepper; cook 4 to 5 minutes or until vegetables are tender. Stir in spinach; cook 2 minutes. Stir in olives. Remove onion mixture to **CROCK-POT**® slow cooker.

2 Combine eggs, cheese, salt and black pepper in large bowl. Pour over vegetables in **CROCK-POT**® slow cooker. Cover; cook on LOW 2½ to 3 hours or on HIGH 1½ to 2 hours or until eggs are set. Cut into wedges. Serve with strawberries, if desired.

Blueberry-Orange French Toast Casserole

MAKES 6 SERVINGS

½ cup sugar
½ cup milk
2 eggs
4 egg whites
1 tablespoon grated orange peel

½ teaspoon vanilla
6 slices whole wheat bread, cut into
   1-inch cubes
1 cup fresh blueberries
Maple syrup (optional)

1 Coat inside of **CROCK-POT**® slow cooker with nonstick cooking spray. Stir sugar and milk in large bowl until sugar is dissolved. Whisk in eggs, egg whites, orange peel and vanilla. Add bread and blueberries; stir to coat.

2 Remove mixture to **CROCK-POT**® slow cooker. Cover; cook on LOW 3 to 4 hours or on HIGH 1½ to 2 hours or until toothpick inserted into center comes out clean.

3 Turn off heat. Let stand 10 minutes. Serve with maple syrup, if desired.

Roasted Pepper and Sourdough Egg Dish

MAKES 6 SERVINGS

3 cups sourdough bread cubes	1 cup cottage cheese
1 jar (12 ounces) roasted red pepper strips, drained	6 eggs
1 cup (4 ounces) shredded Monterey Jack cheese	1 cup milk
1 cup (4 ounces) shredded sharp Cheddar cheese	¼ cup chopped fresh cilantro
	¼ teaspoon black pepper

1 Coat inside of **CROCK-POT**® slow cooker with nonstick cooking spray. Add bread. Arrange roasted peppers evenly over bread cubes; sprinkle with Monterey Jack and Cheddar cheeses.

2 Place cottage cheese in food processor or blender; process until smooth. Add eggs and milk; process just until blended. Stir in cilantro and black pepper.

3 Pour egg mixture into **CROCK-POT**® slow cooker. Cover; cook on LOW 3 to 3½ hours or on HIGH 2 to 2½ hours or until eggs are firm but still moist.

Oatmeal with Maple-Glazed Apples and Cranberries

MAKES 4 SERVINGS

3 cups water

2 cups quick-cooking or old-fashioned oats

¼ teaspoon salt

1 teaspoon unsalted butter

2 medium red or Golden Delicious apples, unpeeled and cut into ½-inch pieces

¼ teaspoon ground cinnamon

2 tablespoons maple syrup

¼ cup dried cranberries

1 Combine water, oats and salt in **CROCK-POT**® slow cooker. Cover; cook on LOW 8 hours.

2 Melt butter in large nonstick skillet over medium heat. Add apples and cinnamon; cook and stir 4 to 5 minutes or until tender. Stir in maple syrup; cook until heated through.

3 Top each oatmeal serving evenly with apple mixture and dried cranberries.

Breakfast Nests

MAKES 4 SERVINGS

1 package (12 ounces) frozen butternut squash spirals, thawed

1 teaspoon vegetable oil

¼ teaspoon salt, plus additional for serving

¼ teaspoon ground nutmeg

¼ teaspoon black pepper, plus additional for serving

4 eggs

1 Line four 6- to 8-ounce ramekins with square of parchment paper; spray parchment with nonstick cooking spray.

2 Combine butternut squash spirals, oil, ¼ teaspoon salt, nutmeg and ¼ teaspoon pepper in medium bowl; toss to coat. Arrange butternut squash spirals evenly in nests in prepared ramekins. Crack one egg over squash in each ramekin. Fill **CROCK-POT**® slow cooker with ¼-inch water; add ramekins.

3 Cover; cook on HIGH 2 hours or until whites are set and yolks are desired doneness. Remove nests from ramekins using parchment to plates, if desired. Season with additional salt and pepper.

Blueberry-Banana Pancakes

MAKES 8 SERVINGS

2 cups all-purpose flour	2 eggs, lightly beaten
⅓ cup sugar	¼ cup (½ stick) unsalted butter, melted
1 tablespoon baking powder	1 teaspoon vanilla
½ teaspoon baking soda	1 cup fresh blueberries
½ teaspoon salt	2 small bananas, sliced
½ teaspoon ground cinnamon	Maple syrup (optional)
1¾ cups milk	

1 Combine flour, sugar, baking powder, baking soda, salt and cinnamon in large bowl; stir to blend. Combine milk, eggs, butter and vanilla in medium bowl; whisk to blend. Pour milk mixture into flour mixture; stir until dry ingredients are moistened. Gently fold in blueberries until mixed.

2 Coat inside of **CROCK-POT**® slow cooker with nonstick cooking spray. Pour batter into **CROCK-POT**® slow cooker. Cover; cook on HIGH 2 hours or until puffed and toothpick inserted into center comes out clean. Cut evenly into eight wedges; top with sliced bananas and maple syrup, if desired.

Party Starters

Chicken and Asiago Stuffed Mushrooms

MAKES 4 TO 5 SERVINGS

20 large white mushrooms, stems removed and reserved

3 tablespoons extra virgin olive oil, divided

¼ cup finely chopped onion

2 cloves garlic, minced

¼ cup Madeira wine

½ pound chicken sausage, casings removed or ground chicken

1 cup grated Asiago cheese

¼ cup seasoned dry bread crumbs

3 tablespoons chopped fresh Italian parsley

½ teaspoon salt

¼ teaspoon black pepper

1 Lightly brush mushroom caps with 1 tablespoon oil; set aside. Finely chop mushroom stems.

2 Heat remaining 2 tablespoons oil in large skillet over medium-high heat. Add onion; cook 1 minute or until just beginning to soften. Add mushroom stems; cook 5 to 6 minutes or until beginning to brown. Stir in garlic; cook 1 minute.

3 Pour in wine; cook 1 minute. Add sausage; cook 3 to 4 minutes or until no longer pink, stirring to break into small pieces. Remove from heat; cool 5 minutes. Stir in cheese, bread crumbs, parsley, salt and pepper.

4 Divide mushroom-sausage mixture evenly among mushroom caps, pressing slightly to compress. Place stuffed mushroom caps in single layer in **CROCK-POT**® slow cooker. Cover; cook on LOW 4 hours or on HIGH 2 hours.

Tip

Stuffed mushrooms are a great way to impress guests with your gourmet cooking skills. These appetizers appear time intensive and fancy, but they are actually simple with the help of a **CROCK-POT**® slow cooker.

Carnitas Tacos

MAKES 12 SERVINGS

1½ pounds boneless pork loin roast, cut into 1-inch cubes
1 onion, finely chopped
½ cup chicken broth
1 tablespoon chili powder
2 teaspoons ground cumin
1 teaspoon dried oregano
½ teaspoon minced canned chipotle peppers in adobo sauce
½ cup pico de gallo
2 tablespoons chopped fresh cilantro
½ teaspoon salt
12 (6-inch) corn tortillas
¾ cup (3 ounces) shredded sharp Cheddar cheese
3 tablespoons sour cream

1 Combine pork, onion, broth, chili powder, cumin, oregano and chipotle peppers in **CROCK-POT®** slow cooker; stir to blend. Cover; cook on LOW 6 hours or on HIGH 3 hours. Pour off excess cooking liquid.

2 Remove pork to large cutting board; shred with two forks. Return to **CROCK-POT®** slow cooker. Stir in pico de gallo, cilantro and salt. Cover; keep warm on LOW or WARM setting.

3 Cut three circles from each tortilla with 2-inch biscuit cutter. Top each evenly with pork, cheese and sour cream. Serve warm.

Tip

Carnitas or "little meats" in Spanish, are a festive way to spice up any gathering. Carnitas traditionally include a large amount of lard, but slow cooking makes the dish healthier by eliminating the need to add lard, oil or fat, while keeping the meat tender and delicious.

Creamy Seafood Dip

MAKES 6 TO 8 SERVINGS

1 package (8 ounces) shredded pepper jack cheese

1 can (6 ounces) lump crabmeat, drained

1 pound cooked shrimp, peeled, deveined and chopped

1 cup whipping cream, divided

1 round sourdough bread loaf (about 1 pound)

1 Place cheese in **CROCK-POT**® slow cooker. Add crabmeat, shrimp and ¾ cup cream; stir to blend. Cover; cook on HIGH 10 to 15 minutes or until cheese is melted.

2 Meanwhile, cut off top of bread and hollow out to create bowl. Cut extra bread into large pieces. Place bread bowl on serving plate. Place extra bread around bowl.

3 Check consistency of dip. Stir in up to ¼ cup additional cream, as needed. Pour into bread bowl.

Parmesan Ranch Snack Mix

MAKES ABOUT 9½ CUPS

3 cups corn or rice cereal squares

2 cups oyster crackers

1 package (5 ounces) bagel chips, broken in half

1½ cups mini pretzel twists

1 cup pistachio nuts

2 tablespoons grated Parmesan cheese

¼ cup (½ stick) butter, melted

1 package (1 ounce) dry ranch salad dressing mix

½ teaspoon garlic powder

1 Combine cereal, crackers, bagel chips, pretzels, pistachios and cheese in **CROCK-POT**® slow cooker; mix gently.

2 Combine butter, salad dressing mix and garlic powder in small bowl. Pour over cereal mixture; toss lightly to coat. Cover; cook on LOW 3 hours.

3 Stir gently. Cook, uncovered, on LOW 30 minutes.

Warm Blue Crab Bruschetta

MAKES 16 SERVINGS

- 4 cups peeled, seeded and diced plum tomatoes
- 1 cup diced white onion
- ⅓ cup olive oil
- 2 tablespoons sugar
- 2 tablespoons balsamic vinegar
- 2 teaspoons minced garlic
- ½ teaspoon dried oregano
- 1 pound lump blue crabmeat, picked over for shells
- 1½ teaspoons kosher salt
- ½ teaspoon cracked black pepper
- ⅓ cup minced fresh basil
- 2 baguettes, sliced and toasted

1 Combine tomatoes, onion, oil, sugar, vinegar, garlic and oregano in **CROCK-POT**® slow cooker; stir to blend. Cover; cook on LOW 2 hours.

2 Stir crabmeat, salt and pepper into **CROCK-POT**® slow cooker, taking care not to break up crabmeat. Cover; cook on LOW 1 hour. Fold in basil. Serve on toasted baguette slices.

Serving Suggestion

Crab topping can also be served on Melba toast or whole grain crackers.

Barbecued Meatballs

MAKES 12 SERVINGS

2 pounds ground beef	½ teaspoon black pepper
1⅓ cups ketchup, divided	1 cup packed brown sugar
3 tablespoons seasoned dry bread crumbs	1 can (6 ounces) tomato paste
1 egg, lightly beaten	¼ cup soy sauce
2 tablespoons dried minced onion	¼ cup cider vinegar
¾ teaspoon garlic salt	1½ teaspoons hot pepper sauce
	Sliced green bell peppers (optional)

1 Preheat oven to 350°F. Combine beef, ⅓ cup ketchup, bread crumbs, egg, dried onion, garlic salt and black pepper in medium bowl; mix lightly but thoroughly. Shape into 1-inch meatballs.

2 Place meatballs in two 15×10-inch jelly-roll pans or shallow roasting pans. Bake 18 minutes or until browned. Remove to **CROCK-POT**® slow cooker using slotted spoon.

3 Mix remaining 1 cup ketchup, brown sugar, tomato paste, soy sauce, vinegar and hot pepper sauce in medium bowl. Pour over meatballs. Cover; cook on LOW 4 hours. Stir in bell peppers during last 15 minutes of cooking, if desired.

Barbecued Franks

Arrange two 12-ounce packages or three 8-ounce packages of cocktail franks in **CROCK-POT**® slow cooker. Combine 1 cup ketchup, brown sugar, tomato paste, soy sauce, vinegar and hot pepper sauce in medium bowl; pour over franks. Cover; cook on LOW 4 hours. Stir in bell peppers during last 15 minutes of cooking. Makes 12 to 14 servings.

Bacon-Wrapped Fingerling Potatoes

MAKES 4 TO 6 SERVINGS

1 pound fingerling potatoes
2 tablespoons olive oil
1 tablespoon minced fresh thyme
½ teaspoon black pepper
¼ teaspoon paprika

½ pound bacon slices, cut crosswise into halves
¼ cup chicken broth
Sprigs fresh thyme (optional)

1 Toss potatoes with oil, minced thyme, pepper and paprika in large bowl. Wrap half slice of bacon tightly around each potato.

2 Heat large skillet over medium heat; add potatoes. Reduce heat to medium-low; cook until lightly browned and bacon has tightened around potatoes. Place potatoes in **CROCK-POT®** slow cooker. Add broth. Cover; cook on HIGH 3 hours. Garnish with thyme sprigs

Sweet and Spicy Sausage Rounds

MAKES ABOUT 16 SERVINGS

1 pound kielbasa sausage, cut into ¼-inch-thick rounds
⅔ cup blackberry jam

⅓ cup steak sauce
1 tablespoon yellow mustard
½ teaspoon ground allspice

Combine sausage, jam, steak sauce, mustard and allspice in **CROCK-POT®** slow cooker; stir to blend. Cover; cook on HIGH 3 hours.

Feta and Mint Spread

MAKES 12 SERVINGS

½ cup plain Greek yogurt*
3 ounces feta cheese, crumbled
2 ounces cream cheese, cubed
2 tablespoons extra virgin olive oil
1 small clove garlic, crushed to a paste
   Baked Pita Chips (recipe follows)
1 tablespoon chopped fresh mint
½ teaspoon grated fresh lemon peel

Carrot and celery sticks
Sprigs fresh mint (optional)

Greek yogurt is yogurt from which much of the liquid (or "whey") has been drained before use. It is available in most major supermarkets. To make your own, place ½ cup plain yogurt in a small colander lined with several layers of damp cheesecloth. Suspend over a large bowl and refrigerate overnight.

1 Coat inside of **CROCK-POT**® "No Dial" food warmer with nonstick cooking spray. Add yogurt, feta cheese, cream cheese, oil and garlic; mix well. Cover; heat 1 hour or until cheese is melted.

2 Meanwhile, prepare Baked Pita Chips.

3 Stir in chopped mint and lemon peel. Serve with Baked Pita Chips, carrot and celery sticks. Garnish with mint sprigs.

Baked Pita Chips

MAKES 36 CHIPS

3 pita bread rounds
1 tablespoon extra virgin olive oil
½ teaspoon dried oregano

¼ teaspoon ground cumin
⅛ teaspoon salt

1 Preheat oven to 375°F. Spray large baking sheet with nonstick cooking spray.

2 Brush one side of each pita round with oil. Sprinkle with oregano, cumin and salt. Cut each pita round into 12 wedges. Place on prepared baking sheet seasoned side up. Bake 8 minutes or until lightly browned. Cool.

Asian Barbecue Skewers

MAKES 4 TO 6 SERVINGS

2 pounds boneless, skinless chicken thighs

½ cup soy sauce

⅓ cup packed brown sugar

2 tablespoons sesame oil

3 cloves garlic, minced

½ cup thinly sliced green onions (optional)

1 tablespoon toasted sesame seeds (optional)*

To toast sesame seeds, spread in small skillet. Shake skillet over medium-low heat 2 minutes or until seeds begin to pop and turn golden brown.

1 Cut each chicken thigh into four pieces, about 1½ inches thick. Thread chicken onto 7-inch-long wooden skewers, folding thinner pieces, if necessary. Place skewers into **CROCK-POT®** slow cooker, layering as flat as possible.

2 Combine soy sauce, brown sugar, oil and garlic in small bowl. Reserve ⅓ cup sauce; set aside. Pour remaining sauce over skewers. Cover; cook on LOW 2 hours. Turn skewers over. Cover; cook on LOW 1 hour.

3 Remove skewers to large serving platter. Discard cooking liquid. Pour reserved sauce over skewers. Sprinkle with green onions and sesame seeds, if desired.

Pepperoni Pizza Dip with Breadstick Dippers

MAKES 8 SERVINGS

1 jar or can (14 ounces) pizza sauce

¾ cup chopped turkey pepperoni

4 green onions, chopped

1 can (2¼ ounces) sliced black olives, drained

½ teaspoon dried oregano

1 cup (4 ounces) shredded mozzarella cheese

1 package (3 ounces) cream cheese, softened

Breadstick Dippers (recipe follows)

1 Combine pizza sauce, pepperoni, green onions, olives and oregano in 2-quart **CROCK-POT®** slow cooker. Cover; cook on LOW 2 hours or on HIGH 1 to 1½ hours or until mixture is heated through.

2 Stir in mozzarella cheese and cream cheese until melted and well blended. Prepare and serve with warm Breadstick Dippers.

Breadstick Dippers

1 package (8 ounces) refrigerated breadstick dough

2 teaspoons melted butter

2 teaspoons minced fresh Italian parsley

Bake breadsticks according to package directions. Brush with melted butter and sprinkle with parsley. Serve with warm dip.

Caramelized Onion Dip

MAKES 12 SERVINGS

1 tablespoon olive oil	½ cup sour cream
1½ cups chopped sweet onion	⅓ cup mayonnaise
1 teaspoon sugar	⅓ cup shredded Swiss cheese
⅛ teaspoon dried thyme	¼ teaspoon beef bouillon granules
¼ teaspoon salt	Potato chips and carrot sticks
2 ounces cream cheese, cubed	

1 Heat oil in medium skillet over medium heat. Add onion, sugar and thyme; cook 12 minutes or until golden, stirring occasionally. Stir in salt.

2 Coat inside of **CROCK-POT**® "No Dial" food warmer. Add onion mixture, cream cheese, sour cream, mayonnaise, Swiss cheese and bouillon; mix well. Cover; heat 1 hour or until warm. Stir to blend. Serve with potato chips and carrot sticks.

Chipotle Turkey Sloppy Joe Sliders

MAKES 12 SLIDERS

1 pound turkey Italian sausage links, casings removed	1 tablespoon minced canned chipotle peppers in adobo sauce, plus 1 tablespoon sauce
1 package (14 ounces) frozen green and red bell pepper strips with onions	2 teaspoons ground cumin
1 can (6 ounces) tomato paste	½ teaspoon dried thyme
1 tablespoon quick-cooking tapioca	12 corn muffins or small dinner rolls, split and toasted

1 Brown sausage in large skillet over medium-high heat 6 to 8 minutes, stirring to break up meat. Remove to **CROCK-POT**® slow cooker using slotted spoon.

2 Stir in pepper strips with onions, tomato paste, tapioca, chipotle peppers with sauce, cumin and thyme. Cover; cook on LOW 8 to 10 hours. Serve on corn muffins.

Sausage and Swiss Chard Stuffed Mushrooms

MAKES 6 TO 8 SERVINGS

4 tablespoons olive oil, divided
½ pound bulk pork sausage
½ onion, finely chopped
2 cups chopped Swiss chard
¼ teaspoon dried thyme
2 tablespoons garlic-and-herb-flavored dry bread crumbs
1½ cups chicken broth, divided

½ teaspoon salt, divided
½ teaspoon black pepper, divided
2 packages (6 ounces *each*) cremini mushrooms, stemmed*
2 tablespoons grated Parmesan cheese
2 tablespoons chopped fresh Italian parsley

Do not substitute white button mushrooms.

1 Coat inside of **CROCK-POT**® slow cooker with nonstick cooking spray. Heat 1 tablespoon oil in medium skillet over medium heat. Add sausage; cook and stir 6 to 8 minutes or until browned. Remove sausage to medium bowl using slotted spoon.

2 Add onion to skillet; cook and stir 3 minutes or until translucent, scraping up any browned bits from bottom of skillet. Stir in chard and thyme; cook 1 to 2 minutes or until chard is wilted. Remove from heat.

3 Stir in sausage, bread crumbs, 1 tablespoon broth, ¼ teaspoon salt and ¼ teaspoon pepper. Brush remaining 3 tablespoons oil over mushrooms. Season with remaining ¼ teaspoon salt and ¼ teaspoon pepper. Fill mushrooms evenly with stuffing.

4 Pour remaining broth into **CROCK-POT**® slow cooker. Arrange stuffed mushrooms in bottom. Cover; cook on HIGH 3 hours. To serve, remove mushrooms using slotted spoon; discard cooking liquid. Combine cheese and parsley in small bowl; sprinkle evenly over mushrooms.

Warm Moroccan-Style Bean Dip

MAKES 4 TO 6 SERVINGS

2 teaspoons canola oil

1 small onion, chopped

2 cloves garlic, minced

2 cans (about 15 ounces *each*) cannellini beans, rinsed and drained

¾ cup canned diced tomatoes

½ teaspoon ground turmeric (optional)

¼ teaspoon salt

¼ teaspoon ground cumin

¼ teaspoon ground cinnamon

¼ teaspoon paprika

¼ teaspoon black pepper

⅛ teaspoon ground cloves

⅛ teaspoon ground red pepper

2 tablespoons plain yogurt

1 tablespoon water

¼ teaspoon dried mint (optional)

Warm pita bread rounds, cut into wedges

1 Heat oil in small skillet over medium-high heat. Add onion; cook and stir 5 minutes or until translucent. Add garlic; cook and stir 30 seconds. Remove to **CROCK-POT**® slow cooker. Stir in beans, tomatoes, tumeric, if desired, salt, cumin, cinnamon, paprika, black pepper, cloves and ground red pepper. Cover; cook on LOW 6 hours.

2 Remove bean mixture and enough cooking liquid to food processor or blender; process using on/off pulsing action until coarsely chopped. (Or use immersion blender.) Remove to large serving bowl.

3 Beat yogurt and cold water in small bowl until well combined. Drizzle over bean dip. Garnish with dried mint. Serve warm with pita wedges.

Tip

Moroccan cuisine has a wide array of dishes beyond the most famous couscous. The cuisine makes use of a wide variety of spices; this reflects the many ethnicities that have influenced the country over the centuries. This spice-filled dip is sure to stimulate guests' taste buds and conversation with its combination of exotic flavors.

Hoisin Sriracha Chicken Wings

MAKES 5 TO 6 SERVINGS

3 pounds chicken wings, tips removed and split at joints

½ cup hoisin sauce

¼ cup plus 1 tablespoon sriracha sauce, divided

2 tablespoons packed brown sugar

Chopped green onions (optional)

1 Coat inside of **CROCK-POT**® slow cooker with nonstick cooking spray. Preheat broiler. Spray large baking sheet with cooking spray. Arrange wings on prepared baking sheet. Broil 6 to 8 minutes or until browned, turning once. Remove wings to **CROCK-POT**® slow cooker.

2 Combine hoisin sauce, ¼ cup sriracha sauce and brown sugar in medium bowl; stir to blend. Pour sauce mixture over wings in **CROCK-POT**® slow cooker; stir to coat. Cover; cook on LOW 3½ to 4 hours. Remove wings to large serving platter; cover with foil to keep warm.

3 Turn **CROCK-POT**® slow cooker to HIGH. Cook, uncovered, on HIGH 10 to 15 minutes or until sauce is thickened. Stir in remaining 1 tablespoon sriracha sauce. Spoon sauce over wings to serve. Garnish with green onions.

Juicy Reuben Sliders

MAKES 24 SLIDERS

1 corned beef brisket (about 1½ pounds), trimmed

2 cups sauerkraut, drained

½ cup beef broth

1 small onion, sliced

1 clove garlic, minced

4 to 6 whole white peppercorns

¼ teaspoon caraway seeds

48 slices cocktail rye bread

12 slices deli Swiss cheese

Dijon mustard (optional)

1 Place corned beef in **CROCK-POT**® slow cooker. Add sauerkraut, broth, onion, garlic, peppercorns and caraway seeds. Cover; cook on LOW 7 to 9 hours.

2 Remove corned beef to large cutting board. Cover; let rest 10 minutes. Cut across grain into 16 slices. Cut each slice into 3 pieces. Place 2 pieces corned beef on each of 24 slices of bread. Place 1 heaping tablespoon sauerkraut on each sandwich. Cut each slice of Swiss cheese into quarters; place 2 quarters on each sandwich. Spread remaining 24 slices of bread with mustard, if desired, and place on top of sandwiches.

Bacon-Wrapped Dates

MAKES 8 TO 10 SERVINGS

4 ounces goat cheese or blue cheese

1 package (8 ounces) dried pitted dates

1 pound thick-cut bacon (about 11 slices), halved

1 Fill **CROCK-POT®** slow cooker with about ½ inch of water. Spoon goat cheese evenly into centers of dates; close. Wrap half slice of bacon around each date; secure with toothpick.

2 Heat large skillet over medium heat. Add wrapped dates; cook and turn 5 to 10 minutes until browned. Remove to **CROCK-POT®** slow cooker.

3 Cover; cook on LOW 2 to 3 hours. Remove toothpicks before serving.

Angelic Deviled Eggs

MAKES 12 SERVINGS

6 eggs

¼ cup cottage cheese

3 tablespoons ranch dressing

2 teaspoons Dijon mustard

2 tablespoons minced fresh chives or dill

1 tablespoon diced well-drained pimientos or roasted red pepper

1 Place eggs in single layer in bottom of **CROCK-POT®** slow cooker; add just enough water to cover tops of eggs. Cover; cook on LOW 3½ hours. Rinse and drain eggs under cold running water; peel when cool enough to handle.

2 Cut eggs in half lengthwise. Remove yolks, reserving 3 yolk halves. Discard remaining yolks or reserve for another use. Place egg whites, cut sides up, on serving plate; cover with plastic wrap. Refrigerate while preparing filling.

3 Combine cottage cheese, dressing, mustard and reserved yolk halves in small bowl; mash with fork until well blended. Stir in chives and pimientos. Spoon cottage cheese mixture into egg whites. Cover; refrigerate at least 1 hour before serving.

Apricot and Brie Dip

MAKES 3 CUPS

½ cup dried apricots, finely chopped
⅓ cup plus 1 tablespoon apricot preserves, divided
¼ cup apple juice

1 round wheel Brie cheese (2 pounds), rind removed and cut into cubes
Crackers or bread

Combine dried apricots, ⅓ cup apricot preserves and apple juice in **CROCK-POT®** slow cooker. Cover; cook on HIGH 40 minutes. Stir in cheese. Cover; cook on HIGH 30 to 40 minutes or until cheese is melted. Stir in remaining 1 tablespoon preserves. Turn **CROCK-POT®** slow cooker to LOW. Serve warm with crackers.

Tomato Topping for Bruschetta

MAKES 8 SERVINGS

6 medium tomatoes, peeled, seeded and diced
2 stalks celery, chopped
2 shallots, chopped
4 pepperoncini peppers, chopped*
2 tablespoons olive oil
2 teaspoons tomato paste

1 teaspoon salt
½ teaspoon black pepper
8 slices country bread or other large round bread
2 cloves garlic, minced

Pepperoncini are pickled peppers sold in jars with brine. They are available in the condiment aisle of large supermarkets.

1 Drain tomatoes in fine-mesh strainer. Combine tomatoes, celery, shallots, pepperoncini peppers, oil, tomato paste, salt and black pepper in **CROCK-POT®** slow cooker; stir gently to blend. Cover; cook on LOW 45 minutes to 1 hour.

2 Toast bread; immediately rub with garlic. Spread tomato topping on bread to serve.

Raspberry-Balsamic Glazed Meatballs

MAKES ABOUT 16 SERVINGS

1 bag (2 pounds) frozen fully cooked meatballs

1 cup raspberry preserves

3 tablespoons sugar

3 tablespoons balsamic vinegar

1 tablespoon plus 1½ teaspoons Worcestershire sauce

¼ teaspoon red pepper flakes

1 tablespoon grated fresh ginger (optional)

1 Coat inside of **CROCK-POT**® slow cooker with nonstick cooking spray. Add frozen meatballs.

2 Combine preserves, sugar, vinegar, Worcestershire sauce and red pepper flakes in small microwavable bowl. Microwave on HIGH 45 seconds; stir. Microwave 15 seconds or until melted. Reserve ½ cup glaze in refrigerator. Pour remaining glaze mixture over meatballs; stir until well coated. Cover; cook on LOW 5 hours or on HIGH 2½ hours.

3 Stir in reserved glaze and ginger, if desired. Cook, uncovered, on HIGH 15 to 20 minutes or until thickened slightly, stirring occasionally.

Quick and Easy Stuffed Mushrooms

MAKES 8 SERVINGS

20 large white mushrooms, stems removed and reserved
1 tablespoon oil
¼ cup finely chopped celery
¼ cup finely chopped onion
1 clove garlic, minced

¼ cup whole wheat dry bread crumbs
1 teaspoon Worcestershire sauce
½ teaspoon dried marjoram
⅛ teaspoon ground red pepper
1½ cups vegetable broth

1 Coat inside of **CROCK-POT®** slow cooker with nonstick cooking spray. Brush mushroom caps with oil; set aside. Finely chop mushroom stems.

2 Spray large skillet with cooking spray; heat over medium heat. Add mushroom stems, celery, onion and garlic; cook and stir 5 minutes or until onion is tender. Remove to large bowl. Stir in bread crumbs, Worcestershire sauce, marjoram and ground red pepper.

3 Fill mushroom caps evenly with mixture, pressing down firmly. Pour broth into **CROCK-POT®** slow cooker. Arrange stuffed mushrooms in bottom. Cover; cook on HIGH 3 hours or until mushrooms are tender. To serve, remove mushrooms with slotted spoon; discard cooking liquid.

Note

Mushrooms can be stuffed up to 1 day ahead. Refrigerate filled mushroom caps, covered, until ready to cook.

Pulled Pork Sliders with Cola Barbecue Sauce

MAKES 16 SLIDERS

1 teaspoon vegetable oil
1 boneless pork shoulder roast
   (3 pounds)*
1 cup cola
¼ cup tomato paste
2 tablespoons packed brown sugar
2 teaspoons Worcestershire sauce
2 teaspoons spicy brown mustard

Hot pepper sauce
Salt
16 dinner rolls or potato rolls, split
   Sliced pickles (optional)

*Unless you have a 5-, 6- or 7-quart
CROCK-POT® slow cooker, cut any roast
larger than 2½ pounds in half so it cooks
completely.*

1 Heat oil in large skillet over medium-high heat. Add pork; cook 5 to 7 minutes or until browned on all sides. Remove to **CROCK-POT®** slow cooker. Pour cola over pork. Cover; cook on LOW 7½ to 8 hours or on HIGH 3½ to 4 hours.

2 Turn off heat. Remove pork to large cutting board; shred with two forks. Let cooking liquid stand 5 minutes. Skim off and discard fat. Whisk tomato paste, brown sugar, Worcestershire sauce and mustard into cooking liquid. Cover; cook on HIGH 15 minutes or until thickened.

3 Stir shredded pork back into **CROCK-POT®** slow cooker. Season with hot pepper sauce and salt. Serve on rolls. Top with pickles, if desired.

Barbecue Beef Sliders

MAKES 6 SERVINGS

- 1 tablespoon packed light brown sugar
- 1 teaspoon ground cumin
- 1 teaspoon chili powder
- 1 teaspoon paprika
- ½ teaspoon salt
- ¼ teaspoon ground red pepper
- 3 pounds beef short ribs

- ½ cup plus 2 tablespoons barbecue sauce, divided
- ¼ cup water
- 12 slider rolls
- ¾ cup prepared coleslaw
- 12 bread and butter pickle chips

1 Coat inside of **CROCK-POT®** slow cooker with nonstick cooking spray. Combine brown sugar, cumin, chili powder, paprika, salt and ground red pepper in small bowl; toss to blend. Rub over ribs; remove to **CROCK-POT®** slow cooker. Pour in ½ cup barbecue sauce and water; turn to coat ribs.

2 Cover; cook on LOW 7 to 8 hours or on HIGH 4 to 4½ hours or until ribs are very tender and meat shreds easily. Remove ribs to large cutting board. Discard bones; remove meat to large bowl. Shred meat using two forks, discarding any large pieces of fat. Stir in remaining 2 tablespoons barbecue sauce and 2 tablespoons liquid from **CROCK-POT®** slow cooker.

3 Arrange bottom half of rolls on platter or work surface. Top each with ¼ cup beef mixture, 1 tablespoon coleslaw and 1 pickle chip. Place roll tops on each.

Tip

It makes cleanup easier when you coat the inside of the **CROCK-POT®** slow cooker with nonstick cooking spray before adding the ingredients. To easily remove any sticky barbecue sauce residue, soak the stoneware in hot soapy water, then scrub it with a plastic or nylon scrubber. Don't use steel wool.

Honey-Glazed Chicken Wings

MAKES 6 SERVINGS

3 tablespoons vegetable oil, divided
3 pounds chicken wings
1 cup honey
½ cup soy sauce
2 tablespoons tomato paste

2 teaspoons water
1 clove garlic, minced
1 teaspoon sugar
1 teaspoon black pepper

1 Heat 1½ tablespoons oil in large skillet over medium heat. Add wings in batches; cook 1 to 2 minutes on each side or until browned. Remove to **CROCK-POT**® slow cooker using slotted spoon.

2 Combine remaining 1½ tablespoons oil, honey, soy sauce, tomato paste, water, garlic, sugar and pepper in medium bowl; stir to blend. Pour sauce over wings. Cover; cook on LOW 6 to 8 hours or on HIGH 3 to 4 hours.

Chipotle Black Bean and Cheese Dip

MAKES 4 CUPS

1 can (about 15 ounces) refried black beans
1 can (about 15 ounces) black beans, rinsed and drained
1 cup salsa
4 ounces 2% milk pasteurized process cheese product, cut into cubes

2 green onions, sliced
1 tablespoon minced canned chipotle peppers in adobo sauce
⅓ cup chopped fresh cilantro (optional)
Multi-grain tortilla chips

1 Coat inside of 2-quart **CROCK-POT**® slow cooker with nonstick cooking spray. Combine beans, salsa, cheese product, green onions and chipotle peppers in **CROCK-POT**® slow cooker.

2 Cover; cook on LOW 2½ to 3 hours or on HIGH 1¼ to 1½ hours or until heated through. Stir in cilantro, if desired. Serve with tortilla chips.

Stuffed Baby Bell Peppers

MAKES 6 SERVINGS

1 tablespoon olive oil
½ medium onion, chopped
½ pound ground beef
½ cup cooked rice
3 tablespoons chopped fresh Italian parsley
2 tablespoons lemon juice

1 tablespoon dried dill weed
1 tablespoon tomato paste, divided
½ teaspoon salt
⅛ teaspoon black pepper
¼ cup beef broth
1 bag yellow and red baby bell peppers (about 2 dozen)

1 Heat oil in medium skillet over medium heat. Add onion; cook and stir 5 minutes or until translucent.

2 Add beef; brown 6 to 8 minutes, stirring to break up meat. Drain fat. Remove to large bowl. Add rice, parsley, lemon juice, dill, 1½ teaspoons tomato paste, salt and black pepper; mix well. Whisk broth and remaining 1½ teaspoons tomato paste in small bowl.

3 Cut lengthwise slit down side of each bell pepper; run under cold water to wash out seeds. Fill each bell pepper with 2 to 3 teaspoons meat mixture. Place filled bell peppers in **CROCK-POT®** slow cooker, filling side up. Add broth mixture. Cover; cook on LOW 5 hours or on HIGH 2½ hours.

Thai Coconut Chicken Meatballs

MAKES 4 TO 5 SERVINGS

1 pound ground chicken
2 green onions, chopped
1 clove garlic, minced
2 teaspoons toasted sesame oil
2 teaspoons mirin
1 teaspoon fish sauce
½ cup unsweetened canned coconut milk

¼ cup chicken broth
2 teaspoons packed brown sugar
1 teaspoon Thai red curry paste
1 tablespoon canola oil
2 teaspoons lime juice
2 tablespoons water
1 tablespoon cornstarch

1 Combine chicken, green onions, garlic, sesame oil, mirin and fish sauce in large bowl; mix well. Shape chicken mixture into 1½-inch meatballs. Combine coconut milk, broth, brown sugar and curry paste in small bowl; stir to blend.

2 Heat canola oil in large skillet over medium-high heat. Working in batches, brown meatballs on all sides. Remove to **CROCK-POT**® slow cooker. Add coconut milk mixture. Cover; cook on HIGH 3½ to 4 hours. Remove meatballs to large bowl. Stir lime juice into **CROCK-POT**® slow cooker.

3 Stir water into cornstarch in small bowl until smooth; whisk into sauce in **CROCK-POT**® slow cooker. Add meatballs; turn to coat. Cook, uncovered, on HIGH 10 to 15 minutes or until sauce is slightly thickened.

Tip

Meatballs that are of equal size will be done at the same time. To ensure your meatballs are the same size, pat seasoned ground meat into an even rectangle and then slice into even rows and columns. Roll each portion into a smooth ball.

Sauced Little Smokies

MAKES 24 SERVINGS

1 bottle (14 ounces) barbecue sauce
¾ cup grape jelly
½ cup packed brown sugar
½ cup ketchup

1 tablespoon prepared mustard
1 teaspoon Worcestershire sauce
3 packages (14 to 16 ounces *each*) miniature cocktail franks

Stir barbecue sauce, jelly, brown sugar, ketchup, mustard and Worcestershire sauce into **CROCK-POT**® slow cooker until combined. Add cocktail franks; stir to coat. Cover; cook on LOW 3 to 4 hours or on HIGH 1 to 2 hours.

Nacho Dip

MAKES 10 CUPS

1 tablespoon vegetable oil
1 onion, chopped
2 pounds ground beef
2 cans (about 15 ounces *each*) black beans, rinsed and drained
1 can (28 ounces) diced tomatoes
1 can (about 15 ounces) refried beans

1 can (about 15 ounces) cream-style corn
3 cloves garlic, minced
1 package (1¼ ounces) taco seasoning mix
Tortilla chips
Queso blanco

1 Heat oil in large skillet over medium-high heat. Add onion; cook 2 to 3 minutes or until translucent. Add beef; brown 6 to 8 minutes, stirring to break up meat. Drain fat.

2 Stir beef mixture, black beans, tomatoes, refried beans, corn, garlic and taco seasoning mix into **CROCK-POT**® slow cooker. Cover; cook on LOW 5 to 6 hours or on HIGH 2½ to 3 hours. Serve on tortilla chips. Sprinkle with queso blanco.

Channa Chat (Indian-Spiced Snack Mix)

MAKES 6 TO 8 SERVINGS

2 teaspoons canola oil

1 medium onion, finely chopped and divided

2 cloves garlic, minced

2 cans (about 15 ounces *each*) chickpeas, rinsed and drained

¼ cup vegetable broth

2 teaspoons tomato paste

¼ teaspoon ground cinnamon

¼ teaspoon ground cumin

¼ teaspoon black pepper

1 whole bay leaf

½ cup balsamic vinegar

1 tablespoon packed brown sugar

1 plum tomato, chopped

½ jalapeño pepper, seeded and minced *or* ¼ teaspoon ground red pepper (optional)*

3 tablespoons chopped fresh cilantro (optional)

*Jalapeño peppers can sting and irritate the skin, so wear rubber gloves when handling peppers and do not touch your eyes.

1 Heat oil in small skillet over medium-high heat. Add half of onion and garlic. Reduce heat to medium; cook and stir 2 minutes or until soft. Remove to **CROCK-POT**® slow cooker. Stir in chickpeas, broth, tomato paste, cinnamon, cumin, black pepper and bay leaf. Cover; cook on LOW 6 hours or on HIGH 3 hours. Remove and discard bay leaf.

2 Remove chickpea mixture with slotted spoon to large bowl. Cool 15 minutes. Meanwhile, combine vinegar and brown sugar in small saucepan; cook and stir over medium-low heat until vinegar is reduced by half and mixture becomes syrupy.

3 Add tomato, remaining onion and jalapeño pepper, if desired, to chickpeas; toss to combine. Drizzle with balsamic syrup and garnish with cilantro.

Creamy Artichoke-Parmesan Dip

MAKES 1½ CUPS

1 teaspoon olive oil

2 tablespoons finely chopped onion

½ can (about 7 ounces) artichoke hearts, drained and chopped

½ cup half-and-half

½ cup (2 ounces) mozzarella cheese

⅓ cup grated Parmesan cheese

⅓ cup mayonnaise

⅛ teaspoon dried oregano

⅛ teaspoon garlic powder

4 pita bread rounds, toasted and cut into wedges

Fresh vegetables (optional)

1 Heat oil in medium saucepan over medium heat. Add onion; cook and stir 3 to 5 minutes or until tender. Add artichokes, half-and-half, cheeses, mayonnaise, oregano and garlic powder; cook and stir 5 to 7 minutes or until mixture comes to a boil.

2 Coat inside of **CROCK-POT®** "No Dial" food warmer with nonstick cooking spray. Fill with warm dip. Serve with pita wedges and vegetables, if desired.

Barley "Caviar"

MAKES 8 APPETIZERS

4½ cups water
¾ cup uncooked pearl barley
1 teaspoon salt, divided
½ cup sliced pimiento-stuffed olives
½ cup finely chopped red bell pepper
1 stalk celery, chopped
1 large shallot, finely chopped
1 jalapeño pepper, minced*

2 tablespoons plus 1 teaspoon olive oil
4 teaspoons white wine vinegar
¼ teaspoon ground cumin
⅛ teaspoon black pepper
8 leaves endive or Bibb lettuce

Jalapeño peppers can sting and irritate the skin, so wear rubber gloves when handling peppers and do not touch your eyes.

1 Add water, barley and ½ teaspoon salt to **CROCK-POT**® slow cooker. Cover; cook on LOW 4 to 5 hours or on HIGH 2½ to 3 hours or until barley is tender and liquid is absorbed.

2 Turn off heat. Stir in olives, bell pepper, celery, shallot and jalapeño pepper. Combine oil, vinegar, remaining ½ teaspoon salt, cumin and black pepper in small bowl; stir to blend. Pour over barley mixture in **CROCK-POT**® slow cooker; stir gently to coat. Let stand 10 minutes. To serve, spoon barley mixture evenly into endive leaves.

Party Mix

MAKES 10 CUPS

3 cups rice squares cereal
2 cups toasted oat ring cereal
2 cups wheat squares cereal
1 cup pistachio nuts or peanuts
1 cup thin pretzel sticks
½ cup (1 stick) butter, melted

1 tablespoon Worcestershire sauce
1 teaspoon seasoned salt
½ teaspoon garlic powder
⅛ teaspoon ground red pepper (optional)

1 Combine cereal, nuts and pretzels in **CROCK-POT**® slow cooker.

2 Combine butter, Worcestershire sauce, seasoned salt, garlic powder and ground red pepper, if desired, in small bowl; stir to blend. Pour over cereal mixture in **CROCK-POT**® slow cooker; toss lightly to coat.

3 Cover; cook on LOW 3 hours, stirring well every 30 minutes. Cook, uncovered, on LOW 30 minutes. Store in airtight container.

Spiced Beer Fondue

MAKES 1½ CUPS

2 tablespoons butter

2 tablespoons all-purpose flour

1 can (8 ounces) light-colored beer, such as pale ale or lager

½ cup half-and-half

1 cup (4 ounces) shredded smoked gouda cheese

2 teaspoons coarse grain mustard

1 teaspoon Worcestershire sauce

⅛ teaspoon salt

⅛ teaspoon ground red pepper

Dash ground nutmeg (optional)

Apple slices and cooked potato wedges

1 Melt butter in medium saucepan over medium heat. Sprinkle with flour; whisk until smooth. Stir in beer and half-and-half; bring to a boil. Cook and stir 2 minutes. Stir in cheese, mustard, Worcestershire sauce, salt and ground red pepper; cook and stir until cheese is melted.

2 Coat inside of **CROCK-POT**® "No-Dial" food warmer with nonstick cooking spray. Fill with warm fondue. Sprinkle with nutmeg, if desired. Serve with apples and potatoes.

Salsa-Style Wings

MAKES 4 SERVINGS

2 tablespoons vegetable oil

1½ pounds chicken wings (about 18 wings)

2 cups salsa

¼ cup packed brown sugar

Sprigs fresh cilantro (optional)

1 Heat oil in large skillet over medium-high heat. Add wings in batches; cook 3 to 4 minutes or until browned on all sides. Remove to **CROCK-POT**® slow cooker.

2 Combine salsa and brown sugar in medium bowl; stir to blend. Pour over wings. Cover; cook on LOW 5 to 6 hours or on HIGH 2 to 3 hours. Serve with salsa mixture. Garnish with cilantro.

Soups and Stews

Chicken Orzo Soup

MAKES 6 TO 8 SERVINGS

- 1 tablespoon vegetable oil
- 1 onion, diced
- 1 bulb fennel, quartered, cored, thinly sliced, tops removed and fronds reserved for garnish
- 2 teaspoons minced garlic
- 8 cups chicken broth

- 2 boneless, skinless chicken breasts (8 ounces *each*)
- 2 carrots, peeled and thinly sliced
- 2 sprigs fresh thyme
- 1 whole bay leaf
  Salt and black pepper
- ½ cup uncooked orzo

1 Heat oil in large skillet over medium heat. Add onion and sliced fennel; cook 8 minutes or until tender. Add garlic; cook and stir 1 minute. Remove to **CROCK-POT**® slow cooker. Add broth, chicken, carrots, thyme, bay leaf, salt and pepper. Cover; cook on HIGH 2 to 3 hours.

2 Remove chicken to large cutting board; shred with two forks. Add orzo to **CROCK-POT**® slow cooker. Cover; cook on HIGH 30 minutes. Stir shredded chicken back into **CROCK-POT**® slow cooker. Remove and discard thyme sprigs and bay leaf. Garnish each serving with fennel fronds.

Chicken and Mushroom Stew

MAKES 6 SERVINGS

4 tablespoons vegetable oil, divided
2 medium leeks (white and light green parts only), halved lengthwise and thinly sliced crosswise
1 carrot, cut into 1-inch pieces
1 stalk celery, diced
6 boneless, skinless chicken thighs (about 2 pounds)
  Salt and black pepper
12 ounces cremini mushrooms, quartered

1 ounce dried porcini mushrooms, rehydrated in 1½ cups hot water and chopped, soaking liquid strained and reserved
1 teaspoon minced garlic
1 sprig fresh thyme
1 whole bay leaf
¼ cup all-purpose flour
½ cup dry white wine
1 cup chicken broth

1 Heat 1 tablespoon oil in large skillet over medium heat. Add leeks; cook 8 minutes or until softened. Remove to **CROCK-POT®** slow cooker. Add carrot and celery.

2 Heat 1 tablespoon oil in same skillet over medium-high heat. Season chicken with salt and pepper. Add chicken in batches; cook 8 minutes or until browned on both sides. Remove to **CROCK-POT®** slow cooker.

3 Heat remaining 2 tablespoons oil in same skillet. Add cremini mushrooms; cook 7 minutes or until mushrooms have released their liquid and started to brown. Add porcini mushrooms, garlic, thyme, bay leaf and flour; cook and stir 1 minute. Add wine; cook and stir until evaporated, scraping up any browned bits from bottom of skillet. Add reserved soaking liquid and broth; bring to a simmer. Pour mixture into **CROCK-POT®** slow cooker.

4 Cover; cook on HIGH 2 to 3 hours. Remove and discard thyme sprig and bay leaf before serving.

Simmered Split Pea Soup

MAKES 6 SERVINGS

3 cans (about 14 ounces *each*) chicken
   broth
1 package (16 ounces) dried split peas,
   rinsed and sorted
8 slices bacon, crisp-cooked, chopped
   and divided
1 onion, chopped

2 carrots, chopped
1 teaspoon black pepper
½ teaspoon dried thyme
1 whole bay leaf

Combine broth, peas, half of bacon, onion, carrots, pepper, thyme and bay leaf in **CROCK-POT**® slow cooker. Cover; cook on LOW 6 to 8 hours. Remove and discard bay leaf. Garnish with remaining half of bacon.

Broccoli Cheddar Soup

MAKES 6 SERVINGS

3 tablespoons butter
1 medium onion, chopped
3 tablespoons all-purpose flour
¼ teaspoon ground nutmeg
¼ teaspoon black pepper
4 cups vegetable broth
1 large bunch broccoli, chopped

1 medium red potato, peeled and
   chopped
1 teaspoon salt
1 whole bay leaf
1½ cups (6 ounces) shredded Cheddar
   cheese, plus additional for garnish
½ cup whipping cream

1 Melt butter in medium saucepan over medium heat. Add onion; cook and stir 6 minutes or until softened. Add flour, nutmeg and pepper; cook and stir 1 minute. Remove to **CROCK-POT**® slow cooker. Stir in broth, broccoli, potato, salt and bay leaf.

2 Cover; cook on HIGH 3 hours. Remove and discard bay leaf. Add soup in batches to food processor or blender; purée until desired consistency. Pour soup back into **CROCK-POT**® slow cooker. Stir in 1½ cups cheese and cream until cheese is melted. Garnish with additional cheese.

Chicken and Vegetable Soup

MAKES 10 SERVINGS

1 tablespoon olive oil

2 medium parsnips, cut into ½-inch pieces

2 medium carrots, cut into ½-inch pieces

2 medium onions, chopped

2 stalks celery, cut into ½-inch pieces

1 whole chicken (3 to 3½ pounds)

4 cups chicken broth

10 sprigs fresh Italian parsley

4 sprigs fresh thyme *or* ½ teaspoon dried thyme

1 Coat inside of **CROCK-POT**® slow cooker with nonstick cooking spray. Heat oil in large skillet over medium-high heat. Add parsnips, carrots, onions and celery; cook and stir 5 minutes or until vegetables are softened. Remove parsnip mixture to **CROCK-POT**® slow cooker. Add chicken, broth, parsley and thyme.

2 Cover; cook on LOW 6 to 7 hours. Remove chicken to large cutting board; let stand 10 minutes. Remove and discard skin and bones from chicken. Shred chicken using two forks. Stir shredded chicken back into **CROCK-POT**® slow cooker.

Beef and Beet Borscht

MAKES 6 TO 8 SERVINGS

6 slices bacon

1 boneless beef chuck roast (1½ pounds), trimmed and cut into ½-inch pieces

1 medium onion, chopped

4 cloves garlic, minced

4 medium beets, peeled and cut into ½-inch pieces

2 large carrots, sliced

3 cups beef broth

6 sprigs fresh dill

3 tablespoons honey

3 tablespoons red wine vinegar

2 whole bay leaves

3 cups shredded green cabbage

1 Heat large skillet over medium heat. Add bacon; cook and stir until crisp. Remove to paper towel-lined plate using slotted spoon; crumble.

2 Return skillet to medium-high heat. Add beef; cook 5 minutes or until browned. Remove beef to **CROCK-POT**® slow cooker.

3 Pour off all but 1 tablespoon drippings from skillet. Add onion and garlic; cook 4 minutes or until onion is softened. Remove onion mixture to **CROCK-POT**® slow cooker. Stir in bacon, beets, carrots, broth, dill, honey, vinegar and bay leaves.

4 Cover; cook on LOW 5 to 6 hours. Stir in cabbage. Cover; cook on LOW 30 minutes. Remove and discard bay leaves before serving.

Butternut Squash, Chickpea and Lentil Stew

MAKES 6 SERVINGS

2 cups peeled and diced butternut squash (½-inch pieces)

2 cups vegetable broth

1 can (about 15 ounces) chickpeas, rinsed and drained

1 can (about 14 ounces) fire-roasted diced tomatoes

1 cup chopped sweet onion

¾ cup dried brown lentils, rinsed and sorted

2 teaspoons ground cumin

¾ teaspoon salt

Olive oil (optional)

Sprigs fresh thyme (optional)

Coat inside of **CROCK-POT®** slow cooker with nonstick cooking spray. Combine squash, broth, chickpeas, tomatoes, onion, lentils, cumin and salt in **CROCK-POT®** slow cooker. Cover; cook on LOW 8 to 9 hours or on HIGH 4 to 4½ hours or until squash and lentils are tender. Ladle into shallow bowls. Drizzle with oil, if desired. Garnish with thyme.

Classic Beef Stew

MAKES 8 SERVINGS

2½ pounds cubed beef stew meat

¼ cup all-purpose flour

2 tablespoons olive oil, divided

3 cups beef broth

16 baby carrots

8 fingerling potatoes, halved crosswise

1 medium onion, chopped

1 ounce dried oyster mushrooms, chopped

2 teaspoons garlic powder

1 teaspoon dried basil

1 teaspoon dried oregano

½ teaspoon dried rosemary

½ teaspoon dried marjoram

½ teaspoon dried sage

½ teaspoon dried thyme

Salt and black pepper (optional)

Chopped fresh Italian parsley (optional)

1 Combine beef and flour in large resealable food storage bag; toss to coat. Heat 1 tablespoon oil in large skillet over medium-high heat. Add half of beef; cook and stir 4 minutes or until browned. Remove to **CROCK-POT**® slow cooker. Repeat with remaining oil and beef.

2 Add broth, carrots, potatoes, onion, mushrooms, garlic powder, basil, oregano, rosemary, marjoram, sage and thyme to **CROCK-POT**® slow cooker; stir to blend.

3 Cover; cook on LOW 10 to 12 hours or on HIGH 5 to 6 hours. Season with salt and pepper, if desired. Garnish with parsley.

Italian Hillside Garden Soup

MAKES 6 SERVINGS

1 tablespoon olive oil

1 cup chopped green bell pepper

1 cup chopped onion

½ cup sliced celery

1 can (about 14 ounces) diced tomatoes with basil, garlic and oregano

1 can (about 15 ounces) navy beans, rinsed and drained

1 medium zucchini, chopped

1 cup frozen cut green beans

2 cans (about 14 ounces *each*) chicken broth

¼ teaspoon garlic powder

1 package (9 ounces) refrigerated sausage- or cheese-filled tortellini pasta

3 tablespoons chopped fresh basil

Grated Asiago or Parmesan cheese (optional)

1 Heat oil in large skillet over medium-high heat. Add bell pepper, onion and celery; cook and stir 4 minutes or until onion is translucent. Remove to **CROCK-POT**® slow cooker.

2 Add tomatoes, navy beans, zucchini, green beans, broth and garlic powder. Cover; cook on LOW 7 hours or on HIGH 3½ hours.

3 Add tortellini. Cover; cook on HIGH 20 to 25 minutes or until pasta is tender. Stir in basil. Garnish with cheese.

Tip

Cooking times are guidelines. **CROCK-POT**® slow cookers, just like ovens, cook differently depending on a variety of factors, including capacity and altitude.

Wild Mushroom Beef Stew

MAKES 8 SERVINGS

1½ to 2 pounds cubed beef stew meat	4 shiitake mushrooms, sliced
2 tablespoons all-purpose flour	1 small white onion, chopped
½ teaspoon salt	1 medium stalk celery, sliced
½ teaspoon black pepper	1 clove garlic, minced
2 medium potatoes, chopped	1 teaspoon paprika
1½ cups beef broth	1 teaspoon Worcestershire sauce
2 medium carrots, sliced	1 whole bay leaf

Place beef in **CROCK-POT**® slow cooker. Combine flour, salt and pepper in small bowl; stir to blend. Place flour mixture in **CROCK-POT**® slow cooker; toss to coat beef. Add potatoes, broth, carrots, mushrooms, onion, celery, garlic, paprika, Worcestershire sauce and bay leaf. Cover; cook on LOW 10 to 12 hours or on HIGH 4 to 6 hours. Remove and discard bay leaf. Stir to blend just before serving.

Note

This classic beef stew is given a twist with the addition of flavorful shiitake mushrooms. If shiitake mushrooms are unavailable in your local grocery store, you can substitute other mushrooms of your choice. For extra punch, add a few dried porcini mushrooms to the stew.

Tip

You may double the amount of meat, mushrooms, carrots, potatoes, onion and celery for a 5-, 6- or 7-quart **CROCK-POT**® slow cooker.

Lamb and Chickpea Stew

MAKES 6 SERVINGS

1 pound lamb stew meat
2 teaspoons salt, divided
2 tablespoons vegetable oil, divided
1 large onion, chopped
1 tablespoon minced garlic
1½ teaspoons ground cumin
1 teaspoon ground turmeric
1 teaspoon ground coriander
1 teaspoon ground cinnamon
¼ teaspoon black pepper

2 cups chicken broth
1 cup diced canned tomatoes, drained
1 cup dried chickpeas, rinsed and sorted
½ cup chopped dried apricots
¼ cup chopped fresh Italian parsley
2 tablespoons honey
2 tablespoons lemon juice
Hot cooked couscous

1 Season lamb with 1 teaspoon salt. Heat 1 tablespoon oil in large skillet over medium-high heat. Add lamb; cook and stir 8 minutes or until browned on all sides. Remove to **CROCK-POT**® slow cooker.

2 Heat remaining 1 tablespoon oil in same skillet over medium heat. Add onion; cook and stir 6 minutes or until softened. Add garlic, remaining 1 teaspoon salt, cumin, turmeric, coriander, cinnamon and pepper; cook and stir 1 minute. Add broth and tomatoes; cook and stir 5 minutes, scraping up any brown bits from bottom of skillet. Remove to **CROCK-POT**® slow cooker. Stir in chickpeas.

3 Cover; cook on LOW 7 hours. Stir in apricots. Cover; cook on LOW 1 hour. Turn off heat. Let stand 10 minutes. Skim off and discard fat. Stir in parsley, honey and lemon juice. Serve over couscous.

Cauliflower Soup

MAKES 8 SERVINGS

2 heads cauliflower, cut into small florets
8 cups chicken broth
¾ cup chopped celery
¾ cup chopped onion

2 teaspoons salt
2 teaspoons black pepper
2 cups milk or whipping cream
1 teaspoon Worcestershire sauce

1 Combine cauliflower, broth, celery, onion, salt and pepper in **CROCK-POT®** slow cooker. Cover; cook on LOW 7 to 8 hours or on HIGH 3 to 4 hours.

2 Pour cauliflower mixture into food processor or blender; process until smooth. Add milk and Worcestershire sauce; process until blended. Pour soup back into **CROCK-POT®** slow cooker. Cover; cook on HIGH 15 to 20 minutes or until heated through.

Potato Cheddar Soup

MAKES 6 SERVINGS

2 pounds new red potatoes, cut into ½-inch cubes
3 cups vegetable broth
¾ cup coarsely chopped carrots
1 medium onion, coarsely chopped

½ teaspoon salt
1 cup half-and-half
¼ teaspoon black pepper
2 cups (8 ounces) shredded Cheddar cheese

1 Place potatoes, broth, carrots, onion and salt in **CROCK-POT®** slow cooker. Cover; cook on LOW 6 to 7 hours or on HIGH 3 to 3½ hours or until vegetables are tender.

2 Stir in half-and-half and pepper. Cover; cook on HIGH 15 minutes. Turn off heat. Remove lid; let stand 5 minutes. Stir in cheese until melted.

Serving Suggestion

Try this soup topped with croutons.

Pozole Rojo

MAKES 8 SERVINGS

4 dried ancho chiles, stemmed and seeded

3 dried guajillo chiles, stemmed and seeded*

2 cups boiling water

2½ pounds boneless pork shoulder, trimmed and cut in half

3 teaspoons salt, divided

1 tablespoon vegetable oil

2 medium onions, chopped

1½ tablespoons minced garlic

2 teaspoons ground cumin

2 teaspoons Mexican oregano**

4 cups chicken broth

2 cans (30 ounces *each*) white hominy, rinsed and drained

Optional toppings: sliced radishes, lime wedges, sliced romaine lettuce, chopped onion, tortilla chips and/or diced avocado

Guajillo chiles can be found in the ethnic section of large supermarkets.

**Mexican oregano has a stronger flavor than regular oregano. It can be found in the spices and seasonings section of most large supermarkets.*

1 Place ancho and guajillo chiles in medium bowl; pour boiling water over top. Weigh down chiles with small plate or bowl; soak 30 minutes.

2 Meanwhile, season pork with 1 teaspoon salt. Heat oil in large skillet over medium-high heat. Add pork; cook 8 to 10 minutes or until browned on all sides. Remove to **CROCK-POT®** slow cooker.

3 Heat same skillet over medium heat. Add onions; cook 6 minutes or until softened. Add garlic, cumin, oregano and remaining 2 teaspoons salt; cook and stir 1 minute. Stir in broth; bring to a simmer, scraping up any browned bits from bottom of skillet. Pour over pork in **CROCK-POT®** slow cooker.

4 Place softened chiles and soaking liquid in food processor or blender; process until smooth. Pour through fine-mesh sieve into medium bowl, pressing with spoon to extract liquid. Discard solids. Stir mixture into **CROCK-POT®** slow cooker.

5 Cover; cook on LOW 5 hours. Stir in hominy. Cover; cook on LOW 1 hour. Turn off heat. Let stand 10 to 15 minutes. Skim off fat and discard. Remove pork to large cutting board; shred with two forks. Ladle hominy mixture into bowls; top each serving with pork and desired toppings.

Ghormeh Sabzi (Persian Green Stew)

MAKES 6 SERVINGS

1½ pounds boneless leg of lamb,
    cut into 1-inch cubes

1 teaspoon ground turmeric

¾ teaspoon salt

½ teaspoon curry powder

½ teaspoon ground black pepper,
    divided

2 tablespoons olive oil, divided

2 medium onions, chopped

1 bag (5 ounces) baby spinach,
    chopped

2 cups chopped fresh Italian parsley

1 cup chopped fresh cilantro

6 green onions, green part only,
    chopped

1½ cups beef broth

1 can (about 15 ounces) cannellini
    beans, rinsed and drained

2 tablespoons fresh lime juice

3 cups hot cooked basmati rice

    Naan bread (optional)

1 Coat inside of **CROCK-POT**® slow cooker with nonstick cooking spray.

2 Combine lamb, turmeric, salt, curry powder and pepper in large bowl. Heat 1 tablespoon oil in large skillet over medium-high heat. Add half of lamb; cook and stir 4 minutes or until browned. Remove to **CROCK-POT**® slow cooker. Repeat with remaining lamb. Add onions and remaining 1 tablespoon oil to skillet; cook 6 to 7 minutes or until onions are starting to brown. Stir in spinach, parsley, cilantro and green onions; cook and stir 2 minutes or until wilted. Add to lamb in **CROCK-POT**® slow cooker; pour broth over all.

3 Cover; cook on LOW 8 hours or on HIGH 4 hours. Add beans. Cover; cook on HIGH 30 minutes. Turn off heat. Stir in lime juice. Serve over rice with naan, if desired.

Summer Vegetable Stew

MAKES 4 SERVINGS

1 cup vegetable broth

1 can (about 15 ounces) chickpeas, rinsed and drained

1 medium zucchini, cut into ½-inch pieces

1 summer squash, cut into ½-inch pieces

4 large plum tomatoes, cut into ½-inch pieces

1 cup frozen corn

½ to 1 teaspoon dried rosemary

¼ cup grated Asiago or Parmesan cheese

1 tablespoon chopped fresh Italian parsley

Combine broth, chickpeas, zucchini, squash, tomatoes, corn and rosemary in **CROCK-POT®** slow cooker; stir to blend. Cover; cook on LOW 8 hours or on HIGH 5 hours. Top each serving evenly with cheese and parsley.

Tip

Layer the ingredients in the order given in this recipe to ensure they will cook properly.

Hearty Lentil Stew

MAKES 6 SERVINGS

1 cup dried lentils, rinsed and sorted

1 package (16 ounces) frozen green beans

2 cups cauliflower florets

1 cup chopped onion

1 cup baby carrots, cut into halves crosswise

3 cups vegetable broth

2 teaspoons ground cumin

¾ teaspoon ground ginger

1 can (15 ounces) chunky tomato sauce with garlic and herbs

½ cup salted peanuts

1 Layer lentils, beans, cauliflower, onion and carrots in **CROCK-POT®** slow cooker. Combine broth, cumin and ginger in large bowl; stir to blend. Pour over vegetables in **CROCK-POT®** slow cooker.

2 Cover; cook on LOW 9 to 11 hours. Stir in tomato sauce. Cover; cook on LOW 10 minutes or until heated through. Sprinkle each serving evenly with peanuts.

Chicken Tortilla Soup

MAKES 4 TO 6 SERVINGS

2 cans (about 14 ounces *each*) diced
  tomatoes

1 can (4 ounces) diced mild green
  chiles, drained

1 cup chicken broth, divided

1 yellow onion, diced

2 cloves garlic, minced

1 teaspoon ground cumin

4 boneless, skinless chicken thighs

Salt and black pepper

4 corn tortillas, sliced into ¼-inch strips

2 tablespoons chopped fresh cilantro

½ cup (2 ounces) shredded Monterey
  Jack cheese

1 avocado, diced and tossed with lime
  juice

Lime juice

1 Combine tomatoes, chiles, ½ cup broth, onion, garlic and cumin in **CROCK-POT**® slow cooker; stir to blend. Add chicken. Cover; cook on LOW 6 hours or on HIGH 3 hours.

2 Remove chicken to large cutting board; shred with two forks. Stir shredded chicken, salt, pepper and additional ½ cup broth, if necessary, into **CROCK-POT**® slow cooker.

3 Just before serving, add tortillas and cilantro to **CROCK-POT**® slow cooker; stir to blend. Top each serving with cheese, avocado and lime juice.

Shrimp and Okra Gumbo

MAKES 6 SERVINGS

1 tablespoon olive oil

8 ounces kielbasa, halved lengthwise and cut into ¼-inch-thick half slices

1 green bell pepper, chopped

1 medium onion, chopped

3 stalks celery, cut into ¼-inch slices

6 green onions, chopped

4 cloves garlic, minced

1 cup chicken broth

1 can (about 14 ounces) diced tomatoes

1 teaspoon Cajun seasoning

½ teaspoon dried thyme

1 pound large raw shrimp, peeled and deveined (with tails on)

2 cups frozen cut okra, thawed

1 Coat inside of **CROCK-POT®** slow cooker with nonstick cooking spray. Heat oil in large skillet over medium-high heat. Add kielbasa; cook and stir 4 minutes or until browned. Remove to **CROCK-POT®** slow cooker using slotted spoon.

2 Return skillet to medium-high heat. Add bell pepper, chopped onion, celery, green onions and garlic; cook and stir 5 to 6 minutes or until vegetables are crisp-tender. Remove to **CROCK-POT®** slow cooker. Stir in broth, tomatoes, Cajun seasoning and thyme.

3 Cover; cook on LOW 4 hours. Stir in shrimp and okra. Cover; cook on LOW 30 to 35 minutes.

Asian Sweet Potato and Corn Stew

MAKES 6 SERVINGS

1 tablespoon vegetable oil

1 large onion, chopped

2 tablespoons peeled minced fresh ginger

½ jalapeño or serrano pepper, seeded and minced*

2 cloves garlic, minced

1 cup frozen corn, thawed

2 teaspoons curry powder

1 can (13½ ounces) unsweetened coconut milk

1 teaspoon cornstarch

4 sweet potatoes, cut into ¾-inch cubes

1 can (about 14 ounces) vegetable broth

1 tablespoon soy sauce

Hot cooked jasmine or long grain rice

Optional toppings: chopped fresh cilantro, coarsely chopped dry-roasted peanuts and/or chopped green onions

Jalapeño and serrano peppers can sting and irritate the skin, so wear rubber gloves when handling peppers and do not touch your eyes.

1 Heat oil in large skillet over medium heat. Add onion, ginger, jalapeño pepper and garlic; cook and stir 5 minutes. Remove from heat. Stir in corn and curry powder.

2 Stir coconut milk into cornstarch in **CROCK-POT®** slow cooker. Stir in potatoes, broth and soy sauce; top with curried corn. Cover; cook on LOW 5 to 6 hours. Stir gently to smooth cooking liquid. Spoon over rice in bowls. Top as desired.

Pumpkin Soup with Crumbled Bacon and Toasted Pumpkin Seeds

MAKES 4 SERVINGS

2 teaspoons olive oil
½ cup raw pumpkin seeds*
3 slices thick-cut bacon
1 medium onion, chopped
1 teaspoon kosher salt
½ teaspoon chipotle chili powder
½ teaspoon black pepper
2 cans (29 ounces *each*) 100% pumpkin purée

4 cups chicken broth
¾ cup apple cider
½ cup whipping cream or half-and-half
   Sour cream (optional)

Raw pumpkin seeds or pepitas may be found in the produce or ethnic food section of your local supermarket.

1 Coat inside of **CROCK-POT**® slow cooker with nonstick cooking spray. Heat oil in small skillet over medium-high heat. Add pumpkin seeds; stir about 1 minute or until seeds begin to pop. Spoon into small bowl; set aside.

2 Add bacon to skillet; cook and stir until crisp. Remove bacon to paper towel-lined plate using slotted spoon. Reserve drippings in skillet. Crumble bacon when cool enough to handle; set aside. Reduce heat to medium. Add onion to skillet; cook 3 minutes or until translucent. Stir in salt, chipotle chili powder and pepper. Remove onion mixture to **CROCK-POT**® slow cooker.

3 Whisk pumpkin, broth and cider into **CROCK-POT**® slow cooker until smooth. Cover; cook on HIGH 4 hours.

4 Turn off heat; remove lid. Whisk in cream. Adjust seasoning as necessary. Strain soup into bowls; garnish with pumpkin seeds, bacon and sour cream.

Curried Vegetable and Cashew Stew

MAKES 8 SERVINGS

1 medium potato, cut into ½-inch cubes	2 teaspoons grated fresh ginger
1 can (about 15 ounces) chickpeas, rinsed and drained	2 teaspoons curry powder
	½ teaspoon salt
1 can (about 14 ounces) diced tomatoes	¼ teaspoon black pepper
1 medium (about ½ pound) eggplant, cut into ½-inch cubes	1 medium zucchini (about 8 ounces), cut into ½-inch cubes
1 medium onion, chopped	2 tablespoons golden raisins
1 cup vegetable broth	½ cup frozen peas
2 tablespoons quick-cooking tapioca	½ cup cashew nuts

1 Combine potato, chickpeas, tomatoes, eggplant, onion, broth, tapioca, ginger, curry powder, salt and pepper in **CROCK-POT**® slow cooker. Cover; cook on LOW 8 to 9 hours.

2 Stir zucchini, raisins, peas and cashews into **CROCK-POT**® slow cooker. Turn **CROCK-POT**® slow cooker to HIGH. Cover; cook on HIGH 1 hour or until zucchini is tender.

Rich and Hearty Drumstick Soup

MAKES 4 SERVINGS

2 turkey drumsticks (about 1¾ pounds *total*)	1 teaspoon minced garlic
4½ cups chicken broth	½ teaspoon poultry seasoning
2 medium carrots, sliced	2 ounces uncooked egg noodles
1 medium stalk celery, thinly sliced	¼ cup chopped fresh Italian parsley
1 cup chopped onion	2 tablespoons butter
	¾ teaspoon salt

1 Coat inside of **CROCK-POT**® slow cooker with nonstick cooking spray. Add turkey, broth, carrots, celery, onion, garlic and poultry seasoning. Cover; cook on HIGH 5 hours.

2 Remove turkey to large cutting board. Add noodles to **CROCK-POT**® slow cooker. Cover; cook on HIGH 30 minutes or until noodles are tender.

3 Meanwhile, cut turkey into 1-inch pieces; discard bones. Stir in turkey, parsley, butter and salt. Cover; cook on HIGH 10 minutes or until heated through.

Super-Easy Chicken Noodle Soup

MAKES 4 SERVINGS

1 can (about 48 ounces) chicken broth

2 boneless, skinless chicken breasts, cut into 1-inch pieces

4 cups water

⅔ cup diced onion

⅔ cup diced celery

⅔ cup diced carrots

⅔ cup sliced mushrooms

½ cup frozen peas

4 cubes chicken bouillon

2 tablespoons butter

1 tablespoon chopped Italian parsley

1 teaspoon salt

1 teaspoon ground cumin

1 teaspoon dried marjoram

1 teaspoon black pepper

2 cups cooked egg noodles

French bread (optional)

Combine broth, chicken, water, onion, celery, carrots, mushrooms, peas, bouillon, butter, parsley, salt, cumin, marjoram and pepper in **CROCK-POT®** slow cooker. Cover; cook on LOW 5 to 7 hours or on HIGH 3 to 4 hours. Stir in noodles during last 30 minutes of cooking. Serve with bread, if desired.

Asian Sugar Snap Pea Soup

MAKES 4 SERVINGS

2 tablespoons peanut or canola oil	1 tablespoon soy sauce
4 to 5 new potatoes, coarsely chopped	1 teaspoon ground coriander
2 green onions, chopped	1 teaspoon ground cumin
1 medium carrot, thinly sliced	1 teaspoon prepared horseradish
1 stalk celery, thinly sliced	⅛ teaspoon ground red pepper
1 leek, thinly sliced	1 cup fresh sugar snap peas, shelled, rinsed and drained
5 cups water	4 cups cooked brown rice
2 cups broccoli, cut into florets	
1 tablespoon lemon juice	

1 Heat oil in large skillet over medium heat. Add potatoes, green onions, carrot, celery and leek; cook and stir 10 to 12 minutes or until vegetables begin to soften.

2 Remove to **CROCK-POT**® slow cooker. Add water, broccoli, lemon juice, soy sauce, coriander, cumin, horseradish and ground red pepper. Cover; cook on LOW 5 to 6 hours or on HIGH 2 to 3 hours.

3 Stir in peas. Cover; cook on HIGH 15 minutes or until peas are crisp-tender. To serve, portion rice into four bowls. Ladle soup over rice and serve immediately.

Beef Fajita Soup

MAKES 8 SERVINGS

1 pound cubed beef stew meat

1 can (about 15 ounces) pinto beans, rinsed and drained

1 can (about 15 ounces) black beans, rinsed and drained

1 can (about 14 ounces) diced tomatoes with roasted garlic

1 can (about 14 ounces) beef broth

1½ cups water

1 green bell pepper, thinly sliced

1 red bell pepper, thinly sliced

1 onion, thinly sliced

2 teaspoons ground cumin

1 teaspoon seasoned salt

1 teaspoon black pepper

Optional toppings: sour cream, shredded cheese and/or chopped olives

Combine beef, beans, tomatoes, broth, water, bell peppers, onion, cumin, salt and black pepper in **CROCK-POT**® slow cooker; stir to blend. Cover; cook on LOW 8 hours. Top as desired.

Kale, Olive Oil and Parmesan Soup

MAKES 4 TO 6 SERVINGS

2 tablespoons olive oil

1 small Spanish onion, sliced

3 cloves garlic, minced

Kosher salt and black pepper

8 cups vegetable broth

2 pounds kale, washed and chopped

Grated Parmesan cheese

Extra virgin olive oil (optional)

1 Heat 2 tablespoons olive oil in large skillet over medium-high heat. Add onion, garlic, salt and pepper; cook and stir 4 to 5 minutes or until onion begins to soften. Remove onion mixture to **CROCK-POT**® slow cooker; add broth. Cover; cook on LOW 3 hours or until heated through.

2 Stir in kale. Turn **CROCK-POT**® slow cooker to HIGH. Cover; cook on HIGH 15 minutes or until heated through. Spoon soup into individual serving bowls. Sprinkle with cheese and drizzle with extra virgin olive oil just before serving, if desired.

Thai-Style Chicken Pumpkin Soup

MAKES 4 TO 6 SERVINGS

1 tablespoon extra virgin olive oil

6 boneless, skinless chicken breasts, cut into 1-inch cubes

1 large white onion, thinly sliced

3 cloves garlic, minced

1 tablespoon minced fresh ginger

½ to ¾ teaspoon red pepper flakes

2 stalks celery, diced

2 carrots, diced

1 can (15 ounces) solid-pack pumpkin*

½ cup creamy peanut butter

4 cups chicken broth

½ cup mango nectar

½ cup fresh lime juice

3 tablespoons rice vinegar

½ cup minced fresh cilantro, divided

½ cup whipping cream

1 tablespoon cornstarch

2 to 4 cups hot cooked rice (preferably jasmine or basmati)

3 green onions, minced

½ cup roasted unsalted peanuts, coarsely chopped

Lime wedges (optional)

Do not use pumpkin pie filling.

1 Heat oil in large skillet over medium heat. Add chicken; cook and stir 3 minutes. Add onion, garlic, ginger and red pepper flakes; cook 1 or 2 minutes or until fragrant. Remove chicken mixture to **CROCK-POT**® slow cooker.

2 Stir in celery, carrots, pumpkin, peanut butter, broth, mango nectar and lime juice. Cover; cook on LOW 8 hours or on HIGH 4 hours.

3 Stir in rice vinegar and ¼ cup cilantro. Stir cream and cornstarch in small bowl; whisk into soup. Simmer, uncovered, on HIGH 10 minutes or until soup is thickened.

4 To serve, put rice in soup bowls. Ladle soup around rice. Sprinkle with remaining ¼ cup cilantro, green onions, peanuts and lime wedge, if desired.

Chicken and Sweet Potato Stew

MAKES 6 SERVINGS

4 boneless, skinless chicken breasts, cut into 1-inch pieces

2 medium sweet potatoes, peeled and cubed

2 medium Yukon Gold potatoes, peeled and cubed

2 medium carrots, cut into ½-inch slices

1 can (28 ounces) whole stewed tomatoes

1 cup chicken broth

1 teaspoon salt

1 teaspoon paprika

1 teaspoon celery seed

½ teaspoon black pepper

⅛ teaspoon ground cinnamon

⅛ teaspoon ground nutmeg

¼ cup fresh basil, chopped

Combine chicken, potatoes, carrots, tomatoes, broth, salt, paprika, celery seed, pepper, cinnamon and nutmeg in **CROCK-POT**® slow cooker; stir to blend. Cover; cook on LOW 6 to 8 hours or on HIGH 3 to 4 hours. Sprinkle with basil just before serving.

Tip

Recipe can be doubled for a 5-, 6- or 7-quart **CROCK-POT**® slow cooker.

Cape Cod Stew

MAKES 8 SERVINGS

2 pounds medium raw shrimp, peeled and deveined

2 pounds fresh cod or other white fish

3 lobsters (1½ to 2½ pounds *each*), uncooked

1 pound mussels or clams, scrubbed

2 cans (about 14 ounces *each*) chopped tomatoes

4 cups beef broth

½ cup chopped onion

½ cup chopped carrot

½ cup chopped fresh cilantro

2 tablespoons sea salt

2 teaspoons minced garlic

2 teaspoons lemon juice

4 whole bay leaves

1 teaspoon dried thyme

½ teaspoon saffron threads

1 Cut shrimp and fish into bite-size pieces and place in large bowl; refrigerate. Remove lobster tails and claws. Chop tail into 2-inch pieces and separate claws at joints. Place lobster and mussels in large bowl; refrigerate.

2 Combine tomatoes, broth, onion, carrot, cilantro, salt, garlic, lemon juice, bay leaves, thyme and saffron in **CROCK-POT**® slow cooker; stir to blend. Cover; cook on LOW 7 hours.

3 Add seafood. Turn **CROCK-POT**® slow cooker to HIGH. Cover; cook on HIGH 45 minutes to 1 hour or until seafood is just cooked through. Remove and discard bay leaves. Discard any mussels that do not open.

Chunky Italian Stew with Beans

MAKES 8 SERVINGS

2 teaspoons olive oil

4 green bell peppers, cut into ¾-inch pieces

2 yellow squash, cut into ¾-inch pieces

2 zucchini, cut into ¾-inch pieces

2 onions, cut into ¾-inch pieces

8 ounces mushrooms, quartered (about 2 cups)

2 cans (about 15 ounces *each*) navy beans, rinsed and drained

2 cans (about 14 ounces *each*) diced tomatoes

2 teaspoons dried oregano

1 teaspoon sugar

1 teaspoon Italian seasoning

¼ teaspoon red pepper flakes (optional)

1½ cups (6 ounces) shredded mozzarella cheese

2 tablespoons grated Parmesan cheese

1 Heat oil in large skillet over medium-high heat. Add bell peppers, squash, zucchini, onions and mushrooms; cook and stir 8 minutes or until onions are translucent. Remove to **CROCK-POT®** slow cooker.

2 Add beans, tomatoes, oregano, sugar, Italian seasoning and red pepper flakes, if desired, to **CROCK-POT®** slow cooker; stir to blend. Cover; cook on LOW 7 to 8 hours. Top with cheeses just before serving.

Curried Lamb and Swiss Chard Soup

MAKES 6 TO 8 SERVINGS

2 tablespoons extra virgin olive oil
1 small red onion, chopped
2 cloves garlic, minced
8 cups water
2 cups Swiss chard, trimmed, cleaned and chopped
2 cups green cabbage, cored, cleaned and chopped
2 cups cannellini beans, rinsed and sorted

2 lamb shanks
1 teaspoon salt
1 teaspoon curry powder
1 teaspoon black pepper
¼ cup lemon juice
1 teaspoon grated lemon peel
Finely chopped fresh Italian parsley (optional)

1 Heat oil in medium skillet over medium heat. Add onion and garlic; cook and stir 3 to 4 minutes or until tender. Remove to **CROCK-POT**® slow cooker.

2 Add water, Swiss chard, cabbage, beans, lamb shanks, salt, curry powder and pepper; stir to blend. Cover; cook on LOW 8 to 10 hours.

3 Remove lamb shanks to large cutting board; let stand 10 minutes. Remove and discard bones from meat. Shred meat; return to **CROCK-POT**® slow cooker. Add lemon juice; stir to blend. Garnish soup with lemon peel and parsley.

Roasted Tomato-Basil Soup

MAKES 6 SERVINGS

2 cans (28 ounces *each*) whole tomatoes, drained, 3 cups liquid reserved

2½ tablespoons packed dark brown sugar

1 medium onion, finely chopped

3 cups vegetable broth

3 tablespoons tomato paste

¼ teaspoon ground allspice

1 can (5 ounces) evaporated milk

¼ cup shredded fresh basil (about 10 large leaves)

Salt and black pepper

Sprigs fresh basil (optional)

1 Preheat oven to 450°F. Line baking sheet with foil; spray with nonstick cooking spray. Arrange tomatoes on foil in single layer. Sprinkle with brown sugar; top with onion. Bake 25 minutes or until tomatoes look dry and light brown. Let tomatoes cool slightly; finely chop.

2 Combine tomato mixture, 3 cups reserved liquid from tomatoes, broth, tomato paste and allspice in **CROCK-POT®** slow cooker; stir to blend. Cover; cook on LOW 8 hours or on HIGH 4 hours.

3 Add evaporated milk and shredded basil; season with salt and pepper. Cover; cook on HIGH 30 minutes or until heated through. Garnish each serving with basil sprig.

Cannellini Minestrone Soup

MAKES 6 SERVINGS

4 cups chicken broth	¼ cup dried cannellini beans, rinsed and sorted
2 cups escarole, cut into ribbons	
1 can (about 14 ounces) diced tomatoes	2 tablespoons chopped fresh chives
1 can (12 ounces) tomato-vegetable juice	1 tablespoon chopped fresh Italian parsley
1 cup chopped green onions	¼ teaspoon salt
1 cup chopped carrots	¼ teaspoon black pepper
1 cup chopped celery	2 ounces uncooked ditalini pasta
1 cup chopped potatoes	

1 Combine broth, escarole, tomatoes, vegetable juice, green onions, carrots, celery, potatoes, beans, chives, parsley, salt and pepper in **CROCK-POT**® slow cooker; stir to blend. Cover; cook on LOW 6 to 8 hours or on HIGH 4 to 6 hours.

2 Stir in pasta. Cover; cook on HIGH 20 minutes or until pasta is tender.

Chipotle Chicken Stew

MAKES 6 SERVINGS

1 pound boneless, skinless chicken thighs, cubed	½ cup orange juice
	1 medium onion, diced
1 can (about 15 ounces) navy beans, rinsed and drained	1 canned chipotle pepper in adobo sauce, minced
1 can (about 15 ounces) black beans, rinsed and drained	1 teaspoon salt
1 can (about 14 ounces) crushed tomatoes, undrained	1 teaspoon ground cumin
	1 whole bay leaf
1½ cups chicken broth	Sprigs fresh cilantro (optional)

1 Combine chicken, beans, tomatoes, broth, orange juice, onion, chipotle pepper, salt, cumin and bay leaf in **CROCK-POT**® slow cooker.

2 Cover; cook on LOW 7 to 8 hours or on HIGH 3½ to 4 hours. Remove and discard bay leaf. Garnish with cilantro.

Cod Fish Stew

MAKES 6 TO 8 SERVINGS

½ pound bacon, coarsely chopped
1 large carrot, diced
1 large onion, diced
2 stalks celery, diced
2 cloves garlic, minced
   Salt and black pepper
3 cups water
2 cups clam juice or fish broth
1 can (28 ounces) plum tomatoes, drained

2 potatoes, diced
½ cup dry white wine
3 tablespoons chopped fresh Italian parsley
3 tablespoons tomato paste
3 saffron threads
2½ pounds fresh cod, skinned and cut into 2-inch pieces

1 Heat medium skillet over medium heat. Add bacon; cook and stir until crisp. Add carrot, onion, celery, garlic, salt and pepper to skillet; cook and stir 6 to 7 minutes or until vegetables soften.

2 Remove bacon and vegetables to **CROCK-POT**® slow cooker using slotted spoon. Stir in water, clam juice, tomatoes, potatoes, wine, parsley, tomato paste and saffron. Cover; cook on LOW 6 to 7 hours or on HIGH 3 to 4 hours.

3 Add cod. Cover; cook on HIGH 10 to 20 minutes or until cod is just cooked through.

Note

Cod is a great fish to use for a soup or stew. The thick creamy white fish becomes a hearty meal when paired with bacon and tomato.

Hearty Chicken Tequila Soup

MAKES 2 TO 4 SERVINGS

1 small onion, cut into 8 wedges	2 tablespoons chopped fresh cilantro, plus additional for garnish
1 cup frozen corn	1 whole fryer chicken (about 3½ pounds)
1 can (about 14 ounces) diced tomatoes with mild green chiles	2 cups chicken broth
2 cloves garlic, minced	3 tablespoons tequila
	¼ cup sour cream

1 Place onion wedges on bottom of **CROCK-POT®** slow cooker. Add corn, tomatoes, garlic and 2 tablespoons cilantro; stir to blend. Place chicken on top of tomato mixture.

2 Pour broth and tequila over chicken and tomato mixture. Cover; cook on LOW 8 to 10 hours.

3 Remove chicken to large cutting board; discard skin and bones. Shred chicken with two forks. Stir shredded chicken back into **CROCK-POT®** slow cooker. Ladle into individual bowls. Top each serving with sour cream; garnish with additional cilantro.

Hearty Chilies

Spicy Turkey Chili

MAKES 6 SERVINGS

2   cans (about 15 ounces *each*) cannellini
    or small white beans, rinsed and
    drained

1   can (about 14 ounces) chicken broth

2   onions, chopped

1   can (about 14 ounces) cream-style corn

1   red bell pepper, chopped

3   cloves garlic, minced

2   jalapeño peppers, seeded and chopped*

2   tablespoons chili powder

2   teaspoons ground cumin

3   boneless, skinless turkey thighs

¾   teaspoon ground red pepper

¾   teaspoon salt

½   teaspoon black pepper

    Optional toppings: tortilla chips,
    sour cream and/or fresh chopped
    cilantro (optional)

*Jalapeño peppers can sting and irritate the
skin, so wear rubber gloves when handling
peppers and do not touch your eyes.*

1 Stir beans, broth, onions, corn, bell pepper, garlic, jalapeño peppers, chili powder and
cumin into **CROCK-POT**® slow cooker until combined. Add turkey. Cover; cook on LOW
7 to 8 hours or on HIGH 3 to 4 hours.

2 Remove turkey to large cutting board; shred with two forks. Stir shredded turkey,
ground red pepper, salt and black pepper into **CROCK-POT**® slow cooker; stir to blend.
Top as desired.

Vegetarian Chili

MAKES 4 SERVINGS

1 tablespoon vegetable oil
1 cup chopped onion
1 cup chopped red bell pepper
2 tablespoons minced jalapeño pepper*
1 clove garlic, minced
1 can (about 28 ounces) stewed
   tomatoes
1 can (about 15 ounces) black beans,
   rinsed and drained
1 can (about 15 ounces) chickpeas,
   rinsed and drained

½ cup frozen corn
¼ cup tomato paste
1 teaspoon sugar
1 teaspoon ground cumin
1 teaspoon dried basil
1 teaspoon chili powder
¼ teaspoon black pepper

Jalapeño peppers can sting and irritate the skin, so wear rubber gloves when handling peppers and do not touch your eyes.

1 Heat oil in large skillet over medium-high heat. Add onion, bell pepper, jalapeño pepper and garlic; cook and stir 5 minutes. Remove onion mixture to **CROCK-POT**® slow cooker using slotted spoon.

2 Add tomatoes, beans, chickpeas, corn, tomato paste, sugar, cumin, basil, chili powder and black pepper; stir to blend. Cover; cook on LOW 4 to 5 hours.

Three-Bean Chili with Chorizo

MAKES 6 TO 8 SERVINGS

2 Mexican chorizo sausages (about 6 ounces *each*), casings removed

1 tablespoon vegetable oil

1 large onion, chopped

1 tablespoon salt

1 tablespoon tomato paste

1 tablespoon minced garlic

1 tablespoon chili powder

1 tablespoon ancho chili powder

2 to 3 teaspoons chipotle chili powder

2 teaspoons ground cumin

1 teaspoon ground coriander

3 cups water

2 cans (about 14 ounces *each*) crushed tomatoes

½ cup dried pinto beans, rinsed and sorted

½ cup dried kidney beans, rinsed and sorted

½ cup dried black beans, rinsed and sorted

Chopped fresh cilantro (optional)

1 Heat large nonstick skillet over medium-high heat. Add sausages; cook 3 to 4 minutes, stirring to break up meat. Remove to **CROCK-POT®** slow cooker using slotted spoon.

2 Wipe out skillet. Heat oil in same skillet over medium heat. Add onion; cook and stir 6 minutes or until softened. Add salt, tomato paste, garlic, chili powders, cumin and coriander; cook and stir 1 minute. Remove to **CROCK-POT®** slow cooker. Stir in water, tomatoes and beans.

3 Cover; cook on LOW 10 hours. Garnish each serving with cilantro.

Hearty Pork and Bacon Chili

MAKES 8 TO 10 SERVINGS

2½ pounds boneless pork shoulder, cut into 1-inch pieces

3½ teaspoons salt, divided

1¼ teaspoons black pepper, divided

1 tablespoon vegetable oil

4 slices thick-cut bacon, diced

2 medium onions, chopped

1 red bell pepper, chopped

¼ cup chili powder

2 tablespoons tomato paste

1 tablespoon minced garlic

1 tablespoon ground cumin

1 tablespoon smoked paprika

1 bottle (12 ounces) pale ale

2 cans (about 14 ounces *each*) diced tomatoes

2 cups water

¾ cup dried kidney beans, rinsed and sorted

¾ cup dried black beans, rinsed and sorted

3 tablespoons cornmeal

Feta cheese and chopped fresh cilantro (optional)

1 Season pork with 1 teaspoon salt and 1 teaspoon black pepper. Heat oil in large skillet over medium-high heat. Add pork in batches; cook 6 minutes or until browned on all sides. Remove to **CROCK-POT®** slow cooker using slotted spoon.

2 Heat same skillet over medium heat. Add bacon; cook and stir until crisp. Remove to **CROCK-POT®** slow cooker using slotted spoon.

3 Pour off all but 2 tablespoons drippings from skillet. Return skillet to medium heat. Add onions and bell pepper; cook and stir 6 minutes or just until softened. Stir in chili powder, tomato paste, garlic, cumin, paprika, remaining 2½ teaspoons salt and remaining ¼ teaspoon black pepper; cook and stir 1 minute. Stir in ale. Bring to a simmer, scraping up any browned bits from bottom of skillet. Pour over pork in **CROCK-POT®** slow cooker. Stir in tomatoes, water, beans and cornmeal.

4 Cover; cook on LOW 10 hours. Turn off heat. Let stand 10 minutes. Skim fat from surface. Garnish each serving with cheese and cilantro.

Black Bean Mushroom Chili

MAKES 4 SERVINGS

1 tablespoon vegetable oil

2 cups (8 ounces) sliced baby bella or button mushrooms

1 cup chopped onion

4 cloves garlic, minced

1 can (about 15 ounces) black beans, rinsed and drained

1 can (about 14 ounces) fire-roasted diced tomatoes

1 cup salsa

1 yellow or green bell pepper, finely diced

2 teaspoons chili powder or ground cumin

Sour cream (optional)

1 Coat inside of **CROCK-POT®** slow cooker with nonstick cooking spray. Heat oil in large skillet over medium heat. Add mushrooms, onion and garlic; cook 8 minutes or until mushrooms have released their liquid and liquid has thickened slightly.

2 Combine mushroom mixture, beans, tomatoes, salsa, bell pepper and chili powder in **CROCK-POT®** slow cooker; stir to blend. Cover; cook on LOW 5 to 6 hours or on HIGH 2½ to 3 hours. Ladle into shallow bowls. Top with sour cream, if desired.

Best Ever Chili

MAKES 8 SERVINGS

1½ pounds ground beef

1 cup chopped onion

2 cans (about 15 ounces *each*) kidney beans, drained and liquid reserved

1½ pounds plum tomatoes, diced

1 can (15 ounces) tomato paste

3 to 6 tablespoons chili powder

Sour cream and chopped green onion (optional)

1 Brown beef and onion in large skillet over medium-high heat 6 to 8 minutes, stirring to break up meat. Remove beef mixture to **CROCK-POT®** slow cooker using slotted spoon.

2 Add beans, tomatoes, tomato paste, 1 cup reserved bean liquid and chili powder to **CROCK-POT®** slow cooker; stir to blend. Cover; cook on LOW 10 to 12 hours. Top each serving with sour cream and green onion, if desired.

Southwest Chipotle Chili

MAKES 12 SERVINGS

3 links chorizo sausage (1 pound *total*), casings removed

1 pound ground beef

3 cans (about 14 ounces *each*) diced tomatoes

1 can (about 15 ounces) dark red kidney beans, rinsed and drained

1 can (about 15 ounces) black beans, rinsed and drained

1 can (about 14 ounces) stewed tomatoes, plus 1 can water

1 can (about 14 ounces) tomato sauce

2 medium green bell peppers, chopped

3 canned chipotle peppers in adobo sauce, chopped, plus 1 tablespoon adobo sauce reserved*

2 to 3 small serrano peppers, chopped*

1 poblano pepper, chopped*

1 medium onion, chopped

2 tablespoons ground red pepper

2 tablespoons chili powder

2 tablespoons hot pepper sauce

1 tablespoon sugar

Salt and black pepper

Chipotle, serrano and poblano peppers can sting and irritate the skin. Wear rubber gloves when handling peppers and do not touch your eyes.

1 Brown chorizo and ground beef in large skillet over medium-high heat 6 to 8 minutes, stirring to break up meat. Drain fat.

2 Combine chorizo and beef, diced tomatoes, beans, stewed tomatoes with water, tomato sauce, bell peppers, chipotle peppers with reserved sauce, serrano peppers, poblano pepper, onion, ground red pepper, chili powder, hot pepper sauce, sugar, salt and black pepper in **CROCK-POT®** slow cooker. Cover; cook on LOW 5 to 6 hours or on HIGH 2 to 3 hours.

White Chicken Chili

MAKES 6 TO 8 SERVINGS

8 ounces dried navy beans, rinsed and sorted	1 teaspoon dried oregano
1 tablespoon vegetable oil	¼ teaspoon black pepper
2 pounds boneless, skinless chicken breasts (about 4)	¼ teaspoon ground red pepper (optional)
2 onions, chopped	4 cups chicken broth
1 tablespoon minced garlic	1 can (4 ounces) fire-roasted diced mild green chiles, rinsed and drained
2 teaspoons ground cumin	¼ cup chopped fresh cilantro
2 teaspoons salt	

1 Place beans in bottom of **CROCK-POT®** slow cooker. Heat oil in large skillet over medium-high heat. Add chicken; cook 8 minutes or until browned on all sides. Remove to **CROCK-POT®** slow cooker.

2 Heat same skillet over medium heat. Add onions; cook 6 minutes or until softened and lightly browned. Add garlic, cumin, salt, oregano, black pepper and ground red pepper, if desired; cook and stir 1 minute. Add broth and chiles; bring to a simmer, stirring to scrape up any browned bits from bottom of skillet. Remove onion mixture to **CROCK-POT®** slow cooker.

3 Cover; cook on LOW 5 hours. Remove chicken to large cutting board; shred with two forks. Return chicken to **CROCK-POT®** slow cooker. Top each serving with cilantro.

Pork Tenderloin Chili

MAKES 8 SERVINGS

1½ to 2 pounds pork tenderloin, cooked and cut into 2-inch pieces

2 cans (about 15 ounces *each*) pinto beans, rinsed and drained

2 cans (about 15 ounces *each*) black beans, rinsed and drained

2 cans (about 14 ounces *each*) whole tomatoes

2 cans (4 ounces *each*) diced mild green chiles

1 package (1¼ ounces) taco seasoning mix

Diced avocado (optional)

Combine pork, beans, tomatoes, chiles and taco seasoning mix in **CROCK-POT®** slow cooker; stir to blend. Cover; cook on LOW 4 hours. Top with avocado, if desired.

Corn and Two Bean Chili

MAKES 4 SERVINGS

1 can (about 15 ounces) pinto or kidney beans, rinsed and drained

1 can (about 15 ounces) black beans, rinsed and drained

1 can (about 14 ounces) fire-roasted diced tomatoes

1 cup salsa

1 cup frozen corn

½ cup minced onion

1 teaspoon chili powder

1 teaspoon ground cumin

½ cup sour cream (optional)

1 cup (4 ounces) shredded Cheddar cheese (optional)

1 Coat inside of **CROCK-POT®** slow cooker with nonstick cooking spray. Combine beans, tomatoes, salsa, corn, onion, chili powder and cumin in **CROCK-POT®** slow cooker; stir to blend.

2 Cover; cook on LOW 5 to 6 hours or on HIGH 2½ to 3 hours. Top each serving with sour cream and cheese, if desired.

Corn Chip Chili

MAKES 6 SERVINGS

1 tablespoon olive oil

1 medium onion, chopped

1 medium red bell pepper, chopped

1 jalapeño pepper, seeded and finely chopped*

4 cloves garlic, minced

2 pounds ground beef

1 can (4 ounces) diced mild green chiles, drained

2 cans (about 14 ounces *each*) fire-roasted diced tomatoes

2 tablespoons chili powder

1½ teaspoons ground cumin

1½ teaspoons dried oregano

¾ teaspoon salt

3 cups corn chips

1 cup (4 ounces) shredded sharp Cheddar cheese

6 tablespoons chopped green onions

Jalapeño peppers can sting and irritate the skin, so wear rubber gloves when handling peppers and do not touch your eyes.

1 Coat inside of **CROCK-POT**® slow cooker with nonstick cooking spray.

2 Heat oil in large skillet over medium-high heat. Add onion, bell pepper, jalapeño pepper and garlic; cook and stir 2 minutes or until softened. Add beef; cook and stir 10 to 12 minutes or until beef is no longer pink and liquid has evaporated. Stir in green chiles; cook 1 minute. Remove beef mixture to **CROCK-POT**® slow cooker using slotted spoon. Stir in tomatoes, chili powder, cumin, oregano and salt.

3 Cover; cook on LOW 6 to 7 hours or on HIGH 3 to 4 hours. Place corn chips evenly into serving bowls; top with chili. Sprinkle evenly with cheese and green onions.

Classic Chili

MAKES 6 SERVINGS

1½ pounds ground beef
1½ cups chopped onion
1 cup chopped green bell pepper
2 cloves garlic, minced
3 cans (about 15 ounces *each*) dark red kidney beans, rinsed and drained
2 cans (about 15 ounces *each*) tomato sauce

1 can (about 14 ounces) diced tomatoes
2 to 3 teaspoons chili powder
1 to 2 teaspoons ground mustard
¾ teaspoon dried basil
½ teaspoon black pepper
1 to 2 dried red chiles (optional)
Shredded Cheddar cheese (optional)
Sprigs fresh cilantro (optional)

1 Brown beef, onion, bell pepper and garlic in large skillet over medium-high heat 6 to 8 minutes, stirring to break up meat. Remove beef mixture to **CROCK-POT®** slow cooker using slotted spoon.

2 Add beans, tomato sauce, tomatoes, chili powder, mustard, basil, black pepper and chiles, if desired, to **CROCK-POT®** slow cooker; stir to blend. Cover; cook on LOW 8 to 10 hours or on HIGH 4 to 5 hours. If used, remove chiles before serving. Top with cheese, if desired. Garnish with cilantro.

Chili Verde

MAKES 4 SERVINGS

¾ pound boneless lean pork loin roast, cut into 1-inch cubes

1 pound fresh tomatillos, husks removed, rinsed and coarsely chopped

1 can (about 15 ounces) Great Northern beans, rinsed and drained

1 can (about 14 ounces) chicken broth

1 large onion, halved and thinly sliced

1 can (4 ounces) diced mild green chiles

6 cloves garlic, sliced

1 teaspoon ground cumin

Salt and black pepper

½ cup lightly packed fresh cilantro, chopped

1 Spray large skillet with nonstick cooking spray. Heat over medium-high heat. Add pork; cook 5 to 7 minutes or until browned on all sides.

2 Combine pork, tomatillos, beans, broth, onion, chiles, garlic, cumin, salt and pepper in **CROCK-POT**® slow cooker. Cover; cook on HIGH 3 to 4 hours.

3 Turn **CROCK-POT**® slow cooker to LOW. Stir in cilantro. Cover; cook on LOW 10 minutes.

Beef Chuck Chili

MAKES 8 TO 10 SERVINGS

½ cup plus 2 tablespoons olive oil, divided

1 boneless beef chuck roast (5 pounds), trimmed*

3 cups finely chopped onions

2 green bell peppers, chopped

4 poblano peppers, seeded and finely chopped**

2 serrano peppers, seeded and minced**

3 jalapeño peppers, seeded and minced**

2 tablespoons minced garlic

1 can (28 ounces) crushed tomatoes, undrained

½ cup Mexican lager

¼ cup hot pepper sauce

1 tablespoon ground cumin

Prepared corn bread

*Unless you have a 5-, 6- or 7-quart CROCK-POT® slow cooker, cut any roast larger than 2½ pounds in half so it cooks completely.

**Poblano, serrano and jalapeño peppers can sting and irritate the skin. Wear rubber gloves when handling peppers and do not touch your eyes.

1 Heat ½ cup oil in large skillet over medium-high heat. Add roast; brown on both sides. Remove to **CROCK-POT®** slow cooker.

2 Heat remaining 2 tablespoons oil in same skillet over low heat. Add onions, peppers and garlic; cook and stir 7 minutes or until onions are tender. Remove to **CROCK-POT®** slow cooker. Stir in tomatoes. Cover; cook on LOW 4 to 5 hours.

3 Remove beef to large cutting board; shred with two forks. Add lager, hot pepper sauce and cumin to cooking liquid. Return beef to cooking liquid; mix well. Serve over corn bread.

Three-Bean Turkey Chili

MAKES 6 TO 8 SERVINGS

1 pound ground turkey

1 small onion, chopped

1 can (28 ounces) diced tomatoes

1 can (about 15 ounces) chickpeas, rinsed and drained

1 can (about 15 ounces) kidney beans, rinsed and drained

1 can (about 15 ounces) black beans, rinsed and drained

1 can (8 ounces) tomato sauce

1 can (4 ounces) diced mild green chiles

1 to 2 tablespoons chili powder

1 Place turkey and onion in large skillet over medium-high heat; cook and stir 6 to 8 minutes or until turkey is browned. Remove to **CROCK-POT**® slow cooker.

2 Add tomatoes, chickpeas, beans, tomato sauce, chiles and chili powder to **CROCK-POT**® slow cooker; stir to blend. Cover; cook on HIGH 6 to 8 hours.

Chorizo Chili

MAKES 6 SERVINGS

1 pound ground beef

8 ounces bulk raw chorizo sausage *or* ½ (15-ounce) package raw chorizo sausage, casings removed*

1 can (about 15 ounces) chili beans in chili sauce

2 cans (about 14 ounces *each*) chili-style diced tomatoes

Optional toppings: sour cream, fresh chives and shredded Cheddar cheese

A highly seasoned Mexican pork sausage.

1 Brown beef and chorizo in large skillet over medium-high heat 6 to 8 minutes, stirring to break up meat. Remove beef mixture to **CROCK-POT**® slow cooker using slotted spoon. Stir beans and tomatoes into **CROCK-POT**® slow cooker.

2 Cover; cook on LOW 7 hours. Turn off heat. Let stand 10 to 12 minutes. Skim fat from surface. Top as desired.

Simple Beef Chili

MAKES 8 SERVINGS

3 pounds ground beef

2 cans (about 14 ounces *each*) diced tomatoes

2 cans (about 15 ounces *each*) kidney beans, rinsed and drained

2 cups chopped onions

1 package (10 ounces) frozen corn

1 cup chopped green bell pepper

1 can (8 ounces) tomato sauce

3 tablespoons chili powder

1 teaspoon garlic powder

½ teaspoon ground cumin

½ teaspoon dried oregano

Prepared corn bread (optional)

1 Brown beef in large skillet over medium-high heat 6 to 8 minutes, stirring to break up meat. Remove to **CROCK-POT®** slow cooker using slotted spoon.

2 Add tomatoes, beans, onions, corn, bell pepper, tomato sauce, chili powder, garlic powder, cumin and oregano to **CROCK-POT®** slow cooker. Cover; cook on LOW 4 hours. Serve with corn bread, if desired.

Tip

The flavor and aroma of crushed or ground herbs and spices may lessen during a longer cooking time. So, when slow cooking in your **CROCK-POT®** slow cooker, be sure to taste and adjust seasonings, if necessary, before serving.

Cincinnati Chili

MAKES 6 SERVINGS

1 tablespoon vegetable oil

2 medium onions, chopped

2 pounds ground beef

1 can (28 ounces) diced tomatoes

1 cup tomato sauce

½ cup water

3 cloves garlic, minced

1 tablespoon unsweetened cocoa powder

1 tablespoon chili powder

2½ teaspoons ground cinnamon

2 teaspoons salt

1½ teaspoons ground cumin

1½ teaspoons Worcestershire sauce

1¼ teaspoons ground allspice

¾ teaspoon ground red pepper

12 ounces cooked spaghetti

Optional toppings: chopped onions, shredded Cheddar cheese, kidney beans and/or oyster crackers

1 Heat oil in large skillet over medium-high heat. Add onions; cook 2 to 3 minutes or until translucent. Add beef; cook 6 to 8 minutes or until beef is browned, stirring to break up meat. Drain fat. Remove beef mixture to **CROCK-POT®** slow cooker using slotted spoon.

2 Stir tomatoes, tomato sauce, water, garlic, cocoa, chili powder, cinnamon, salt, cumin, Worcestershire sauce, allspice and ground red pepper into **CROCK-POT®** slow cooker.

3 Cover; cook on LOW 7 to 8 hours or on HIGH 3½ to 4 hours. Spoon chili over spaghetti. Top as desired.

Hearty Chili Mac

MAKES 4 SERVINGS

1 pound ground beef
1 can (about 14 ounces) diced
   tomatoes, drained
1 cup chopped onion
1 tablespoon chili powder
1 clove garlic, minced

½ teaspoon salt
½ teaspoon ground cumin
½ teaspoon dried oregano
¼ teaspoon red pepper flakes
¼ teaspoon black pepper
2 cups hot cooked elbow macaroni

1 Brown beef in large skillet over medium-high heat 6 to
8 minutes, stirring to break up meat. Drain fat. Remove
to **CROCK-POT**® slow cooker.

2 Add tomatoes, onion, chili powder, garlic, salt, cumin,
oregano, red pepper flakes and black pepper to
CROCK-POT® slow cooker; mix well. Cover; cook on
LOW 4 hours.

3 Stir in macaroni. Cover; cook on LOW 1 hour.

Savory Chicken and Oregano Chili

MAKES 8 SERVINGS

3 cans (about 15 ounces *each*) cannellini
   beans, rinsed and drained
3½ cups chicken broth
2 cups chopped cooked chicken
2 medium red bell peppers, chopped
1 medium onion, chopped

1 can (4 ounces) diced mild green
   chiles, drained
3 cloves garlic, minced
2 teaspoons ground cumin
1 teaspoon salt
1 tablespoon minced fresh oregano

Place beans, broth, chicken, bell peppers, onion, chiles,
garlic, cumin and salt in **CROCK-POT**® slow cooker;
stir to blend. Cover; cook on LOW 8 to 10 hours or on
HIGH 4 to 5 hours. Stir in oregano just before serving.

Merlot Beef Chili with Horseradish Sour Cream

MAKES 4 SERVINGS

1 tablespoon olive oil

1 pound boneless beef chuck roast, cut into ½-inch cubes

1 can (about 14 ounces) stewed tomatoes with Italian seasonings, undrained

1 can (about 10 ounces) condensed beef broth, undiluted

1 can (8 ounces) tomato sauce

½ cup chopped onion

½ cup chopped green bell pepper

¼ cup Merlot or dry red wine

2 cloves garlic, minced

1 tablespoon chili powder

2 teaspoons sugar

¾ teaspoon instant coffee granules

½ teaspoon black pepper

2 whole bay leaves

¾ cup sour cream

3 tablespoons prepared horseradish

1 teaspoon salt

1 Heat oil in large skillet over high heat. Add beef; cook and stir 6 to 8 minutes or until browned. Remove to **CROCK-POT**® slow cooker using slotted spoon. Stir stewed tomatoes, broth, tomato sauce, onion, bell pepper, wine, garlic, chili powder, sugar, coffee granules, black pepper and bay leaves into **CROCK-POT**® slow cooker. Cover; cook on LOW 12 hours or on HIGH 6 hours.

2 Meanwhile, combine sour cream, horseradish and salt in small bowl; stir to blend. Cover and refrigerate.

3 Remove and discard bay leaves. Top with sour cream mixture just before serving.

Mama's Beer Chili

MAKES 4 TO 6 SERVINGS

1 can (28 ounces) crushed tomatoes

1 package (10 ounces) frozen corn

1 can (about 15 ounces) kidney beans, rinsed and drained

1 cup beer (preferably dark)

⅓ cup honey

⅓ cup diced mild green chiles

3 tablespoons chili powder

3 tablespoons hot pepper sauce

3 cubes beef bouillon

1 to 2 tablespoons all-purpose flour

1 teaspoon curry powder

2 tablespoons olive oil

1 large onion (preferably Vidalia), diced

4 cloves garlic, crushed

1½ to 2 pounds ground turkey

Sliced green onions (optional)

1 Combine tomatoes, corn, beans, beer, honey, chiles, chili powder, hot pepper sauce, bouillon cubes, flour and curry powder in **CROCK-POT**® slow cooker; stir to blend.

2 Heat oil in large skillet over medium-low heat. Add diced onion; cook and stir 5 minutes. Add garlic; cook and stir 2 minutes. Add turkey; cook and stir 6 to 8 minutes or until turkey is no longer pink. Remove to **CROCK-POT**® slow cooker.

3 Cover; cook on LOW 8 to 10 hours or on HIGH 4 to 6 hours. Garnish each serving with green onions.

Chili with Turkey and Beans

MAKES 4 SERVINGS

2 cans (about 15 ounces *each*) red kidney beans, rinsed and drained

2 cans (about 14 ounces *each*) whole tomatoes, drained

1 pound cooked ground turkey

1 can (about 15 ounces) black beans, rinsed and drained

1 can (about 15 ounces) tomato sauce

1 cup finely chopped onion

1 cup finely chopped celery

1 cup finely chopped carrot

½ cup amaretto (optional)

3 tablespoons chili powder

1 tablespoon Worcestershire sauce

4 teaspoons ground cumin

2 teaspoons ground red pepper

1 teaspoon salt

Shredded Cheddar cheese (optional)

Combine kidney beans, whole tomatoes, turkey, black beans, tomato sauce, onion, celery, carrot, amaretto, if desired, chili powder, Worcestershire sauce, cumin, ground red pepper and salt in **CROCK-POT®** slow cooker; stir to blend. Cover; cook on HIGH 7 hours. Top with cheese, if desired.

Dynamite Chili

MAKES 6 SERVINGS

½ pound ground beef
  Salt and black pepper
2 cans (about 14 ounces *each*) Italian-style stewed tomatoes
1 can (about 15 ounces) light red kidney beans, rinsed and drained
1 can (about 15 ounces) dark red kidney beans, rinsed and drained
1½ cups water
1 large onion, thinly sliced
½ cup chopped red bell pepper

½ cup chopped yellow bell pepper
2 cloves garlic, minced
2 tablespoons ground chili powder
1 tablespoon dried parsley flakes
1 tablespoon ground coriander
1 tablespoon ground cumin
1 teaspoon red pepper flakes
  Optional toppings: diced green onions, sour cream and/or shredded Cheddar cheese

1 Season beef with salt and black pepper. Brown beef in large skillet over medium-high heat 6 to 8 minutes, stirring to break up meat. Drain fat.

2 Add beef, tomatoes, beans, water, onion, bell peppers, garlic, chili powder, parsley flakes, coriander, cumin and red pepper flakes to **CROCK-POT®** slow cooker. Cover; cook on LOW 4 to 6 hours or on HIGH 2 to 3 hours. Top as desired.

Chili and Cheese "Baked" Potato Supper

MAKES 4 SERVINGS

4 russet potatoes (about 2 pounds), unpeeled

2 cups prepared meatless chili

½ cup (2 ounces) shredded Cheddar cheese

2 green onions, sliced

¼ cup sour cream (optional)

1 Prick potatoes in several places with fork. Wrap potatoes in foil. Place in **CROCK-POT**® slow cooker. Cover; cook on LOW 8 to 10 hours or on HIGH 4 to 5 hours.

2 Carefully unwrap potatoes and place on serving dish. Place chili in medium microwavable dish; microwave on HIGH 3 to 5 minutes. Split potatoes and spoon chili on top. Sprinkle with cheese, onions and sour cream, if desired.

White Bean Chili

MAKES 6 SERVINGS

1 pound ground chicken

3 cups coarsely chopped celery

1 can (28 ounces) whole tomatoes, undrained and coarsely chopped

1 can (about 15 ounces) Great Northern beans, rinsed and drained

1½ cups coarsely chopped onions

1 cup chicken broth

3 cloves garlic, minced

4 teaspoons chili powder

1½ teaspoons ground cumin

¾ teaspoon ground allspice

¾ teaspoon ground cinnamon

½ teaspoon black pepper

1 Spray large skillet with nonstick cooking spray; heat over medium-high heat. Add chicken; cook 6 to 8 minutes or until browned, stirring to break up meat.

2 Combine chicken, celery, tomatoes, beans, onions, broth, garlic, chili powder, cumin, allspice, cinnamon and pepper in **CROCK-POT**® slow cooker; stir to blend. Cover; cook on LOW 5 to 6 hours.

Sweet Potato and Black Bean Chipotle Chili

MAKES 8 TO 10 SERVINGS

1 tablespoon vegetable oil

2 large onions, diced

3 tablespoons chili powder

2 tablespoons tomato paste

1 tablespoon chipotle chili powder

1 tablespoon minced garlic

2 teaspoons salt

1 teaspoon ground cumin

1 cup water

2 large sweet potatoes, peeled and cut into ½-inch pieces (about 2 pounds)

2 cans (about 15 ounces *each*) black beans, rinsed and drained

2 cans (28 ounces *each*) crushed tomatoes

Optional toppings: sliced green onions, shredded Cheddar cheese and/or tortilla chips

1 Heat oil in large skillet over medium-high heat. Add onions; cook 8 minutes or until lightly browned and softened. Add chili powder, tomato paste, chipotle chili powder, garlic, salt and cumin; cook and stir 1 minute. Add water, scraping up any brown bits from bottom of skillet. Remove to **CROCK-POT**® slow cooker. Add sweet potatoes, beans and tomatoes.

2 Cover; cook on LOW 8 hours or on HIGH 4 hours. Ladle into individual bowls. Top with desired toppings.

Mole Chili

MAKES 4 TO 6 SERVINGS

2 corn tortillas, each cut into 4 wedges

1½ pounds boneless beef chuck roast, cut into 1-inch pieces

¾ teaspoon salt

½ teaspoon black pepper

3 tablespoons olive oil, divided

2 medium onions, chopped

5 cloves garlic, minced

1 cup beef broth

1 can (about 14 ounces) fire-roasted diced tomatoes

2 tablespoons chili powder

1 tablespoon ground ancho chile

1 teaspoon ground cumin

1 teaspoon dried oregano

¾ teaspoon ground cinnamon

1 can (about 15 ounces) red kidney beans, rinsed and drained

2 ounces semisweet chocolate, chopped

Queso fresco and chopped fresh cilantro (optional)

1 Coat inside of **CROCK-POT**® slow cooker with nonstick cooking spray. Place tortillas in food processor or blender; process to fine crumbs. Set aside.

2 Season beef with salt and pepper. Heat 1 tablespoon oil in large skillet over medium-high heat. Add half of beef to skillet; cook 4 minutes or until browned. Remove to **CROCK-POT**® slow cooker. Repeat with remaining beef and 1 tablespoon oil.

3 Heat remaining 1 tablespoon oil in skillet. Add onions and garlic; cook 2 minutes or until beginning to soften. Pour broth into skillet, scraping up any browned bits from bottom of skillet. Remove to **CROCK-POT**® slow cooker. Stir in reserved tortilla crumbs, tomatoes, chili powder, ancho chile, cumin, oregano and cinnamon.

4 Cover; cook on LOW 8 to 8½ hours or on HIGH 4 to 4½ hours. Stir in beans. Cover; cook on LOW 30 minutes. Turn off heat. Stir in chocolate until melted. Top with queso fresco and cilantro, if desired.

Black and White Chili

MAKES 6 SERVINGS

1 pound boneless, skinless chicken breasts, cut into ¾-inch pieces

1 cup chopped onion

1 can (about 15 ounces) Great Northern beans, rinsed and drained

1 can (about 15 ounces) black beans, rinsed and drained

1 can (about 14 ounces) stewed tomatoes

2 tablespoons Texas-style chili seasoning mix

1 Spray large skillet with nonstick cooking spray; heat over medium heat. Add chicken and onion; cook and stir 5 minutes or until chicken is browned.

2 Combine chicken mixture, beans, tomatoes and chili seasoning mix in **CROCK-POT®** slow cooker; stir to blend. Cover; cook on LOW 4 to 4½ hours.

Serving Suggestion

For a change of pace, this delicious chili is excellent served over cooked rice or pasta.

Mediterranean Chili

MAKES 6 SERVINGS

2 cans (about 28 ounces *each*) chickpeas, rinsed and drained

1 can (28 ounces) diced tomatoes

1 can (about 14 ounces) vegetable broth

2 onions, chopped

10 kalamata olives, chopped

4 cloves garlic, chopped

2 teaspoons ground cumin

¼ teaspoon ground red pepper

½ cup chopped fresh mint

1 teaspoon dried oregano

½ teaspoon grated lemon peel

1 cup crumbled feta cheese

Sprigs fresh mint (optional)

1 Combine chickpeas, tomatoes, broth, onions, olives, garlic, cumin and ground red pepper in **CROCK-POT®** slow cooker; stir to blend. Cover; cook on LOW 7 to 8 hours or on HIGH 3½ hours.

2 Stir in chopped mint, oregano and lemon peel; top each serving with feta. Garnish with mint sprigs.

Turkey Chili

MAKES 6 SERVINGS

2 tablespoons olive oil, divided
1½ pounds ground turkey
2 medium onions, chopped
1 medium red bell pepper, chopped
1 medium green bell pepper, chopped
5 cloves garlic, minced
1 jalapeño pepper, finely chopped*
2 cans (about 14 ounces *each*) fire-roasted diced tomatoes

4 teaspoons chili powder
1 teaspoon ground cumin
1 teaspoon dried oregano
½ teaspoon salt

*Jalapeño peppers can sting and irritate the skin, so wear rubber gloves when handling peppers and do not touch your eyes.

1 Heat 1 tablespoon oil in large skillet over medium-high heat. Add turkey; cook 7 to 8 minutes, stirring to break up meat. Remove to **CROCK-POT**® slow cooker using slotted spoon.

2 Heat remaining 1 tablespoon oil in same skillet over medium-high heat. Add onions, bell peppers, garlic and jalapeño pepper; cook and stir 4 to 5 minutes or until softened. Stir in tomatoes, chili powder, cumin, oregano and salt; cook 1 minute. Remove onion mixture to **CROCK-POT**® slow cooker. Cover; cook on LOW 6 hours.

Beef and Black Bean Chili

MAKES 4 SERVINGS

1 tablespoon vegetable oil

1 pound boneless beef round steak, cut into 1-inch cubes

1 package (14 ounces) frozen green and red bell pepper strips with onions

1 can (about 15 ounces) black beans, rinsed and drained

1 can (about 14 ounces) fire-roasted diced tomatoes

2 tablespoons chili powder

1 tablespoon minced garlic

2 teaspoons ground cumin

½ ounce semisweet chocolate, chopped

Hot cooked rice

Shredded Cheddar cheese (optional)

1 Heat oil in large skillet over medium-high heat. Brown beef 6 to 8 minutes on all sides. Remove to **CROCK-POT**® slow cooker using slotted spoon.

2 Stir pepper strips with onions, beans, tomatoes, chili powder, garlic and cumin into **CROCK-POT**® slow cooker. Cover; cook on LOW 8 to 9 hours. Turn off heat; stir in chocolate until melted. Serve over rice; garnish with cheese.

Chipotle Vegetable Chili with Chocolate

MAKES 6 SERVINGS

2 tablespoons olive oil
1 medium onion, chopped
1 medium green bell pepper, chopped
1 medium red bell pepper, chopped
1 cup frozen corn
1 can (28 ounces) diced tomatoes
1 can (about 15 ounces) black beans, rinsed and drained

1 can (about 15 ounces) pinto beans, rinsed and drained
1 tablespoon chili powder
1 teaspoon ground cumin
½ teaspoon chipotle chili powder
1 ounce semisweet chocolate, chopped

1 Heat oil in large skillet over medium-high heat. Add onion and bell peppers; cook and stir 4 minutes or until softened. Stir in corn; cook 3 minutes. Remove to **CROCK-POT®** slow cooker.

2 Stir tomatoes, beans, chili powder, cumin and chipotle chili powder into **CROCK-POT®** slow cooker. Cover; cook on LOW 6 to 7 hours. Stir chocolate into **CROCK-POT®** slow cooker until melted.

Kick'n Chili

MAKES 6 SERVINGS

2 pounds ground beef

1 onion, chopped

2 cloves garlic, minced

3 cans (about 14 ounces *each*) diced tomatoes with mild green chiles

1 jar (16 ounces) salsa

1 tablespoon *each* salt, ground cumin, chili powder, paprika, dried oregano and black pepper

2 teaspoons red pepper flakes

¼ teaspoon ground red pepper

1 Brown beef, onion and garlic in large skillet over medium-high heat 6 to 8 minutes, stirring to break up meat. Remove beef mixture to **CROCK-POT**® slow cooker using slotted spoon.

2 Add tomatoes, salsa, cumin, chili powder, paprika, oregano, red pepper flakes, salt, ground red pepper and black pepper to **CROCK-POT**® slow cooker; stir to blend. Cover; cook on LOW 4 to 6 hours.

Chunky Chili

MAKES 4 SERVINGS

1 pound ground beef
1 medium onion, chopped
2 cans (about 14 ounces *each*) diced tomatoes
1 can (about 15 ounces) pinto beans, rinsed and drained
½ cup prepared salsa

1 tablespoon chili powder
1½ teaspoons ground cumin
Salt and black pepper
Optional toppings: shredded Cheddar cheese, diced onions and sliced pitted black olives

1 Cook beef and onion in large skillet over medium-high heat until beef is browned and onion is tender, stirring to break up meat. Drain and discard fat.

2 Place beef mixture, tomatoes, beans, salsa, chili powder and cumin in **CROCK-POT**® slow cooker; stir. Cover; cook on LOW 5 to 6 hours. Season with salt and pepper. Top as desired.

Tip

Tapping or spinning the cover until the condensation falls off will allow you to see inside the **CROCK-POT**® slow cooker without removing the lid.

Beef and Lamb

Classic Slow-Cooked Pot Roast

MAKES 6 SERVINGS

1 tablespoon olive oil

1 boneless beef chuck roast (about 3 pounds)*

1 medium onion, chopped

2 pounds new potatoes, cut into wedges

1 pound carrots, cut lengthwise and halved

1 cup beef broth

1½ teaspoons salt

1 teaspoon dried rosemary

1 teaspoon dried thyme

1 teaspoon black pepper

Sprigs fresh thyme and rosemary (optional)

Unless you have a 5-, 6- or 7-quart CROCK-POT® slow cooker, cut any roast larger than 2½ pounds in half so it cooks completely.

1 Heat oil in large skillet over medium heat. Add beef; cook 5 to 7 minutes or until browned on both sides. Remove beef to **CROCK-POT®** slow cooker.

2 Add onion, potatoes, carrots, broth, salt, dried rosemary, dried thyme and pepper to **CROCK-POT®** slow cooker. Cover; cook on LOW 8 hours or on HIGH 4 hours. Garnish with fresh thyme and rosemary sprigs.

Portuguese Madeira Beef Shanks

MAKES 4 SERVINGS

1 large white onion, diced

1 green bell pepper, diced

½ cup diced celery

½ cup minced fresh Italian parsley

2 jalapeño peppers, seeded and minced*

4 cloves garlic, minced

4 medium beef shanks, bone in (about 3 pounds *total*)

1 tablespoon fresh rosemary, minced

1 teaspoon salt

1 cup beef broth

1 cup dry Madeira wine

4 cups hot cooked rice

Horseradish sauce (optional)

Jalapeño peppers can sting and irritate the skin, so wear rubber gloves when handling peppers and do not touch your eyes.

1 Combine onion, bell pepper, celery, parsley, jalapeño peppers and garlic in **CROCK-POT®** slow cooker; stir to blend.

2 Rub beef shanks with rosemary and salt. Place shanks on top of vegetables. Pour broth and wine over shanks and vegetables. Cover; cook on LOW 7 to 9 hours.

3 To serve, spoon 1 cup rice into each soup plate. Top rice with beef shank. Spoon vegetable sauce over shanks. Serve with horseradish sauce, if desired.

Moroccan-Style Lamb Shoulder Chops with Couscous

MAKES 4 SERVINGS

4 lamb blade chops (about 2½ pounds)
Salt and black pepper
1 tablespoon olive oil
1 onion, chopped
1 clove garlic, minced
1 teaspoon grated fresh ginger
¼ teaspoon ground cinnamon
½ teaspoon ground turmeric
1 whole bay leaf

1 can (about 14 ounces) diced tomatoes, undrained
1 cup canned chickpeas, rinsed and drained
½ cup water
2 tablespoons lemon juice
Hot cooked couscous
Lemon wedges (optional)

1 Coat inside of **CROCK-POT**® slow cooker with nonstick cooking spray. Season lamb chops with salt and pepper. Heat oil in large skillet over medium-high heat. Add lamb chops; cook 5 to 7 minutes or until browned on all sides. Remove to **CROCK-POT**® slow cooker.

2 Add onion to same skillet; cook and stir 2 to 3 minutes or until softened. Add garlic, ginger, cinnamon, turmeric, salt, pepper and bay leaf; cook and stir 30 seconds. Stir in tomatoes with juice, chickpeas, water and lemon juice; simmer 2 minutes. Pour mixture over lamb. Cover; cook on HIGH 3½ to 4 hours or until lamb is tender.

3 Remove and discard bay leaf. Serve lamb chops over couscous with sauce and vegetables. Serve with lemon wedges, if desired.

Tip

Adding fresh lemon or lime juice just before serving enhances the flavor of many dishes. Try it with other dishes prepared in your **CROCK-POT**® slow cooker.

Royal Round Steak

MAKES 6 SERVINGS

1 to 2 tablespoons oil
1 to 2 pounds boneless beef round
   steak, cut into 1-inch pieces
1 package (about 1 ounce) dry onion
   soup mix

2 cans (10¾ ounces *each*) cream of
   mushroom soup, undiluted
Hot cooked egg noodles

1 Heat oil in large skillet over medium-high heat. Add beef; cook 6 to 8 minutes or until browned on all sides.

2 Combine dry soup mix and canned soup in medium bowl. Pour into **CROCK-POT**® slow cooker. Add browned meat. Cover; cook on HIGH 6 to 7 hours.

3 To serve, spoon over noodles.

Easy Salisbury Steak

MAKES 4 SERVINGS

1½ pounds ground beef
1 egg
½ cup plain dry bread crumbs
1 package (about 1 ounce) dry onion
   soup mix*

1 can (10½ ounces) golden mushroom
   soup, undiluted

You may pulse onion soup mix in a small food processor or coffee grinder for a finer grind, if desired.

1 Coat inside of **CROCK-POT**® slow cooker with nonstick cooking spray. Combine beef, egg, bread crumbs and dry soup mix in large bowl. Form mixture evenly into four 1-inch thick patties.

2 Heat large skillet over medium-high heat. Add patties; cook 2 minutes per side until lightly browned. Remove to **CROCK-POT**® slow cooker, in single layer. Pour mushroom soup evenly over patties. Cover; cook on LOW 3 to 3½ hours.

Meatballs and Spaghetti Sauce

MAKES 6 TO 8 SERVINGS

2 pounds ground beef
1 cup plain dry bread crumbs
1 onion, chopped
2 eggs, beaten
¼ cup minced fresh Italian parsley
4 teaspoons minced garlic, divided
½ teaspoon ground mustard

½ teaspoon black pepper
4 tablespoons olive oil, divided
1 can (28 ounces) whole tomatoes
½ cup chopped fresh basil
1 teaspoon sugar
Salt and black pepper
Hot cooked spaghetti

1 Combine beef, bread crumbs, onion, eggs, parsley, 2 teaspoons garlic, ground mustard and ½ teaspoon pepper in large bowl; mix well. Form into walnut-sized balls. Heat 2 tablespoons oil in large skillet over medium heat. Add meatballs; cook 6 to 8 minutes until browned on all sides. Remove to **CROCK-POT**® slow cooker.

2 Combine tomatoes, basil, remaining 2 tablespoons oil, remaining 2 teaspoons garlic, sugar, salt and black pepper in medium bowl; stir to blend. Pour over meatballs, turn to coat. Cover; cook on LOW 3 to 5 hours or on HIGH 1½ to 2 hours. Serve over spaghetti.

Tip

Recipe can be doubled for a 5-, 6- or 7-quart **CROCK-POT**® slow cooker.

Shepherd's Pie

MAKES 6 SERVINGS

- 1 **pound ground beef**
- 1 **pound ground lamb**
- 1 **package (12 ounces) frozen chopped onions**
- 2 **teaspoons minced garlic**
- 1 **package (16 ounces) frozen peas and carrots**

- 1 **can (about 14 ounces) diced tomatoes, drained**
- 3 **tablespoons quick-cooking tapioca**
- 2 **teaspoons dried oregano**
  Salt and black pepper
- 2 **packages (24 ounces *each*) prepared mashed potatoes**

1 Brown beef and lamb in large nonstick skillet over medium-high heat 6 to 8 minutes, stirring to break up meat. Drain fat. Remove to **CROCK-POT**® slow cooker using slotted spoon. Return skillet to heat. Add onions and garlic; cook and stir 5 to 7 minutes or until onions are tender. Remove to **CROCK-POT**® slow cooker using slotted spoon.

2 Stir peas and carrots, tomatoes, tapioca, oregano, salt and pepper into **CROCK-POT**® slow cooker. Cover; cook on LOW 7 to 8 hours.

3 Top with prepared mashed potatoes. Cover; cook on LOW 30 minutes or until potatoes are heated through.

Southwest-Style Meat Loaf

MAKES 6 SERVINGS

1½ pounds ground beef

2 eggs

1 small onion, chopped (about ½ cup)

½ medium green bell pepper, chopped (about ½ cup)

½ cup plain dry bread crumbs

¾ cup chunky salsa, divided

1½ teaspoons ground cumin

¾ cup (3 ounces) shredded Mexican cheese blend

¾ teaspoon salt

¼ teaspoon black pepper

1 Combine beef, eggs, onion, bell pepper, bread crumbs, ¼ cup salsa, cumin, cheese, salt and black pepper in large bowl; mix well. Form mixture into 9×5-inch loaf.

2 Fold two long pieces of foil in half lengthwise. (Each should be about 24 inches long.) Crisscross pieces on work surface, coat with nonstick cooking spray and set meat loaf on top. Use ends of foil as handles to gently lower meat loaf into **CROCK-POT**® slow cooker, letting ends hang over the top. Top meat loaf with remaining ½ cup salsa.

3 Cover; cook on LOW 7 to 8 hours or on HIGH 3 to 4 hours or until meat loaf is firm and cooked through. Remove meat loaf to large cutting board; let stand 5 minutes before slicing.

Pantry Beef Stroganoff

MAKES 4 SERVINGS

1 pound cubed beef stew meat	1 can (10¾ ounces) condensed cream of mushroom soup
3 tablespoons all-purpose flour, divided	½ cup beef broth
1½ teaspoons dried thyme	¾ cup sour cream
½ teaspoon black pepper	3 cups hot cooked egg noodles
1 tablespoon vegetable or olive oil	Minced fresh Italian parsley (optional)
½ cup chopped onion	

1 Coat inside of **CROCK-POT®** slow cooker with nonstick cooking spray. Place beef, 2 tablespoons flour, thyme and pepper in large resealable food storage bag; shake to coat beef. Heat oil in large skillet over medium heat. Add half of beef; cook 4 to 5 minutes or until browned on all sides, turning occasionally. Remove to large plate. Repeat with remaining half of beef.

2 Add onion to same skillet; cook and stir 5 to 7 minutes or until softened. Add beef, onion, soup and broth to **CROCK-POT®** slow cooker; mix well.

3 Cover; cook on LOW 6 to 7 hours or on HIGH 3 to 4 hours. Whisk remaining 1 tablespoon flour into sour cream in medium bowl. Whisk in ¼ cup of liquid from **CROCK-POT®** slow cooker. Return mixture to **CROCK-POT®** slow cooker; stir to blend. Cover; cook on HIGH 10 minutes or until sauce is thickened. Serve over noodles. Garnish with parsley.

Texas-Style Barbecued Brisket

MAKES 10 TO 12 SERVINGS

3 tablespoons Worcestershire sauce
1 tablespoon chili powder
1 teaspoon celery salt
1 teaspoon black pepper
1 teaspoon liquid smoke
2 cloves garlic, minced

1 beef brisket (3 to 4 pounds), trimmed*
2 whole bay leaves
1¾ cups prepared barbecue sauce

Unless you have a 5-, 6- or 7-quart CROCK-POT® slow cooker, cut any roast larger than 2½ pounds in half so it cooks completely.

1 Combine Worcestershire sauce, chili powder, celery salt, pepper, liquid smoke and garlic in small bowl; stir to blend. Spread mixture on all sides of beef. Place beef in large resealable food storage bag; seal bag. Refrigerate 24 hours.

2 Place beef, marinade and bay leaves in **CROCK-POT®** slow cooker. Cover; cook on LOW 7 hours.

3 Remove beef to large cutting board. Pour cooking liquid into 2-cup measure; let stand 5 minutes. Skim off and discard fat. Remove and discard bay leaves. Stir 1 cup cooking liquid into barbecue sauce in medium bowl. Discard any remaining cooking liquid.

4 Return beef and barbecue sauce mixture to **CROCK-POT®** slow cooker. Cover; cook on LOW 1 hour or until meat is fork-tender. Remove beef to cutting board. Cut across grain into ¼-inch-thick slices. Serve with sauce.

Spicy Sausage Bolognese Sauce

MAKES 6 SERVINGS

2 tablespoons olive oil, divided	½ teaspoon black pepper
1 pound ground beef	3 tablespoons tomato paste
1 pound hot Italian sausage, casings removed	1 tablespoon minced garlic
¼ pound pancetta, diced	2 cans (28 ounces *each*) diced tomatoes, drained
1 large onion, finely diced	¾ cup whole milk
2 medium carrots, finely diced	¾ cup dry red wine
1 large stalk celery, finely diced	1 pound hot cooked spaghetti (optional)
½ teaspoon salt	½ cup grated Parmesan cheese (optional)

1 Heat 1 tablespoon oil in large skillet over medium-high heat. Brown beef and sausage 6 to 8 minutes, stirring to break up meat. Drain fat. Remove to **CROCK-POT**® slow cooker. Wipe out skillet with paper towels; return to heat.

2 Add remaining 1 tablespoon oil to skillet. Add pancetta; cook until crisp and brown, stirring occasionally. Remove to **CROCK-POT**® slow cooker with slotted spoon.

3 Reduce heat to medium. Add onion, carrots, celery, salt and pepper to skillet; cook and stir until onion is translucent and carrots and celery are just tender. Stir in tomato paste and garlic; cook and stir 1 minute. Add onion mixture to **CROCK-POT**® slow cooker.

4 Stir tomatoes, milk and wine into **CROCK-POT**® slow cooker. Cover; cook on LOW 6 hours. Reserve 5 cups sauce for another use. Toss remaining 6 cups sauce with spaghetti, if desired. Sprinkle with cheese just before serving, if desired.

Braised Fruited Lamb

MAKES 6 TO 8 SERVINGS

6 tablespoons extra virgin olive oil	½ cup white vinegar or dry white wine
4 pounds lamb shanks	¼ cup raspberry jam
2 tablespoons salt	½ teaspoon ground allspice
2 tablespoons black pepper	½ teaspoon ground cinnamon
1 cup dried apricots	Hot cooked mashed sweet potatoes (optional)
1 cup dried figs	
1½ cups water	

1 Preheat broiler. Brush oil on lamb shanks; season with salt and pepper. Place shanks on large baking sheet; broil 5 minutes per side. Remove to **CROCK-POT**® slow cooker. Add dried fruits.

2 Combine water, vinegar, jam, allspice and cinnamon in small bowl; stir to blend. Pour over lamb shanks. Cover; cook on LOW 8 to 9 hours or on HIGH 4 to 5 hours.

Easy Beef Burgundy

MAKES 4 TO 6 SERVINGS

1½ pounds boneless beef round steak, cut into 1-inch pieces	1 can (4 ounces) sliced mushrooms, drained
1 can (10¾ ounces) condensed cream of mushroom soup, undiluted	1 package (about 1 ounce) dry onion soup mix
1 cup dry red wine	1 tablespoon minced garlic
1 onion, chopped	Hot cooked egg noodles (optional)

Combine beef, mushroom soup, wine, onion, mushrooms, dry soup mix and garlic in **CROCK-POT**® slow cooker. Cover; cook on LOW 6 to 8 hours or until beef is tender. Serve over noodles, if desired.

Cajun Pot Roast

MAKES 6 SERVINGS

1 boneless beef chuck roast (3 pounds)*

1 to 2 tablespoons Cajun seasoning

1 tablespoon vegetable oil

1 can (about 14 ounces) diced tomatoes

1 can (about 14 ounces) diced tomatoes with mild green chiles

1 medium onion, chopped

1 cup chopped rutabaga

1 cup chopped mushrooms

1 cup chopped turnip

1 cup chopped parsnip

1 cup chopped green bell pepper

1 cup green beans

1 cup sliced carrots

1 cup corn

2 tablespoons hot pepper sauce

1 teaspoon sugar

½ teaspoon black pepper

¾ cup water

Unless you have a 5-, 6- or 7-quart CROCK-POT® slow cooker, cut any roast larger than 2½ pounds in half so it cooks completely.

1 Coat inside of **CROCK-POT®** slow cooker with nonstick cooking spray. Season roast with Cajun seasoning. Heat oil in large skillet over medium-high heat. Add roast; cook 5 minutes on each side until browned.

2 Place roast, tomatoes, onion, rutabaga, mushrooms, turnip, parsnip, bell pepper, green beans, carrots, corn, hot pepper sauce, sugar and black pepper in **CROCK-POT®** slow cooker. Pour in water. Cover; cook on LOW 6 hours.

Pot Roast with Bacon and Mushrooms

MAKES 6 TO 8 SERVINGS

6 slices bacon

1 boneless beef chuck roast
    (2½ to 3 pounds), trimmed*

¾ teaspoon salt, divided

¼ teaspoon black pepper

¾ cup chopped shallots

8 ounces sliced white mushrooms

¼ ounce dried porcini mushrooms
    (optional)

4 cloves garlic, minced

1 teaspoon dried oregano

1 cup beef broth

2 tablespoons tomato paste

Roasted Cauliflower
    (recipe follows, optional)

*Unless you have a 5-, 6- or 7-quart
CROCK-POT® slow cooker, cut any roast
larger than 2½ pounds in half so it cooks
completely.*

1 Heat large skillet over medium heat. Add bacon; cook and stir until crisp. Remove to paper towel-lined plate using slotted spoon; crumble.

2 Pour off all but 2 tablespoons drippings from skillet. Season roast with ½ teaspoon salt and pepper. Heat same skillet over medium-high heat. Add roast; cook 8 minutes or until well browned. Remove to large plate. Add shallots, white mushrooms, porcini mushrooms, if desired, garlic, oregano and remaining ¼ teaspoon salt; cook 3 to 4 minutes or until softened. Remove shallot mixture to **CROCK-POT®** slow cooker.

3 Stir bacon into **CROCK-POT®** slow cooker. Place roast on top of vegetables. Combine broth and tomato paste in small bowl; stir to blend. Pour broth mixture over roast. Cover; cook on LOW 8 hours. Prepare Roasted Cauliflower, if desired. Remove roast to large cutting board. Let stand 10 minutes before slicing. Top each serving with vegetables and cooking liquid. Serve with Roasted Cauliflower, if desired.

Roasted Cauliflower

Preheat oven to 375°F. Break 1 head cauliflower into florets onto large baking sheet; coat with olive oil. Roast 20 minutes. Turn; roast 15 minutes. Makes 6 servings.

Spicy Shredded Beef Tacos

MAKES 6 TO 8 SERVINGS

1 boneless beef chuck roast
  (2½ pounds)
1¼ teaspoons salt, divided
1 teaspoon *each* ground cumin, garlic
  powder and smoked paprika
2 tablespoons olive oil, divided
2 cups beef broth
1 red bell pepper, sliced
1 tomato, cut into wedges

½ onion, sliced
2 cloves garlic, minced
1 to 2 canned chipotle peppers in
  adobo sauce
Juice of 1 lime
Corn or flour tortillas, warmed
Optional toppings: sliced bell peppers,
  avocado, diced onion, lime wedges
  and/or chopped fresh cilantro

1 Season beef with 1 teaspoon salt, cumin, garlic powder and smoked paprika. Heat
1 tablespoon oil in large skillet over medium-high heat. Add beef; cook 5 minutes on
each side until browned. Remove to **CROCK-POT**® slow cooker.

2 Pour in broth. Cover; cook on LOW 8 to
9 hours or on HIGH 4 to 5 hours.

3 Meanwhile, preheat oven to 425°F.
Combine bell pepper, tomato, onion
and garlic on large baking sheet. Drizzle
with remaining 1 tablespoon oil. Roast
40 minutes or until vegetables are
tender. Place vegetables, chipotle
pepper, lime juice and remaining
¼ teaspoon salt in food processor or
blender; blend until smooth.

4 Remove beef to large cutting board;
shred with two forks. Combine shredded
meat with 1 cup cooking liquid. Discard
remaining cooking liquid. Serve on
tortillas with sauce. Top as desired.

Greek-Style Meatballs and Spinach

MAKES 4 SERVINGS

½ cup old-fashioned oats
¼ cup minced onion
1 clove garlic, minced
¼ teaspoon dried oregano
⅛ teaspoon black pepper
1 egg
8 ounces ground lamb

1 cup beef broth
¼ teaspoon salt
½ cup plain nonfat yogurt
1 teaspoon all-purpose flour
4 cups fresh baby spinach, coarsely chopped
1⅓ cups hot cooked egg noodles

1 Combine oats, onion, garlic, oregano and pepper in medium bowl; whisk in egg. Add lamb; mix well but do not knead. Shape mixture into 16 balls. Place in **CROCK-POT®** slow cooker. Add broth and salt. Cover; cook on LOW 6 hours.

2 Stir yogurt into flour in small bowl. Spoon about ¼ cup hot liquid from **CROCK-POT®** slow cooker into yogurt mixture; stir until smooth. Whisk yogurt mixture into **CROCK-POT®** slow cooker. Add spinach. Cover; cook on LOW 10 minutes or until heated through. Serve over noodles.

Delicious Pepper Steak

MAKES 8 SERVINGS

2 tablespoons toasted sesame oil
2 pounds beef round steak, cut into strips
½ medium red bell pepper, sliced
½ medium green bell pepper, sliced
½ medium yellow bell pepper, sliced
1 medium onion, sliced
14 grape tomatoes
⅓ cup hoisin sauce

¼ cup water
3 tablespoons all-purpose flour
3 tablespoons soy sauce
2 teaspoons garlic powder
1 teaspoon ground cumin
1 teaspoon dried oregano
1 teaspoon paprika
⅛ teaspoon ground red pepper
Hot cooked rice (optional)

1 Heat oil in large skillet over medium-high heat. Add beef in batches; cook 4 to 5 minutes or until browned. Remove to large paper towel-lined plate.

2 Add bell peppers, onion and tomatoes to **CROCK-POT**® slow cooker. Combine hoisin sauce, water, flour, soy sauce, garlic powder, cumin, oregano, paprika and ground red pepper in medium bowl; stir to blend. Add to **CROCK-POT**® slow cooker. Add beef. Cover; cook on LOW 8 to 9 hours or on HIGH 4 to 4½ hours. Serve with rice, if desired.

Italian-Style Pot Roast

MAKES 6 TO 8 SERVINGS

2 teaspoons minced garlic

1 teaspoon salt

1 teaspoon dried basil

1 teaspoon dried oregano

¼ teaspoon red pepper flakes

1 boneless beef bottom round rump roast or chuck shoulder roast (about 2½ to 3 pounds)*

1 large onion, quartered and thinly sliced

1½ cups tomato-basil or marinara pasta sauce

2 cans (about 15 ounces *each*) cannellini or Great Northern beans, rinsed and drained

¼ cup shredded fresh basil (optional)

Unless you have a 5-, 6- or 7-quart CROCK-POT® slow cooker, cut any roast larger than 2½ pounds in half so it cooks completely.

1 Combine garlic, salt, dried basil, oregano and red pepper flakes in small bowl; rub over roast.

2 Place onion slices in **CROCK-POT®** slow cooker. Top roast with onion slices and pasta sauce. Cover; cook on LOW 8 to 9 hours or until roast is fork-tender.

3 Remove roast to large cutting board. Cover loosely with foil; let stand 10 to 15 minutes. Turn off heat. Let liquid in **CROCK-POT®** slow cooker stand 5 minutes to allow fat to rise. Skim off and discard fat.

4 Turn **CROCK-POT®** slow cooker to LOW. Stir beans into liquid. Cover; cook on LOW 15 to 30 minutes or until beans are heated through. Slice roast across the grain into thin slices. Serve with bean mixture. Garnish with fresh basil.

So Simple Supper!

MAKES 8 SERVINGS

1 boneless beef chuck shoulder roast, trimmed (3 to 4 pounds)*

3 cups water

1 package (about 1 ounce) dry onion soup mix

1 package (about 1 ounce) dry au jus gravy mix

1 package (about 1 ounce) dry mushroom gravy mix

Assorted vegetables (potatoes, carrots, pearl onions and celery)

*Unless you have a 5-, 6- or 7-quart CROCK-POT® slow cooker, cut any roast larger than 2½ pounds in half so it cooks completely.

1 Place beef in **CROCK-POT®** slow cooker. Combine water, dry soup mix and dry gravy mixes in large bowl; stir to blend. Pour gravy mixture over beef in **CROCK-POT®** slow cooker. Cover; cook on LOW 4 hours.

2 Add vegetables. Cover; cook on LOW 4 hours.

Beef and Veal Meat Loaf

MAKES 6 SERVINGS

1 tablespoon olive oil	1 pound ground veal
1 small onion, chopped	1 egg
½ red bell pepper, chopped	3 tablespoons tomato paste
3 cloves garlic, minced	1 teaspoon salt
1 teaspoon dried oregano	½ teaspoon black pepper
1 pound ground beef	

1 Coat inside of **CROCK-POT**® slow cooker with nonstick cooking spray. Heat oil in large skillet over medium-high heat. Add onion, bell pepper, garlic and oregano; cook and stir 5 minutes or until vegetables are softened. Remove onion mixture to large bowl; cool 6 minutes.

2 Combine beef, veal, egg, tomato paste, salt and black pepper in large bowl with onion mixture; mix well. Form into 9×5-inch loaf; place in **CROCK-POT**® slow cooker.

3 Cover; cook on LOW 5 to 6 hours. Remove meat loaf to large cutting board; let stand 10 minutes before slicing.

Pepper Steak

MAKES 6 TO 8 SERVINGS

2 tablespoons vegetable oil
3 pounds boneless beef top sirloin steak, cut into strips
5 to 6 cloves garlic, minced
1 medium onion, chopped
½ cup soy sauce
2 teaspoons sugar

1 teaspoon salt
½ teaspoon ground ginger
½ teaspoon black pepper
3 green bell peppers, cut into strips
¼ cup cold water
1 tablespoon cornstarch
Hot cooked rice

1 Heat oil in large skillet over medium heat. Brown steak strips in batches. Add garlic; cook and stir 2 minutes. Remove steak strips, garlic and pan juices to **CROCK-POT®** slow cooker.

2 Add onion, soy sauce, sugar, salt, ginger and black pepper to **CROCK-POT®** slow cooker; stir to blend. Cover; cook on LOW 6 to 8 hours or until meat is tender (up to 10 hours). Add bell pepper strips during final hour of cooking.

3 Stir water into cornstarch in small bowl until smooth; whisk into cooking liquid. Turn **CROCK-POT®** slow cooker to HIGH. Cook, uncovered, on HIGH 15 minutes or until thickened. Serve with rice.

Tip

Cooking times are guidelines. **CROCK-POT®** slow cookers, just like ovens, cook differently depending on a variety of factors. For example, cooking times will be longer at higher altitudes. You may need to slightly adjust cooking times.

Slow Cooker Steak Fajitas

MAKES 4 SERVINGS

1 beef flank steak (about 1 pound)
1 medium onion, cut into strips
½ cup medium salsa, plus additional
  for serving
2 tablespoons chopped fresh cilantro
2 tablespoons fresh lime juice
2 cloves garlic, minced

1 tablespoon chili powder
1 teaspoon ground cumin
½ teaspoon salt
1 small green bell pepper, cut into strips
1 small red bell pepper, cut into strips
  Flour tortillas, warmed

1 Cut flank steak lengthwise in half, then crosswise into thin strips; place meat in **CROCK-POT®** slow cooker. Combine onion, ½ cup salsa, cilantro, lime juice, garlic, chili powder, cumin and salt in **CROCK-POT®** slow cooker. Cover; cook on LOW 5 to 6 hours.

2 Add bell peppers. Cover; cook on LOW 1 hour.

3 Serve with tortillas and additional salsa, if desired.

Tip

CROCK-POT® slow cooker recipes calling for raw meats should cook a minimum of 3 hours on LOW for food safety reasons. When in doubt, use an instant-read thermometer to ensure the meat has reached the recommended internal temperature for safe consumption.

Short Ribs and Mashed Buttermilk Potatoes

MAKES 8 SERVINGS

5 pounds beef short ribs (10 pieces)	4 cloves garlic, chopped
2½ pounds red potatoes	2 teaspoons salt, divided
2 cups dry red wine	¼ teaspoon black pepper
1 can (about 14 ounces) beef broth	1 cup buttermilk
1 large onion, chopped	2 tablespoons butter
2 carrots, chopped	1 teaspoon ground thyme
2 stalks celery, chopped	½ teaspoon dried rosemary
2 tablespoons tomato paste	2 tablespoons all-purpose flour

1 Heat large nonstick skillet over medium-high heat. Add ribs in batches; cook 5 to 6 minutes or until browned. Remove to **CROCK-POT®** slow cooker using slotted spoon.

2 Add potatoes, wine, broth, onion, carrots, celery, tomato paste, garlic, 1 teaspoon salt and pepper to **CROCK-POT®** slow cooker. Cover; cook on LOW 10 to 11 hours or on HIGH 5 to 7 hours.

3 Turn off heat. Remove potatoes to large bowl using slotted spoon. Add buttermilk, butter and remaining 1 teaspoon salt; mash until smooth. Remove ribs to large serving dish using slotted spoon.

4 Let cooking liquid stand 5 minutes. Skim off and discard fat. Turn **CROCK-POT®** slow cooker to HIGH. Stir in thyme and rosemary. Cook, uncovered, on HIGH 15 minutes. Stir ⅓ cup liquid into flour in small bowl until smooth; whisk into cooking liquid. Cover; cook on HIGH 10 to 15 minutes or until thickened. Serve gravy over ribs and potatoes.

Sauvignon Blanc Beef with Beets and Thyme

MAKES 6 SERVINGS

1 pound red or yellow beets, scrubbed and quartered

2 tablespoons extra virgin olive oil

1 boneless beef chuck roast (about 3 pounds)*

1 medium yellow onion, peeled and quartered

2 cloves garlic, minced

5 sprigs fresh thyme

1 whole bay leaf

2 whole cloves

1 cup chicken broth

1 cup Sauvignon Blanc or dry white wine

2 tablespoons tomato paste

Salt and black pepper

Unless you have a 5-, 6- or 7-quart CROCK-POT® slow cooker, cut any roast larger than 2½ pounds in half so it cooks completely.

1 Layer beets evenly in **CROCK-POT**® slow cooker.

2 Heat oil in large skillet over medium heat. Brown roast on all sides 4 to 5 minutes. Add onion and garlic during last few minutes of browning. Remove to **CROCK-POT**® slow cooker.

3 Add thyme, bay leaf and cloves to **CROCK-POT**® slow cooker. Combine broth, wine, tomato paste, salt and pepper in medium bowl; stir to blend. Pour over roast and beets in **CROCK-POT**® slow cooker. Cover; cook on LOW 8 to 10 hours or until roast is fork-tender and beets are tender. Remove and discard bay leaf before serving.

Maple Whiskey-Glazed Beef Brisket

MAKES 4 TO 6 SERVINGS

1 teaspoon ground red pepper
1 tablespoon coarse salt
½ teaspoon black pepper
1½ to 2 pounds beef brisket, scored with a knife on both sides
2 tablespoons olive oil
½ cup maple syrup
¼ cup whiskey

2 tablespoons packed brown sugar
1 tablespoon tomato paste
Juice of 1 orange
2 cloves garlic, crushed
4 (⅟₁₆-inch-thick) slices fresh ginger
4 (½×1½-inch-thick *each*) slices orange peel

1 Combine ground red pepper, salt and black pepper in small mixing bowl. Rub over brisket. Place brisket in large resealable food storage bag.

2 Combine oil, syrup, whiskey, brown sugar, tomato paste, orange juice, garlic, ginger and orange peel in small bowl; stir to blend. Pour mixture over brisket in resealable food storage bag. Marinate brisket in refrigerator at least 2 hours or overnight.

3 Remove brisket and marinade to **CROCK-POT**® slow cooker. Cover, cook on LOW 7 to 9 hours, turning brisket once or twice. Adjust seasonings to taste. Slice thinly across the grain and serve.

Herbed Pot Roast with Fingerling Potatoes

MAKES 8 SERVINGS

1 boneless beef chuck roast (3 pounds)*
¼ cup all-purpose flour
2 tablespoons olive oil
16 baby carrots
8 fingerling potatoes, halved crosswise
1 medium onion, chopped
2 teaspoons garlic powder
1 teaspoon dried basil
1 teaspoon dried oregano

½ teaspoon dried rosemary
½ teaspoon dried marjoram
½ teaspoon dried sage
½ teaspoon dried thyme
¼ teaspoon black pepper
1½ cups beef broth

Unless you have a 5-, 6- or 7-quart CROCK-POT® slow cooker, cut any piece of meat larger than 2½ pounds in half so it cooks completely.

1 Combine beef and flour in large bowl; toss to coat. Heat oil in large skillet over medium-high heat. Remove beef from flour, reserving flour. Add beef to skillet; cook 6 to 8 minutes or until browned.

2 Meanwhile, add carrots, potatoes, onion, garlic powder, basil, oregano, rosemary, marjoram, sage, thyme and pepper to **CROCK-POT®** slow cooker. Combine reserved flour with broth in small bowl; add to **CROCK-POT®** slow cooker. Top with beef.

3 Cover; cook on LOW 10 to 12 hours or on HIGH 5 to 6 hours. Remove beef to large cutting board. Cover loosely with foil; let stand 10 to 15 minutes before evenly slicing into eight pieces. Serve with gravy and vegetables.

Lamb Shanks and Garlic Eggplant

MAKES 4 SERVINGS

2 pounds eggplant, cut into 1-inch-thick slices
1 medium onion, chopped
12 cloves garlic, crushed
3 lamb shanks (1 pound *each*)
1 teaspoon salt

¼ teaspoon black pepper
½ cup dry red wine
1 can (about 14 ounces) fire-roasted diced tomatoes
Pita bread rounds (optional)

1 Preheat broiler. Place eggplant on large baking sheet; spray with nonstick cooking spray. Broil 6 to 8 minutes or until golden brown. Turn and coat with nonstick cooking spray; broil 6 to 8 minutes or until golden brown. Remove to **CROCK-POT®** slow cooker.

2 Spray large skillet with cooking spray; heat over medium-high heat. Add onion; cook 5 to 6 minutes or until golden. Sprinkle onion and garlic over eggplant.

3 Season lamb shanks with salt and pepper. Cook in same skillet over medium-high heat 5 to 7 minutes or until browned on all sides. Remove to **CROCK-POT®** slow cooker using slotted spoon.

4 Add wine to skillet; cook and stir until reduced by half. Stir in tomatoes; pour over lamb. Cover; cook on LOW 7 to 8 hours or on HIGH 3 to 4 hours.

5 Turn off heat. Remove lamb and vegetables from **CROCK-POT®** slow cooker to large cutting board. Use fork to slide meat off bones. Let cooking liquid stand 5 minutes. Skim off and discard fat. Serve lamb and vegetables with cooking liquid. Serve with pita bread rounds, if desired.

Garlic and Mushroom Roast with Savory Gravy

MAKES 8 TO 10 SERVINGS

3 to 4 pounds boneless beef chuck
    roast, cut into ½-inch strips*
Salt and black pepper
¼ cup all-purpose flour
1 to 2 tablespoons vegetable oil
1 to 2 jars (12 ounces *each*) beef gravy
1 to 2 cans (4 ounces *each*) mushrooms,
    drained

1 medium onion, thinly sliced
3 cloves garlic, sliced
Hot cooked rice or couscous
Chopped fresh Italian parsley (optional)

*Unless you have a 5-, 6- or 7-quart
CROCK-POT® *slow cooker, cut any roast*
larger than 2½ pounds in half so it cooks
completely.

1 Season roast with salt and pepper; coat with flour. Heat oil in large skillet over medium-high heat. Brown roast 5 minutes on each side.

2 Place roast, gravy, mushrooms, onion and garlic in **CROCK-POT**® slow cooker. Cover; cook on LOW 8 to 10 hours. Serve over rice. Garnish with parsley.

Beef and Quinoa Stuffed Cabbage Rolls

MAKES 4 SERVINGS

8 large green cabbage leaves, veins
    trimmed at bottom of each leaf
1 pound ground beef
1½ cups cooked quinoa

1 medium onion, chopped
1 cup tomato juice, divided
Salt and black pepper

1 Heat salted water in large saucepan over high heat; bring to a boil. Add cabbage leaves; return to boil. Cook 2 minutes. Drain and let cool.

2 Combine beef, quinoa, onion, ¼ cup tomato juice, salt and pepper in large bowl; mix well. Place cabbage leaf on large work surface; top center with 2 to 3 tablespoons beef mixture. Starting at stem end, roll up jelly-roll style, folding sides in as you go. Repeat with remaining cabbage rolls and beef mixture.

3 Place cabbage rolls seam side down and side by side in single layer in **CROCK-POT**® slow cooker. Pour in remaining ¾ cup tomato juice. Cover; cook on LOW 5 to 6 hours.

Asian Beef with Mandarin Oranges

MAKES 6 SERVINGS

2 tablespoons vegetable oil

2 pounds boneless beef chuck roast, cut into ½-inch strips

1 onion, thinly sliced

1 head bok choy, chopped

1 green bell pepper, sliced

1 can (5 ounces) sliced water chestnuts, drained

1 package (about 3 ounces) shiitake mushrooms, sliced

⅓ cup soy sauce

2 teaspoons minced fresh ginger

¼ teaspoon salt

2 cups beef broth

1 can (11 ounces) mandarin oranges, drained and syrup reserved

2 tablespoons cornstarch

6 cups steamed rice

1 Heat oil in large skillet over medium-high heat. Add beef in batches; cook and stir 5 to 7 minutes or until browned on all sides. Remove to **CROCK-POT**® slow cooker.

2 Add onion to skillet; cook and stir over medium heat 3 minutes or until softened. Add bok choy, bell pepper, water chestnuts, mushrooms, soy sauce, ginger and salt; cook and stir 5 minutes or until bok choy is wilted. Remove to **CROCK-POT**® slow cooker.

3 Pour broth into large bowl. Stir reserved mandarin orange syrup into cornstarch in medium bowl until smooth; whisk into broth. Pour broth mixture into **CROCK-POT**® slow cooker. Cover; cook on LOW 10 hours or on HIGH 5 to 6 hours.

4 Stir in mandarin oranges. To serve, spoon over rice in shallow serving bowls.

Italian Braciole

MAKES 6 SERVINGS

2 pounds beef round steak, thinly sliced

2 slices whole grain bread, toasted and crumbled

½ cup chopped onion

¼ cup grated Parmesan cheese

2 cloves garlic

3 tablespoons olive oil, divided

1 teaspoon Italian seasoning

1 egg

½ teaspoon salt

½ teaspoon black pepper

1 jar (24 to 26 ounces) tomato-basil pasta sauce

Hot cooked pasta (optional)

Chopped fresh Italian parsley (optional)

1 Coat inside of **CROCK-POT®** slow cooker with nonstick cooking spray. Place beef on large cutting board. Pound into ¼-inch thickness; cut evenly into two pieces.

2 Combine bread, onion, cheese, garlic, 2 tablespoons oil, Italian seasoning, egg, salt and pepper in food processor or blender; pulse just until mixture is moistened but still chunky. Divide bread mixture evenly over steak pieces; roll tightly to enclose filling. Tie each with kitchen string to secure.

3 Heat remaining 1 tablespoon oil in large skillet over medium heat. Add steak rolls; cook and turn 6 minutes or until browned on all sides. Pour ½ cup pasta sauce into bottom of **CROCK-POT®** slow cooker; top with steak rolls. Top with remaining pasta sauce. Cover; cook on LOW 4 to 5 hours. Cut steak rolls evenly into 14 pieces. Serve over pasta, if desired. Garnish with parsley.

Perfect Poultry

Chicken Scaloppine in Alfredo Sauce

MAKES 6 SERVINGS

2 tablespoons all-purpose flour	1 tablespoon butter
¼ teaspoon salt	1 tablespoon olive oil
¼ teaspoon black pepper	1 cup Alfredo pasta sauce
6 boneless, skinless chicken tenderloins (about 1 pound), cut lengthwise in half	1 package (12 ounces) uncooked spinach noodles

1 Place flour, salt and pepper in large bowl; stir to combine. Add chicken; toss to coat. Heat butter and oil in large skillet over medium-high heat. Add chicken; cook 3 minutes per side or until browned. Remove chicken to **CROCK-POT**® slow cooker.

2 Add pasta sauce to **CROCK-POT**® slow cooker. Cover; cook on LOW 1 to 1½ hours.

3 Meanwhile, cook noodles according to package directions. Drain; place in large shallow bowl. Spoon chicken and sauce over noodles.

Chicken Enchilada Roll-Ups

MAKES 6 SERVINGS

6 boneless, skinless chicken breasts (about 1½ pounds)

½ cup plus 2 tablespoons all-purpose flour, divided

½ teaspoon salt

2 tablespoons butter

1 cup chicken broth

1 onion, diced

¼ to ½ cup sliced canned jalapeño peppers

½ teaspoon dried oregano

2 tablespoons whipping cream or milk

6 (7- to 8-inch) flour tortillas

6 thin slices American cheese or American cheese with jalapeño peppers

1 Cut each chicken breast lengthwise into 2 or 3 strips. Combine ½ cup flour and salt in large resealable food storage bag. Add chicken strips; shake to coat. Melt butter in large skillet over medium heat. Add chicken strips in batches; cook 2 to 3 minutes per side or until browned. Remove to **CROCK-POT**® slow cooker.

2 Add broth to skillet, stirring to scrape up any browned bits from bottom of skillet. Pour broth mixture into **CROCK-POT**® slow cooker. Add onion, jalapeño peppers and oregano. Cover; cook on LOW 7 to 8 hours or on HIGH 3 to 4 hours.

3 Blend remaining 2 tablespoons flour and cream in small bowl until smooth; whisk into chicken mixture. Cook, uncovered, on HIGH 15 minutes or until thickened. Spoon chicken mixture onto center of flour tortillas. Top each with cheese slice. Fold up tortillas and serve.

Beer Chicken

MAKES 4 TO 6 SERVINGS

2	tablespoons olive oil	1	medium onion, chopped
1	cut-up whole chicken (3 to 5 pounds)	1	tablespoon chopped fresh rosemary
10	new potatoes, halved	1	teaspoon salt
1	can (12 ounces) beer	½	teaspoon black pepper
2	medium carrots, chopped into 1-inch pieces	2	tablespoons water
1	cup chopped celery	2	tablespoons all-purpose flour

1 Heat oil in large skillet over medium heat. Add chicken; cook 5 to 7 minutes on each side or until browned. Remove to **CROCK-POT**® slow cooker.

2 Add potatoes, beer, carrots, celery, onion, rosemary, salt and pepper to **CROCK-POT**® slow cooker. Cover; cook on HIGH 5 hours.

3 Remove vegetables and chicken to large bowl using slotted spoon; keep warm. Stir water into flour in small bowl until smooth; whisk into cooking liquid. Cook, uncovered, on HIGH 10 to 15 minutes or until sauce is thickened. Serve chicken and vegetables with sauce.

Spanish Paella with Chicken and Sausage

MAKES 4 SERVINGS

4 chicken thighs (about 2 pounds *total*)	1½ cups chicken broth
Salt and black pepper	1 can (about 14 ounces) stewed
1 tablespoon olive oil	tomatoes, undrained
1 package (14 ounces) smoked sausage,	1 cup uncooked Arborio rice
sliced into rounds	1 pinch saffron (optional)
1 large onion, chopped	½ cup frozen peas, thawed
1 clove garlic, minced	

1 Season chicken with salt and pepper. Heat oil in large skillet over medium-high heat. Add chicken; cook 5 to 7 minutes or until browned on all sides. Remove chicken to large plate using slotted spoon. Add sausage to skillet; cook and stir 5 minutes or until browned. Remove sausage to plate with chicken using slotted spoon.

2 Add onion to same skillet; cook 3 to 5 minutes or until translucent. Add garlic; cook and stir 1 minute. Stir onion mixture, broth, tomatoes with juice, rice and saffron, if desired, into **CROCK-POT**® slow cooker. Top with chicken and sausage. Cover; cook on LOW 6 to 8 hours or on HIGH 3 to 4 hours.

3 Remove chicken pieces to serving platter; fluff rice with fork. Stir peas into rice. Spoon rice into bowls; top with chicken.

Easy Parmesan Chicken

MAKES 4 SERVINGS

8 ounces mushrooms, sliced
1 medium onion, cut into thin wedges
1 tablespoon olive oil
4 boneless, skinless chicken breasts
1 jar (24 to 26 ounces) pasta sauce
½ teaspoon dried basil
¼ teaspoon dried oregano

1 whole bay leaf
½ cup (2 ounces) shredded mozzarella cheese
¼ cup grated Parmesan cheese
Hot cooked spaghetti
Chopped fresh basil (optional)

1 Place mushrooms and onion in **CROCK-POT**® slow cooker.

2 Heat oil in large skillet over medium-high heat. Add chicken; cook 5 to 6 minutes on each side or until browned. Place chicken in **CROCK-POT**® slow cooker. Pour pasta sauce over chicken; add dried basil, oregano and bay leaf. Cover; cook on LOW 6 to 7 hours or on HIGH 3 to 4 hours. Remove and discard bay leaf.

3 Sprinkle chicken with cheeses. Cook, uncovered, on LOW 10 minutes or until cheeses are melted. Serve over spaghetti and garnish with fresh basil.

Tip

Dairy products should be added at the end of the cooking time, because they will curdle if cooked in the **CROCK-POT**® slow cooker for a long time.

Slow Cooker Turkey Breast

MAKES 4 TO 6 SERVINGS

½ to 1 teaspoon garlic powder
½ to 1 teaspoon paprika
1 boneless turkey breast (4 to 6 pounds)*

1 tablespoon dried parsley flakes

Unless you have a 5-, 6- or 7-quart CROCK-POT® slow cooker, cut any piece of meat larger than 2½ pounds in half so it cooks completely.

1 Combine garlic powder and paprika in small bowl; rub onto turkey. Place turkey in **CROCK-POT®** slow cooker. Sprinkle with parsley flakes. Cover; cook on LOW 6 to 8 hours or on HIGH 3 to 4 hours.

2 Remove turkey to large cutting board. Cover loosely with foil; let stand 10 to 15 minutes before slicing.

Slow-Cooked Chicken Adobo

MAKES 6 SERVINGS

3 pounds bone-in chicken thighs
Garlic powder
Paprika (optional)
Black pepper
1 tablespoon plus 1 teaspoon vegetable oil, divided
1 large onion, sliced
6 cloves garlic

½ cup apple cider vinegar
1 (1-inch) piece fresh ginger, cut into thick slices
2 tablespoons soy sauce or tamari sauce
2 whole bay leaves
Cooked green beans (optional)

1 Season chicken with garlic powder, paprika, if desired, and pepper. Heat 1 tablespoon oil in large skillet over medium-high heat. Brown chicken 3 to 4 minutes on each side.

2 Pour remaining 1 teaspoon oil in **CROCK-POT®** slow cooker. Combine chicken, onion, garlic, vinegar, ginger, soy sauce and bay leaves in **CROCK-POT®** slow cooker. Cover; cook on LOW 8 hours or on HIGH 4 hours. Remove and discard ginger and bay leaves. Serve with green beans, if desired.

Mini Puttanesca Meatballs and Spaghetti

MAKES 8 SERVINGS

- 1 pound ground turkey
- ¼ cup seasoned dry bread crumbs
- 1 egg
- 1 jar (24 to 26 ounces) marinara sauce
- ½ cup coarsely chopped pitted kalamata olives

- 2 tablespoons drained capers
- ½ to ¾ teaspoon red pepper flakes
- 6 ounces hot cooked spaghetti
- ¼ cup fresh basil or Italian parsley slivers (optional)

1 Preheat oven to 425°F. Combine turkey, bread crumbs and egg in large bowl; mix well. Shape into 24 (1-inch) meatballs; place on foil-lined baking sheet. Bake 15 to 18 minutes or until browned and no longer pink in center.

2 Coat inside of 2-quart **CROCK-POT**® slow cooker with nonstick cooking spray. Combine marinara sauce, olives, capers and red pepper flakes in **CROCK-POT**® slow cooker; stir to blend. Add meatballs; turn to coat. Cover; cook on LOW 3 to 4 hours or on HIGH 1½ to 2 hours. Serve sauce and meatballs with spaghetti. Garnish with basil.

Chicken Parmesan with Eggplant

MAKES 6 TO 8 SERVINGS

6 boneless, skinless chicken breasts	2 small eggplants, cut into ¾-inch-thick slices
2 eggs	1½ cups grated Parmesan cheese
2 teaspoons salt	2¼ cups tomato-basil pasta sauce
2 teaspoons black pepper	1 pound (16 ounces) sliced or shredded mozzarella cheese
2 cups seasoned dry bread crumbs	Sprigs fresh basil (optional)
½ cup olive oil	
½ cup (1 stick) butter	

1 Slice chicken breasts in half lengthwise. Cut each half lengthwise again to get four ¾-inch slices.

2 Combine eggs, salt and pepper in medium bowl; whisk to blend. Place bread crumbs in separate medium bowl. Dip chicken in egg mixture; turn to coat. Then coat chicken with bread crumbs, covering both sides evenly.

3 Heat oil and butter in large skillet over medium heat. Add breaded chicken; cook 6 to 8 minutes until browned on both sides. Remove to paper towel-lined plate to drain excess oil.

4 Layer half of eggplant, ¾ cup Parmesan cheese and 1 cup sauce in bottom of **CROCK-POT**® slow cooker. Top with half of chicken, remaining half of eggplant, remaining ¾ cup Parmesan cheese and ¼ cup sauce. Arrange remaining half of chicken on sauce; top with remaining 1 cup sauce and mozzarella cheese. Cover; cook on LOW 6 hours or on HIGH 2 to 4 hours. Garnish with fresh basil.

Chicken Marsala with Fettuccine

MAKES 6 TO 8 SERVINGS

4 boneless, skinless chicken breasts
1 tablespoon vegetable oil
1 onion, chopped
½ cup Marsala wine
2 packages (6 ounces *each*) sliced cremini mushrooms
½ cup chicken broth
2 teaspoons Worcestershire sauce

½ teaspoon salt
½ teaspoon black pepper
½ cup whipping cream
2 tablespoons cornstarch
8 ounces fettuccine, cooked and drained
2 tablespoons chopped fresh Italian parsley (optional)

1 Coat inside of **CROCK-POT®** slow cooker with nonstick cooking spray. Arrange chicken in single layer in **CROCK-POT®** slow cooker.

2 Heat oil in large skillet over medium heat. Add onion; cook and stir 5 to 7 minutes or until translucent. Add wine; cook 2 minutes or until mixture reduces slightly. Stir in mushrooms, broth, Worcestershire sauce, salt and pepper. Pour mixture over chicken. Cover; cook on HIGH 1½ to 1¾ hours or until chicken is cooked through.

3 Remove chicken to large cutting board. Cover loosely with foil to keep warm. Stir cream into cornstarch in small bowl until smooth; whisk into cooking liquid. Cover; cook on HIGH 15 minutes or until thickened. Slice chicken. Place fettuccine in large serving bowl. Top with chicken and sauce. Garnish with parsley.

Tip

Skinless chicken is usually best for recipes using the **CROCK-POT®** slow cooker, because the skin can shrivel and curl during cooking.

Caribbean Jerk Chicken

MAKES 6 SERVINGS

6 boneless, skinless chicken thighs
1 small yellow onion
¼ cup chicken broth
¼ cup soy sauce
1 large jalapeño pepper, seeded*
2 teaspoons minced garlic
1 teaspoon ground ginger
1 teaspoon dried thyme

¼ teaspoon ground cloves
⅛ teaspoon ground allspice
⅛ teaspoon ground cinnamon
  Hot cooked rice (optional)

Jalapeño peppers can sting and irritate the skin, so wear rubber gloves when handling peppers and do not touch your eyes.

1 Coat inside of **CROCK-POT**® slow cooker with nonstick cooking spray; add chicken.

2 Combine onion, broth, soy sauce, jalapeño pepper, garlic, ginger, thyme, cloves, allspice and cinnamon in food processor or blender; process until well blended. Pour onion mixture over chicken in **CROCK-POT**® slow cooker.

3 Cover; cook on HIGH 3 hours. Serve with rice, if desired.

Turkey Stroganoff

MAKES 4 SERVINGS

4 cups sliced mushrooms

2 stalks celery, thinly sliced

2 medium shallots *or* ½ small onion, minced

1 cup chicken broth

½ teaspoon dried thyme

¼ teaspoon black pepper

2 turkey tenderloins, turkey breasts *or* boneless, skinless chicken thighs (about 10 ounces *each*), cut into 1-inch pieces

½ cup sour cream

1 tablespoon plus 1 teaspoon all-purpose flour

¼ teaspoon salt (optional)

1⅓ cups hot cooked egg noodles

1 Spray large skillet with nonstick cooking spray; heat over medium heat. Add mushrooms, celery and shallots; cook and stir 5 minutes or until mushrooms and shallots are tender. Spoon into **CROCK-POT**® slow cooker. Stir broth, thyme and pepper into **CROCK-POT**® slow cooker. Stir in turkey. Cover; cook on LOW 5 to 6 hours.

2 Mix sour cream into flour in small bowl. Spoon 2 tablespoons liquid from **CROCK-POT**® slow cooker into sour cream mixture; stir well. Stir sour cream mixture into **CROCK-POT**® slow cooker. Cover; cook on LOW 10 minutes.

3 Season with salt, if desired. Spoon noodles onto each plate to serve. Top with turkey mixture.

Chicken Meatballs in Spicy Tomato Sauce

MAKES 4 SERVINGS

3 tablespoons olive oil, divided	3 tablespoons tomato paste
1 medium onion, chopped	2 teaspoons salt, divided
6 cloves garlic, minced	1½ pounds ground chicken
1½ teaspoons dried basil	2 egg yolks
¼ teaspoon red pepper flakes	1 teaspoon dried oregano
2 cans (about 14 ounces *each*) diced tomatoes	¼ teaspoon black pepper

1 Heat 2 tablespoons oil in large skillet over medium-high heat. Add onion, garlic, basil and red pepper flakes; cook and stir 5 minutes or until onion is softened. Remove half of mixture to **CROCK-POT**® slow cooker. Stir in diced tomatoes, tomato paste and 1 teaspoon salt.

2 Remove remaining onion mixture to large bowl. Add chicken, egg yolks, oregano, remaining 1 teaspoon salt and black pepper; mix well. Form mixture into 24 (1-inch) balls.

3 Heat remaining 1 tablespoon oil in large skillet. Add meatballs in batches; cook 7 minutes or until browned. Remove to **CROCK-POT**® slow cooker using slotted spoon. Cover; cook on LOW 4 to 5 hours.

Mexican Chicken

MAKES 2 TO 4 SERVINGS

2 to 4 boneless, skinless chicken breasts
1 medium onion, sliced
1 can (10¾ ounces) condensed cream of chicken soup, undiluted
1 can (10 ounces) Mexican-style diced tomatoes with mild green chiles
1 package (8 ounces) pasteurized process cheese product, cubed
Hot cooked spaghetti

1 Place chicken, onion, soup and tomatoes with chiles in **CROCK-POT®** slow cooker. Cover; cook on LOW 6 to 8 hours or on HIGH 4 hours.

2 Break up chicken into pieces. Add cheese product. Cover; cook on HIGH 10 minutes or until cheese is melted. Serve over spaghetti.

Fresh Herbed Turkey Breast

MAKES 8 SERVINGS

2 tablespoons butter, softened
¼ cup fresh sage, minced
¼ cup fresh tarragon, minced
1 clove garlic, minced
1 teaspoon black pepper
½ teaspoon salt
1 split boneless turkey breast (about 4 pounds)
1 tablespoon plus 1½ teaspoons cornstarch

1 Combine butter, sage, tarragon, garlic, pepper and salt in small bowl. Rub butter mixture over turkey breast.

2 Place turkey breast in **CROCK-POT®** slow cooker. Cover; cook on LOW 8 to 10 hours or on HIGH 4 to 5 hours.

3 Remove turkey breast to serving platter; cover loosely with foil to keep warm. Slowly whisk cornstarch into cooking liquid; cook on HIGH 10 minutes or until thickened and smooth. Slice turkey breast. Serve with sauce.

Pomegranate Chicken

MAKES 6 SERVINGS

4 cups pomegranate juice

2 cups walnuts,* toasted

1 tablespoon vegetable oil

1 large onion, finely diced

3 pounds chicken wings

2 tablespoons sugar

¼ teaspoon ground cinnamon

1¼ teaspoons kosher salt

¼ teaspoon black pepper

Hot cooked couscous (optional)

Pomegranate seeds (optional)

To toast walnuts, spread in single layer in heavy-bottomed skillet. Cook and stir 1 to 2 minutes over medium heat until nuts are lightly browned. Remove from skillet immediately.

1 Pour pomegranate juice into small saucepan; bring to a boil over high heat. Boil 18 to 20 minutes or until juice is reduced to 2 cups.

2 Meanwhile, place walnuts in food processor; pulse until finely ground. Remove to **CROCK-POT®** slow cooker.

3 Heat oil in large skillet over medium-high heat. Add onion; cook 6 minutes or until translucent. Add wings, onion, pomegranate juice, sugar, cinnamon, salt and pepper to **CROCK-POT®** slow cooker.

4 Cover; cook on HIGH 3 to 4 hours. Serve over couscous, if desired; garnish with pomegranate seeds.

Indian-Style Curried Drumsticks

MAKES 4 TO 6 SERVINGS

12 chicken drumsticks, skin removed
    (about 3 pounds)
 1 whole cinnamon stick
 2 tablespoons vegetable oil
 1 large onion, diced
 3 tablespoons tomato paste
 1 tablespoon ground cumin
 1 tablespoon grated fresh ginger
 1 tablespoon minced garlic

 2 teaspoons salt
 2 teaspoons ground turmeric
 1 teaspoon ground coriander
 ½ teaspoon black pepper
 8 medium red potatoes, cut in half
    (about 1¾ pounds *total*)
1¼ cups chicken broth
 1 cup frozen peas

1 Place drumsticks and cinnamon stick in **CROCK-POT**® slow cooker. Heat oil in medium saucepan over medium heat. Add onion; cook and stir 3 minutes or until softened. Add tomato paste, cumin, ginger, garlic, salt, turmeric, coriander and pepper; cook and stir 2 minutes. Add onion mixture, potatoes and broth to **CROCK-POT**® slow cooker. Cover; cook on LOW 6 hours.

2 Remove chicken and potatoes to large serving platter using slotted spoon. Stir peas into **CROCK-POT**® slow cooker. Cover; cook on LOW 5 minutes or until peas are heated through. Serve drumsticks and potatoes topped with curry.

Sweet and Sour Chicken

MAKES 4 SERVINGS

1 pound boneless, skinless chicken thighs, cut into 1-inch pieces

¼ cup chicken broth

2 tablespoons soy sauce

2 tablespoons hoisin sauce

1 tablespoon cider vinegar

1 tablespoon tomato paste

2 teaspoons packed brown sugar

1 clove garlic, minced

¼ teaspoon black pepper

2 teaspoons cornstarch

2 tablespoons snipped fresh chives
Hot cooked rice
Sliced cooked carrots (optional)

1 Combine chicken, broth, soy sauce, hoisin sauce, vinegar, tomato paste, brown sugar, garlic and pepper in **CROCK-POT**® slow cooker; stir to blend. Cover; cook on LOW 2½ to 3½ hours.

2 Remove chicken to large cutting board with slotted spoon. Cover loosely with foil to keep warm. Stir 2 tablespoons cooking liquid into cornstarch in small bowl until smooth; add to **CROCK-POT**® slow cooker. Stir in chives. Turn **CROCK-POT**® slow cooker to HIGH. Stir 2 minutes or until sauce is slightly thickened. Serve chicken and sauce over rice with carrots, if desired.

Southwestern Turkey Breast

MAKES 6 SERVINGS

1 can (about 15 ounces) black beans, rinsed and drained

1 can (about 14 ounces) fire-roasted diced tomatoes

1 large onion, coarsely chopped

1 canned chipotle pepper in adobo sauce, chopped

1¼ teaspoons ground cumin, divided

1¼ teaspoons ground coriander, divided

¾ teaspoon ground cinnamon, divided

½ teaspoon salt

1 whole bone-in turkey breast (6 to 7 pounds), skin removed

¼ cup fresh cilantro, chopped

2 teaspoons fresh lime juice

1 teaspoon grated lime peel, finely chopped

Lime wedges and/or sprigs fresh cilantro (optional)

1 Stir beans, tomatoes, onion, chipotle pepper, 1 teaspoon cumin, 1 teaspoon coriander, ½ teaspoon cinnamon and salt into **CROCK-POT®** slow cooker. Place turkey on top. Cover; cook on LOW 6 hours or on HIGH 3 hours.

2 Remove turkey. Stir remaining ¼ teaspoon cumin, ¼ teaspoon coriander, ¼ teaspoon cinnamon, chopped cilantro, lime juice and lime peel into **CROCK-POT®** slow cooker until combined. Serve bean mixture alongside turkey. Garnish with lime wedges and cilantro sprigs.

Cashew Chicken

MAKES 6 SERVINGS

6 boneless, skinless chicken breasts
1½ cups cashew nuts
1 cup sliced mushrooms
1 cup sliced celery
1 can (10¾ ounces) condensed cream of mushroom soup, undiluted

¼ cup chopped green onions
2 tablespoons butter
1½ tablespoons soy sauce
Hot cooked rice

Combine chicken, cashews, mushrooms, celery, soup, green onions, butter and soy sauce in **CROCK-POT®** slow cooker. Cover; cook on LOW 6 to 8 hours or on HIGH 4 to 6 hours. Serve over rice.

Sweet Jalapeño Mustard Turkey Thighs

MAKES 6 SERVINGS

3 turkey thighs, skin removed
¾ cup honey mustard
½ cup orange juice
1 to 2 fresh jalapeño peppers, seeded and finely chopped*
1 tablespoon cider vinegar

1 teaspoon Worcestershire sauce
1 clove garlic, minced
½ teaspoon grated orange peel

Jalapeño peppers can sting and irritate the skin, so wear rubber gloves when handling peppers and do not touch your eyes.

Combine turkey, mustard, orange juice, jalapeño peppers, vinegar, Worcestershire sauce, garlic and orange peel in **CROCK-POT®** slow cooker. Cover; cook on LOW 5 to 6 hours.

Picadillo Chicken Thighs

MAKES 4 SERVINGS

4 large or 8 small bone-in, skinless chicken thighs (about 2½ pounds)
½ to 1 teaspoon chili powder
¼ teaspoon ground cinnamon
1 cup salsa, divided

⅓ cup golden raisins
1 tablespoon cold water
1 tablespoon cornstarch
Hot cooked aparagus (optional)

1 Coat inside of **CROCK-POT**® slow cooker with nonstick cooking spray. Season chicken with chili powder and cinnamon.

2 Spoon ¼ cup salsa into **CROCK-POT**® slow cooker. Stir raisins into remaining ¾ cup salsa. Arrange chicken, overlapping as necessary, in **CROCK-POT**® slow cooker; top with salsa mixture. Cover; cook on LOW 5 to 6 hours or on HIGH 2½ to 3 hours. Remove chicken to serving plates; cover loosely with foil to keep warm.

3 Stir water into cornstarch in small bowl until smooth. Whisk into sauce in **CROCK-POT**® slow cooker. Cover; cook on HIGH 10 minutes or until sauce is thickened. Spoon sauce over chicken. Serve with aspargus, if desired.

Turkey Breast with Sweet Cranberry Sauce

MAKES 8 SERVINGS

1 fresh or thawed bone-in turkey breast (6 to 7 pounds), rinsed and patted dry*

1 can (16 ounces) whole berry cranberry sauce

1 package (about 1 ounce) dry onion soup mix

Grated peel and juice of 1 orange

3 tablespoons soy sauce

2 to 3 tablespoons cornstarch

1 tablespoon sugar

1 teaspoon cider vinegar

Salt

Substitute 2 (3½-pound) bone-in turkey breast halves, if necessary.

1 Coat inside of **CROCK-POT**® slow cooker with nonstick cooking spray. Place turkey in bottom, meat side up. Combine cranberry sauce, dry soup mix, orange peel and orange juice in medium bowl. Pour over turkey. Cover; cook on HIGH 3½ hours.

2 Scoop cranberry mixture off of turkey into cooking liquid. Remove turkey to large cutting board. Cover loosely with foil; let stand 15 minutes before slicing.

3 Stir soy sauce into cornstarch in small bowl until smooth. Stir into cooking liquid with sugar, vinegar and salt. Cover; cook on HIGH 15 minutes or until thickened slightly. Serve sauce over sliced turkey.

Chicken Cacciatore

MAKES 6 SERVINGS

2 tablespoons olive oil, divided
1 medium onion, chopped
1 medium green bell pepper, chopped
1 package (8 ounces) button mushrooms
1 teaspoon garlic powder
1 teaspoon dried rosemary
½ teaspoon dried thyme
½ teaspoon red pepper flakes

2 cans (about 14 ounces *each*) diced tomatoes with basil and oregano
1 can (6 ounces) tomato paste
6 boneless, skinless chicken breasts (about 4 pounds)
  Salt and black pepper
  Shredded mozzarella cheese (optional)
  Hot cooked noodles (optional)

1 Coat inside of **CROCK-POT®** slow cooker with nonstick cooking spray.

2 Heat 1 tablespoon oil in large skillet over medium-high heat. Add onion, bell pepper, mushrooms, garlic powder, rosemary, thyme and red pepper flakes; cook and stir 5 to 7 minutes until onion is softened. Remove mixture to **CROCK-POT®** slow cooker. Stir in diced tomatoes and tomato paste.

3 Heat remaining 1 tablespoon oil over medium-high heat. Season chicken with salt and black pepper. Add chicken; cook 3 to 5 minutes on each side until browned. Remove to **CROCK-POT®** slow cooker. Cover; cook on LOW 6 hours.

4 Top with cheese and serve over noodles, if desired.

Turkey Spinach Lasagna

MAKES 8 SERVINGS

¾ cup chopped onion

2 cloves garlic, minced

1 pound ground turkey

1 teaspoon Italian seasoning

¼ teaspoon black pepper

1 container (15 ounces) ricotta cheese

1 cup (4 ounces) Italian shredded cheese blend, divided

12 ounces no-boil lasagna noodles

1 package (10 ounces) frozen chopped spinach, thawed and pressed dry

1 jar (24 to 26 ounces) chunky marinara sauce

½ cup water

1 Spray large skillet with nonstick cooking spray; heat over medium heat. Add onion and garlic; cook and stir 4 minutes. Add turkey; cook and stir until no longer pink, stirring to break up meat. Season with Italian seasoning and pepper; remove from heat. Set aside.

2 Combine ricotta cheese and ½ cup Italian cheese in small bowl; mix well.

3 Layer half of uncooked noodles, breaking in half to fit and overlap as necessary, in **CROCK-POT**® slow cooker. Spread half of meat mixture and half of spinach over noodles. Top with half of marinara sauce and ¼ cup water. Gently spread cheese mixture on top. Repeat layers with remaining noodles, meat mixture, spinach, marinara sauce and ¼ cup water.

4 Cover; cook on LOW 4 hours. Sprinkle top with remaining ½ cup Italian cheese. Cover; cook on LOW 10 to 15 minutes or until cheese is melted. Divide evenly into eight pieces.

Chicken Provençal

MAKES 8 SERVINGS

2 pounds boneless, skinless chicken thighs, each cut into quarters

2 medium red bell peppers, cut into ¼-inch-thick slices

1 medium yellow bell pepper, cut into ¼-inch-thick slices

1 onion, thinly sliced

1 can (28 ounces) plum tomatoes, drained

3 cloves garlic, minced

¼ teaspoon salt

¼ teaspoon dried thyme

¼ teaspoon ground fennel seed

3 strips orange peel

½ cup chopped fresh basil

Combine chicken, bell peppers, onion, tomatoes, garlic, salt, thyme, fennel seed and orange peel in **CROCK-POT**® slow cooker; stir to blend. Cover; cook on LOW 7 to 9 hours or on HIGH 4 to 6 hours. Sprinkle with basil just before serving.

Serving Suggestions

This Southern French chicken dish contrasts the citrus with sweetness. Serve with a crusty French baguette and seasonal vegetables.

Note

Recipe can be doubled for a 5-, 6- or 7-quart **CROCK-POT**® slow cooker.

Coconut-Curry Chicken Thighs

MAKES 4 SERVINGS

8 chicken thighs (about 2 to 2½ pounds)
½ teaspoon salt
¼ teaspoon black pepper
1 tablespoon olive oil
1 medium onion, chopped
1 medium red bell pepper, chopped
3 cloves garlic, minced
1 tablespoon grated fresh ginger

1 can (13½ ounces) unsweetened coconut milk
3 tablespoons honey
1 tablespoon Thai red curry paste
2 teaspoons Thai roasted red chili paste
2 tablespoons chopped fresh cilantro (optional)
½ cup chopped cashew nuts (optional)

1 Coat inside of **CROCK-POT**® slow cooker with nonstick cooking spray. Season chicken with salt and black pepper. Heat oil in large skillet over medium-high heat. Add chicken; cook 6 to 8 minutes until browned. Remove to **CROCK-POT**® slow cooker.

2 Pour off all but 1 tablespoon fat from skillet. Heat skillet over medium-high heat. Add onion, bell pepper, garlic and ginger; cook and stir 1 to 2 minutes or until vegetables begin to soften. Remove skillet from heat. Stir in coconut milk, honey, curry paste and chili paste until smooth. Pour coconut mixture over chicken in **CROCK-POT**® slow cooker.

3 Cover; cook on LOW 4 hours. Serve chicken with sauce. Garnish each serving with cilantro and cashews.

Chicken and Biscuits

MAKES 4 SERVINGS

4 boneless, skinless chicken breasts, cut into 1-inch pieces

1 can (10¾ ounces) condensed cream of chicken soup

1 package (10 ounces) frozen peas and carrots

1 package (7½ ounces) refrigerated biscuits

1 Place chicken in **CROCK-POT**® slow cooker; pour in soup. Cover; cook on LOW 4 hours.

2 Stir in peas and carrots. Cover; cook on LOW 30 minutes or until vegetables are heated through.

3 Meanwhile, bake biscuits according to package directions. Spoon chicken and vegetable mixture over biscuits to serve.

Turkey Ropa Vieja

MAKES 4 SERVINGS

12 ounces turkey tenderloin (2 large or 3 small) or boneless, skinless chicken thighs

1 can (8 ounces) tomato sauce

2 medium tomatoes, chopped

1 small yellow onion, thinly sliced

1 small green bell pepper, chopped

4 pimiento-stuffed green olives, sliced

1 clove garlic, minced

¾ teaspoon ground cumin

½ teaspoon dried oregano

⅛ teaspoon black pepper

2 teaspoons lemon juice

¼ teaspoon salt

Green olives (optional)

1 cup hot cooked rice and black beans (optional)

1 Place turkey in **CROCK-POT**® slow cooker. Add tomato sauce, tomatoes, onion, bell pepper, sliced olives, garlic, cumin, oregano and black pepper. Cover; cook on LOW 6 to 7 hours.

2 Remove turkey to large cutting board; shred with two forks. Return turkey to **CROCK-POT**® slow cooker. Stir in lemon juice and salt. Serve with olives, rice and beans, if desired.

Chicken Teriyaki

MAKES 4 SERVINGS

1 pound boneless, skinless chicken tenders

24 cherry tomatoes

1 can (6 ounces) pineapple juice

¼ cup soy sauce

1 tablespoon sugar

1 tablespoon minced fresh ginger

1 tablespoon minced garlic

1 tablespoon vegetable oil

1 tablespoon molasses

2 cups hot cooked rice

Chopped fresh chives (optional)

Combine chicken, tomatoes, pineapple juice, soy sauce, sugar, ginger, garlic, oil and molasses in **CROCK-POT**® slow cooker; stir to blend. Cover; cook on LOW 2 hours or until chicken is tender. Serve chicken and sauce over rice. Garnish with chives.

Indian-Style Apricot Chicken

MAKES 4 TO 6 SERVINGS

6 skinless chicken thighs (about 2 pounds)
¼ teaspoon salt, plus additional for seasoning
¼ teaspoon black pepper, plus additional for seasoning
1 tablespoon vegetable oil
1 large onion, chopped
2 cloves garlic, minced
2 tablespoons grated fresh ginger

½ teaspoon ground cinnamon
⅛ teaspoon ground allspice
1 can (about 14 ounces) diced tomatoes
1 cup chicken broth
1 package (8 ounces) dried apricots
Pinch saffron threads (optional)
Hot cooked basmati rice
2 tablespoons chopped fresh Italian parsley (optional)

1 Coat inside of **CROCK-POT**® slow cooker with nonstick cooking spray. Season chicken with ¼ teaspoon salt and ¼ teaspoon pepper. Heat oil in large skillet over medium-high heat. Add chicken; cook 5 to 7 minutes or until browned on all sides. Remove to **CROCK-POT**® slow cooker.

2 Add onion to skillet; cook and stir 3 to 5 minutes or until translucent. Stir in garlic, ginger, cinnamon and allspice; cook and stir 15 to 30 seconds or until mixture is fragrant. Add tomatoes and broth; cook 2 to 3 minutes or until mixture is heated through. Pour into **CROCK-POT**® slow cooker.

3 Add apricots and saffron, if desired. Cover; cook on LOW 5 to 6 hours or on HIGH 3 to 4 hours. Season with additional salt and pepper, if desired. Serve with basmati rice and garnish with parsley.

Note

To skin chicken easily, grasp skin with paper towel and pull away. Repeat with fresh paper towel for each piece of chicken, discarding skins and towels.

Chicken Fajitas with Barbecue Sauce

MAKES 4 SERVINGS

1 can (8 ounces) tomato sauce
⅓ cup chopped green onions
¼ cup ketchup
2 tablespoons water
2 tablespoons orange juice
2 cloves garlic, finely chopped
1 tablespoon cider vinegar
1 tablespoon chili sauce
½ teaspoon vegetable oil

Dash Worcestershire sauce
10 ounces boneless, skinless chicken breasts, cut into ½-inch strips
2 green or red bell peppers, thinly sliced
1 cup sliced onion
2 cups tomato wedges
4 (6-inch) flour tortillas, warmed
Lime wedges (optional)

1 Combine tomato sauce, green onions, ketchup, water, orange juice, garlic, vinegar, chili sauce, oil and Worcestershire sauce in **CROCK-POT®** slow cooker; stir to blend. Cover; cook on HIGH 1½ hours.

2 Spray large skillet with nonstick cooking spray; heat over medium heat. Add chicken; cook and stir 5 to 7 minutes.

3 Turn **CROCK-POT®** slow cooker to LOW. Add chicken, bell peppers and sliced onion to **CROCK-POT®** slow cooker; stir to blend. Cover; cook on LOW 3 to 4 hours.

4 Add tomato wedges to **CROCK-POT®** slow cooker. Cover; cook on LOW 30 to 45 minutes or until heated through. Serve with tortillas and lime wedges, if desired.

Spicy Orange Chicken Nuggets

MAKES 8 TO 9 SERVINGS

1 bag (28 ounces) frozen popcorn chicken bites

1½ cups prepared honey teriyaki marinade

¾ cup orange juice concentrate

⅔ cup water

1 tablespoon orange marmalade

½ teaspoon hot chile sauce or sriracha

Hot cooked rice with peas and corn (optional)

1 Preheat oven to 450°F. Spread chicken evenly on medium baking sheet. Bake 12 to 14 minutes or until crisp. (Do not brown.) Remove to **CROCK-POT**® slow cooker.

2 Combine teriyaki marinade, juice concentrate, water, marmalade and chile sauce in medium bowl; stir to blend. Pour over chicken. Cover; cook on LOW 3 to 3½ hours. Serve with rice, if desired.

Shredded Chicken Tacos

MAKES 4 SERVINGS

2 pounds boneless, skinless chicken thighs

½ cup prepared mango salsa, plus additional for serving

Lettuce (optional)

8 (6-inch) yellow corn tortillas, warmed

1 Coat inside of **CROCK-POT®** slow cooker with nonstick cooking spray. Add chicken and ½ cup salsa. Cover; cook on LOW 4 to 5 hours or on HIGH 2½ to 3 hours.

2 Remove chicken to large cutting board; shred with two forks. Stir shredded chicken back into **CROCK-POT®** slow cooker. To serve, divide chicken and lettuce, if desired, evenly among tortillas. Serve with additional salsa.

Lemon and Herb Turkey Breast

MAKES 4 SERVINGS

1 split turkey breast (about 3 pounds)

½ cup lemon juice

½ cup dry white wine

6 cloves garlic, minced

¼ teaspoon salt

¼ teaspoon dried parsley flakes

¼ teaspoon dried tarragon

¼ teaspoon dried rosemary

¼ teaspoon dried sage

¼ teaspoon black pepper

Sprigs fresh sage and rosemary (optional)

Lemon slices (optional)

1 Place turkey in **CROCK-POT®** slow cooker. Combine lemon juice, wine, garlic, salt, parsley flakes, tarragon, dried rosemary, dried sage and pepper in medium bowl; stir to blend. Pour lemon juice mixture over turkey in **CROCK-POT®** slow cooker.

2 Cover; cook on LOW 8 to 10 hours or on HIGH 4 to 5 hours. Garnish with fresh sage, fresh rosemary and lemon slices.

Basque Chicken with Peppers

MAKES 4 TO 6 SERVINGS

1 cut-up whole chicken (about 4 pounds)
2 teaspoons salt, divided
1 teaspoon black pepper, divided
1½ tablespoons olive oil
1 onion, chopped
1 medium green bell pepper, cut into strips
1 medium yellow bell pepper, cut into strips
1 medium red bell pepper, cut into strips

8 ounces small brown mushrooms, halved
1 can (about 14 ounces) stewed tomatoes
½ cup chicken broth
½ cup Rioja wine
3 ounces tomato paste
2 cloves garlic, minced
1 sprig fresh marjoram
1 teaspoon smoked paprika
4 ounces chopped prosciutto

1 Season chicken with 1 teaspoon salt and ½ teaspoon black pepper. Heat oil in large skillet over medium-high heat. Add chicken in batches; cook 6 to 8 minutes or until browned on all sides. Remove to **CROCK-POT**® slow cooker.

2 Heat same skillet over medium-low heat. Add onion; cook and stir 3 minutes or until softened. Add bell peppers and mushrooms; cook 3 minutes. Add tomatoes, broth, wine, tomato paste, garlic, marjoram, remaining 1 teaspoon salt, paprika and remaining ½ teaspoon black pepper to skillet; bring to a simmer. Simmer 3 to 4 minutes; pour over chicken in **CROCK-POT**® slow cooker.

3 Cover; cook on LOW 5 to 6 hours or on HIGH 3 to 4 hours. Ladle vegetables and sauce over chicken. Sprinkle with prosciutto.

Fish and Shellfish

Asian Lettuce Wraps

MAKES 6 SERVINGS

2 teaspoons canola oil

1½ pounds boneless, skinless chicken breasts or pork shoulder, chopped into ¼-inch pieces

2 leeks, trimmed and chopped into ¼-inch pieces

1 cup shiitake mushrooms, stems removed and caps chopped into ¼-inch pieces

1 stalk celery, chopped into ¼-inch pieces

1 tablespoon oyster sauce

1 tablespoon soy sauce

1 teaspoon dark sesame oil

¼ teaspoon black pepper

2 tablespoons water

1 bag (8 ounces) coleslaw or broccoli slaw mix

½ red bell pepper, cut into thin strips

½ pound large raw shrimp, peeled, deveined and cut into ¼-inch pieces

3 tablespoons dry roasted peanuts, coarsely chopped

Hoisin sauce

12 crisp romaine lettuce leaves, with white rib removed, patted dry

Fresh whole chives

1 Heat canola oil in large skillet over medium-high heat. Add chicken; cook 6 to 8 minutes or until browned on all sides. Remove to **CROCK-POT**® slow cooker. Add leeks, mushrooms, celery, oyster sauce, soy sauce, sesame oil, black pepper and water to **CROCK-POT**® slow cooker. Toss slaw and bell pepper in medium bowl; place in single layer on top of chicken.

2 Cover; cook on LOW 4 to 5 hours or on HIGH 2 to 2½ hours. Stir in shrimp during last 20 minutes of cooking. When shrimp are pink and opaque, remove mixture to large bowl. Add chopped peanuts; mix well.

3 To serve, spread about 1 teaspoon hoisin sauce on each lettuce leaf. Add 1 to 2 tablespoons meat mixture and tightly roll; secure by tying chives around rolled leaves.

Simple Salmon with Fresh Salsa

MAKES 4 SERVINGS

- 4 salmon fillets (about 4 ounces *each*), rinsed and patted dry
- 1 teaspoon salt, divided
- ½ teaspoon dried thyme, crumbled
- ¼ teaspoon black pepper
- ½ cup chicken broth
- 1 medium cucumber, peeled, seeded and chopped
- ½ large green bell pepper, chopped
- ½ cup finely chopped radishes
- ½ cup quartered grape tomatoes
- ¼ cup chopped fresh cilantro
- 3 tablespoons fresh lime juice
- 2 tablespoons finely chopped red onion
  Hot cooked green beans (optional)

1 Season salmon with ½ teaspoon salt, thyme and black pepper. Pour broth into **CROCK-POT**® slow cooker; add salmon. Cover; cook on LOW 3 hours.

2 Meanwhile, combine cucumber, bell pepper, radishes, tomatoes, cilantro, lime juice, onion and remaining ½ teaspoon salt in medium bowl. Cover; refrigerate until ready to serve.

3 To serve, place salmon on serving plates; top with salsa. Serve with green beans, if desired.

Seafood Cioppino

MAKES 4 SERVINGS

1 tablespoon olive oil	1 bottle (8 ounces) clam juice
1 medium bulb fennel, thinly sliced	16 little neck clams, scrubbed
1 medium onion, chopped	24 mussels, scrubbed
4 cloves garlic, minced	1 pound cod fillet, cut into 8 pieces
1 teaspoon dried basil	8 ounces large raw shrimp, peeled and deveined (with tails on)
¼ teaspoon saffron threads, crushed (optional)	½ teaspoon salt
1 can (about 14 ounces) diced tomatoes	⅛ teaspoon black pepper

1 Coat inside of **CROCK-POT**® slow cooker with nonstick cooking spray. Heat oil in large skillet over medium-high heat. Add fennel, onion, garlic, basil and saffron, if desired; cook and stir 4 to 5 minutes or until vegetables are softened. Remove onion mixture to **CROCK-POT**® slow cooker. Stir in tomatoes and clam juice.

2 Cover; cook on HIGH 2 to 3 hours. Add clams. Cover; cook on HIGH 30 minutes. Add mussels. Cover; cook on HIGH 15 minutes.

3 Season cod and shrimp with salt and pepper. Place on top of shellfish. Cover; cook on HIGH 25 to 30 minutes until clams and mussels have opened, fish is cooked through and shrimp are pink and opaque. Discard any unopened clams or mussels.

Salmon Chowder

MAKES 6 SERVINGS

1 can (about 15 ounces) cream-style corn	1 package (8 ounces) cream cheese
1 can (about 14 ounces) chicken broth	½ teaspoon grated lemon peel
8 ounces small red potatoes, chopped	1 salmon fillet (about 1½ pounds), skinned and cut into 6 pieces
1 red onion, finely chopped	⅓ cup chopped fresh dill (optional)
¼ teaspoon salt	Lemon wedges (optional)
½ teaspoon black pepper	

1 Stir corn, broth, potatoes, onion, salt and pepper into **CROCK-POT®** slow cooker. Cover; cook on LOW 4 hours or on HIGH 2 hours or until potatoes are fork-tender.

2 Whisk cream cheese and lemon peel into **CROCK-POT®** slow cooker until smooth. Top with salmon. Cover; cook on LOW 45 minutes to 1 hour or until fillets are just cooked through and flake when tested with fork. Remove fillets from **CROCK-POT®** slow cooker. Ladle soup into bowls; top each with salmon fillet. Garnish each bowl with dill and lemon wedge.

Cajun Chicken and Shrimp Creole

MAKES 6 SERVINGS

1 pound skinless chicken thighs
1 red bell pepper, chopped
1 large onion, chopped
1 stalk celery, diced
1 can (about 14 ounces) diced tomatoes
1 clove garlic, minced
1 tablespoon sugar
1 teaspoon paprika

1 teaspoon Cajun seasoning
1 teaspoon salt
1 teaspoon black pepper
1 pound medium raw shrimp, peeled and deveined
1 tablespoon fresh lemon juice
Hot pepper sauce
1 cup hot cooked rice

1 Place chicken thighs in **CROCK-POT**® slow cooker. Add bell pepper, onion, celery, tomatoes, garlic, sugar, paprika, Cajun seasoning, salt and black pepper. Cover; cook on LOW 7 to 9 hours or on HIGH 3 to 4 hours.

2 Add shrimp, lemon juice and hot pepper sauce to **CROCK-POT**® slow cooker. Cover; cook on LOW 1 hour or on HIGH 30 minutes. Serve over rice.

Tip

Recipe can be doubled for a 5-, 6- or 7-quart **CROCK-POT**® slow cooker.

Mom's Tuna Casserole

MAKES 8 SERVINGS

2 cans (12 ounces *each*) solid albacore
  tuna, drained and flaked

3 cups diced celery

3 cups crushed potato chips, divided

6 hard-cooked eggs, chopped

1 can (10½ ounces) condensed cream of
  mushroom soup, undiluted

1 can (10½ ounces) condensed cream
  of celery soup, undiluted

1 cup mayonnaise

1 teaspoon dried tarragon

1 teaspoon black pepper

1 Combine tuna, celery, 2½ cups potato chips, eggs, soups, mayonnaise, tarragon and
pepper in **CROCK-POT**® slow cooker; stir to blend. Cover; cook on LOW 5 to 7 hours.

2 Sprinkle with remaining ½ cup potato chips before serving.

Tip

Don't use your **CROCK-POT**® slow cooker to reheat leftover
foods. Remove cooled leftover food to resealable food storage
bags or storage containers with tight-fitting lids; refrigerate. Use
a microwave oven, stove top or oven for reheating.

Caribbean Shrimp with Rice

MAKES 4 SERVINGS

1 package (12 ounces) frozen raw
  shrimp (with tails on)

½ cup chicken broth

1 clove garlic, minced

1 teaspoon chili powder

½ teaspoon salt

½ teaspoon dried oregano

1 cup frozen peas, thawed

½ cup diced tomatoes

2 cups cooked long grain rice

1 Combine shrimp, broth, garlic, chili powder, salt and oregano in
CROCK-POT® slow cooker. Cover; cook on LOW 2 hours.

2 Add peas and tomatoes. Cover; cook on LOW 5 minutes. Stir
in rice. Cover; cook on LOW 5 minutes or until rice is heated
through.

Slow-Cooked Bouillabaisse

MAKES 6 SERVINGS

3 stalks celery, chopped

2 medium carrots, chopped

1 medium bulb fennel, cored and chopped

1 medium onion, thinly sliced

3 cups chicken broth

1 bottle (8 ounces) clam juice

1 cup crushed tomatoes

¼ cup tomato paste

½ teaspoon saffron threads, crushed

⅛ teaspoon ground red pepper

12 little neck clams, scrubbed

1 pound cod fillet, cut into 1-inch pieces

12 mussels, scrubbed

½ pound large raw shrimp, peeled and deveined (with tails on)

1 Combine celery, carrots, fennel, onion, broth, clam juice, crushed tomatoes, tomato paste, saffron and ground red pepper in **CROCK-POT®** slow cooker; stir to blend. Cover; cook on LOW 8 hours or on HIGH 4 hours.

2 Stir clams into **CROCK-POT®** slow cooker. Cover; cook on HIGH 10 minutes. Stir in cod, mussels and shrimp. Cover; cook on HIGH 30 minutes or until seafood is cooked through. Divide among six bowls.

Seafood and Tomato Herb Ragoût

MAKES 6 TO 8 SERVINGS

1 can (28 ounces) crushed tomatoes, undrained

1 can (8 ounces) tomato sauce

1 cup water

1 cup dry white wine

1 leek, chopped

1 green bell pepper, chopped

½ cup chopped celery

⅓ cup chopped fresh Italian parsley, plus additional for garnish

¼ cup extra virgin olive oil

3 cloves garlic, minced

2 tablespoons chopped fresh basil

1 tablespoon chopped fresh thyme

1 tablespoon chopped fresh oregano

1 teaspoon salt

½ teaspoon paprika

¼ teaspoon ground red pepper

1 pound orange roughy fillets or other white fish, such as cod or haddock, cubed

12 medium raw shrimp, peeled and deveined

12 scallops, cleaned

1 Stir all ingredients except fish, shrimp and scallops into **CROCK-POT**® slow cooker until well combined. Cover; cook on LOW 6 to 8 hours or on HIGH 3 to 4 hours.

2 Add fish, shrimp and scallops to **CROCK-POT**® slow cooker. Cover; cook on HIGH 15 to 30 minutes or until seafood is just cooked through. Garnish with additional parsley.

Sweet and Sour Shrimp with Pineapple

MAKES 4 SERVINGS

3 cans (8 ounces *each*) pineapple chunks

2 packages (6 ounces *each*) frozen snow peas

⅓ cup plus 2 teaspoons sugar

¼ cup cornstarch

2 cubes chicken bouillon

2 cups boiling water

4 teaspoons soy sauce

1 teaspoon ground ginger

1 pound medium raw shrimp, peeled and deveined (with tails on)*

¼ cup cider vinegar

Hot cooked rice

*Or 1 pound frozen medium raw shrimp, peeled, deveined and unthawed.

1 Drain pineapple chunks, reserving 1 cup juice. Place pineapple and snow peas in **CROCK-POT**® slow cooker.

2 Combine sugar and cornstarch in medium saucepan. Dissolve bouillon cubes in boiling water in small bowl; add to saucepan. Mix in reserved pineapple juice, soy sauce and ginger; bring to a boil and cook 1 minute. Pour mixture into **CROCK-POT**® slow cooker. Cover; cook on LOW 4½ to 5½ hours.

3 Add shrimp and vinegar. Cover; cook on LOW 30 minutes or until shrimp are cooked through. Serve over rice.

Cheesy Shrimp on Grits

MAKES 6 SERVINGS

1 cup finely chopped green bell pepper
1 cup finely chopped red bell pepper
½ cup thinly sliced celery
1 bunch green onions, chopped and divided
¼ cup (½ stick) butter, cubed
1¼ teaspoons seafood seasoning
2 whole bay leaves

¼ teaspoon ground red pepper
1 pound medium raw shrimp, peeled and deveined
5⅓ cups water
1⅓ cups quick-cooking grits
2 cups (8 ounces) shredded sharp Cheddar cheese
¼ cup whipping cream or half-and-half

1 Coat inside of **CROCK-POT**® slow cooker with nonstick cooking spray. Add bell peppers, celery, all but ½ cup green onions, butter, seafood seasoning, bay leaves and ground red pepper. Cover; cook on LOW 4 hours or on HIGH 2 hours.

2 Add shrimp. Cover; cook on HIGH 15 minutes.

3 Meanwhile, bring water to a boil in medium saucepan. Add grits; cook according to package directions.

4 Remove and discard bay leaves. Stir in cheese, cream and remaining ½ cup green onions. Cook, uncovered, on HIGH 5 minutes or until cheese is melted. Serve over grits.

Serving Suggestion

This dish is also delicious served over polenta.

Tip

Seafood is delicate and should be added to the **CROCK-POT**® slow cooker during the last 15 to 30 minutes of the cooking time on HIGH, and during the last 30 to 45 minutes if you're cooking on LOW. This type of seafood overcooks easily, becoming tough and rubbery.

Shrimp Louisiana-Style

MAKES 3 TO 4 SERVINGS

1 pound medium raw shrimp, unpeeled (with tails on)	1 teaspoon minced garlic
½ cup (1 stick) butter, cubed	½ teaspoon salt
⅓ cup lemon juice	½ teaspoon black pepper
1 tablespoon Worcestershire sauce	1½ teaspoons grated lemon peel, plus additional for garnish
1 teaspoon seafood seasoning	Hot cooked rice (optional)

1 Coat inside of **CROCK-POT**® slow cooker with nonstick cooking spray. Add shrimp, butter, lemon juice, Worcestershire sauce, seafood seasoning, garlic, salt and pepper; mix well. Cover; cook on HIGH 1¼ hours.

2 Turn off heat. Stir in 1½ teaspoons lemon peel. Let stand, uncovered, 5 minutes. Serve in shallow soup bowls over rice, if desired. Garnish with additional grated lemon peel.

Braised Sea Bass with Aromatic Vegetables

MAKES 6 SERVINGS

2 tablespoons butter or olive oil	Salt and black pepper
2 bulbs fennel, thinly sliced	6 sea bass fillets or other firm-fleshed white fish (2 to 3 pounds *total*)
3 large carrots, julienned	
3 large leeks, cleaned and thinly sliced	

1 Melt butter in large skillet over medium-high heat. Add fennel, carrots and leeks; cook and stir 6 to 8 minutes or until beginning to soften and lightly brown. Season with salt and pepper. Arrange half of vegetables in bottom of **CROCK-POT**® slow cooker.

2 Season bass with salt and pepper; place on top of vegetables in **CROCK-POT**® slow cooker. Top with remaining vegetables. Cover; cook on LOW 2 to 3 hours or on HIGH 1 to 1½ hours.

Salmon and Bok Choy

MAKES 8 SERVINGS

1 cup vegetable broth
2 cloves garlic, finely chopped
2 teaspoons ground ginger
¼ teaspoon red pepper flakes
3 small heads bok choy, stems and leaves sliced

3 pounds salmon fillets
¼ cup soy sauce
¼ cup packed brown sugar
2 tablespoons lemon juice
½ teaspoon Chinese five-spice powder
4 cups cooked brown rice

1 Combine broth, garlic, ginger and red pepper flakes in **CROCK-POT**® slow cooker. Add bok choy stems. Cover; cook on LOW 4 to 6 hours or on HIGH 1½ hours or until fork-tender.

2 Stir bok choy leaves into **CROCK-POT**® slow cooker; top with salmon. Cover; cook on LOW 30 minutes or until fish is cooked through.

3 Meanwhile, whisk soy sauce, brown sugar, lemon juice and five-spice powder in small saucepan. Bring to a boil. Reduce heat; simmer until reduced to ⅓ cup. Serve salmon and bok choy on rice with sauce.

Cod Tapenade

MAKES 4 SERVINGS

4 cod fillets or other firm white fish
(2 to 3 pounds *total*)
Salt and black pepper

2 lemons, thinly sliced
Tapenade (recipe follows)

1 Season cod with salt and pepper. Arrange half of lemon slices in bottom of **CROCK-POT®** slow cooker. Top with cod; cover with remaining lemon slices. Cover; cook on HIGH 1 hour or until fish is just cooked through. Prepare Tapenade.

2 Remove fish to serving plates; discard lemon. Top with Tapenade.

Tapenade

MAKES ABOUT 1 CUP

½ pound pitted kalamata olives
2 tablespoons chopped fresh thyme
or Italian parsley
2 tablespoons capers, drained
2 tablespoons anchovy paste

1 clove garlic
¼ teaspoon grated orange peel
⅛ teaspoon ground red pepper
½ cup olive oil

Place olives, thyme, capers, anchovy paste, garlic, orange peel and ground red pepper in food processor or blender; pulse to roughly chop. Add oil; pulse briefly to form a chunky paste.

Tip

In a hurry? Substitute store-brought tapenade for homemade!

Seafood Bouillabaisse

MAKES 4 SERVINGS

½ bulb fennel, chopped

1 medium onion, chopped

2 cloves garlic, minced

1 can (28 ounces) tomato purée

2 cans (12 ounces *each*) beer

2 cups water

8 ounces clam juice

1 whole bay leaf

½ teaspoon salt

¼ teaspoon black pepper

½ pound red snapper, cut into 1-inch pieces

8 mussels, scrubbed and debearded

8 cherrystone clams

8 large raw shrimp, unpeeled and rinsed (with tails on)

4 lemon wedges

1 Spray large skillet with nonstick cooking spray; heat over medium-high heat. Add fennel, onion and garlic; cook and stir 5 minutes or until onion is soft and translucent. Remove fennel mixture to **CROCK-POT**® slow cooker. Add tomato purée, beer, water, clam juice, bay leaf, salt and pepper to **CROCK-POT**® slow cooker. Cover; cook on LOW 6 to 8 hours or on HIGH 3 to 4 hours.

2 Add fish, mussels, clams and shrimp to **CROCK-POT**® slow cooker. Cover; cook on LOW 15 minutes or until fish flakes when tested with fork. Discard any mussels and clams that do not open.

3 Remove and discard bay leaf. Ladle broth into wide soup bowls; top with fish, mussels, clams and shrimp. Squeeze lemon over each serving.

Saffron-Scented Shrimp Paella

MAKES 4 TO 6 SERVINGS

3 tablespoons olive oil, divided	1 large pinch saffron threads
1½ cups chopped onions	1 cup dry white wine
4 cloves garlic, thinly sliced	8 cups chicken broth
Salt	4 cups uncooked rice
1 cup roasted red bell pepper, diced	25 large raw shrimp, peeled and deveined (with tails on)
1 cup chopped tomato	White pepper
1 whole bay leaf	

1 Heat 2 tablespoons oil in large skillet over medium heat. Add onions, garlic and salt; cook and stir 5 minutes or until translucent. Add bell pepper, tomato, bay leaf and saffron; cook and stir 3 to 5 minutes or until heated through. Add wine; cook until liquid is reduced by half. Add broth. Bring to a simmer. Adjust seasonings, if desired, and stir in rice. Remove to **CROCK-POT**® slow cooker. Cover; cook on HIGH 30 minutes to 1 hour or until liquid is absorbed.

2 Toss shrimp in remaining 1 tablespoon oil in large bowl. Season with salt and white pepper. Place shrimp on rice in **CROCK-POT**® slow cooker. Cover; cook on HIGH 10 minutes or until shrimp are pink and opaque. Remove and discard bay leaf.

Hoppin' John

MAKES 6 SERVINGS

1 pound andouille or smoked sausage, sliced

2½ cups chicken broth, divided

2 cans (about 15 ounces *each*) black-eyed peas, rinsed and drained

1 box (about 8 ounces) dirty rice mix

½ cup salsa

½ to ¾ cup lump crabmeat

Sliced green onions (optional)

1 Cook and stir sausage in large skillet over medium heat 5 minutes or until browned. Drain fat. Remove sausage to **CROCK-POT**® slow cooker with slotted spoon. Return skillet to heat. Pour in ½ cup broth; cook and stir 3 to 5 minutes, scraping up any browned bits from skillet. Pour over sausage.

2 Stir peas, rice mix, remaining broth and salsa into **CROCK-POT**® slow cooker. Cover; cook on LOW 3 to 4 hours or until rice is tender. Add crabmeat; stir until well combined. Cover; cook on LOW 5 minutes or until heated through. Garnish with green onions.

Paella

MAKES 8 SERVINGS

4 cups boneless, skinless chicken breasts, cut into 1-inch cubes

1 cup chopped onion

1 cup chopped tomatoes

4 teaspoons chopped pimentos

1 teaspoon salt

1 teaspoon black pepper

½ teaspoon dried oregano

¼ teaspoon saffron threads

4 cups cooked rice

4 cups shucked whole clams or canned clams

1 pound large raw shrimp, peeled and deveined (with tails on)

1 cup or 2 cans (8 ounces *each*) lobster meat

8 ounces scallops

1 Place chicken, onion, tomatoes, pimentos, salt, pepper, oregano and saffron in **CROCK-POT**® slow cooker. Cover; cook on LOW 6 hours or on HIGH 2 to 4 hours.

2 Add rice, clams, shrimp, lobster and scallops. Cover; cook on HIGH 15 minutes, or until shrimp are pink and opaque.

Shrimp and Pepper Bisque

MAKES 4 SERVINGS

1 can (about 14 ounces) chicken broth

1 bag (12 ounces) frozen bell pepper stir-fry mix, thawed

½ pound frozen cauliflower florets, thawed

1 stalk celery, sliced

1 tablespoon seafood seasoning

½ teaspoon dried thyme

12 ounces medium raw shrimp, peeled and deveined

2 cups half-and-half

2 to 3 green onions, finely chopped

1 Combine broth, stir-fry mix, cauliflower, celery, seafood seasoning and thyme in **CROCK-POT®** slow cooker. Cover; cook on LOW 8 hours or on HIGH 4 hours.

2 Stir in shrimp. Cover; cook on HIGH 15 minutes or until shrimp are pink and opaque. Purée soup in batches in blender or food processor. Return to **CROCK-POT®** slow cooker. Stir in half-and-half. Ladle into bowls and sprinkle with green onions.

Tip

For a creamier, smoother consistency, strain through several layers of damp cheesecloth.

Sweet and Sour Shrimp

MAKES 4 TO 6 SERVINGS

1 can (16 ounces) sliced peaches in syrup, undrained

½ cup chopped green onions

½ cup chopped red bell pepper

½ cup chopped green bell pepper

½ cup chopped celery

⅓ cup vegetable broth

¼ cup soy sauce

2 tablespoons rice wine vinegar

2 tablespoons dark sesame oil

1 teaspoon red pepper flakes

¼ cup water

2 tablespoons cornstarch

1 package (6 ounces) snow peas

1 pound cooked medium shrimp

1 cup cherry tomatoes, cut into halves

½ cup toasted walnut pieces*

Hot cooked rice

To toast walnuts, spread in single layer in heavy skillet. Cook and stir over medium heat 1 to 2 minutes or until nuts are lightly browned.

1 Place peaches with syrup, green onions, bell peppers, celery, broth, soy sauce, vinegar, oil and red pepper flakes in **CROCK-POT®** slow cooker. Cover; cook on LOW 3 to 4 hours or on HIGH 2 to 3 hours or until vegetables are tender.

2 Stir water into cornstarch in small bowl until smooth; whisk into vegetable mixture. Stir in snow peas. Cover; cook on HIGH 15 minutes or until thickened.

3 Add shrimp, tomatoes and walnuts to **CROCK-POT®** slow cooker. Cover; cook on HIGH 5 minutes or until shrimp are pink and opaque. Serve over rice.

Salmon with Beer

MAKES 4 SERVINGS

4 salmon fillets (6 ounces *each*)
  Salt and black pepper
1 cup Italian dressing
3 tablespoons olive oil
1 yellow bell pepper, sliced
1 red bell pepper, sliced
1 orange bell pepper, sliced

1 large onion, sliced
2 cloves garlic, minced
1 teaspoon lemon peel
½ teaspoon dried basil
2 cups spinach, stems removed
¾ cup amber ale
½ lemon, cut into quarters

1 Season both sides of fillets with salt and black pepper. Place fillets in baking dish; pour Italian dressing over fillets. Cover; refrigerate 30 minutes or up to 2 hours. Discard marinade.

2 Pour oil into **CROCK-POT**® slow cooker; lay salmon fillets on top of oil, stacking as necessary. Top with bell peppers, onion, garlic, lemon peel and basil. Cover with spinach. Pour in ale. Cover; cook on HIGH 1½ hours.

3 Remove fillets to large serving platter; top with vegetables. Squeeze lemon over salmon.

Southwestern Salmon Po' Boys

MAKES 4 SERVINGS

1 red bell pepper, sliced

1 green bell pepper, sliced

1 onion, sliced

½ teaspoon Southwest chipotle seasoning

¼ teaspoon salt

¼ teaspoon black pepper

4 salmon fillets (about 6 ounces *each*), rinsed and patted dry

½ cup Italian dressing

¼ cup water

4 large French sandwich rolls, split *or* French bread cut into 6-inch pieces and split

Chipotle mayonnaise*

Fresh cilantro (optional)

If unavailable, combine ¼ cup mayonnaise with ½ teaspoon adobo sauce or substitute regular mayonnaise.

1 Coat inside of **CROCK-POT**® slow cooker with nonstick cooking spray. Arrange half of sliced bell peppers and onion in bottom.

2 Combine chipotle seasoning, salt and black pepper in small bowl; rub over both sides of salmon. Place salmon on top of vegetables in **CROCK-POT**® slow cooker. Pour Italian dressing over salmon and top with remaining bell peppers and onion. Add water. Cover; cook on HIGH 1½ hours.

3 Toast rolls, if desired. Spread tops with chipotle mayonnaise and garnish with cilantro. Spoon 1 to 2 tablespoons cooking liquid onto roll bottoms. Place 1 salmon fillet on each roll (remove skin first, if desired). Top with vegetable mixture.

Shrimp Fondue Dip

MAKES 1¾ CUPS

- 3 tablespoons butter, divided
- 8 ounces small raw shrimp, peeled and deveined
- 1 teaspoon seafood seasoning
- ¼ teaspoon ground red pepper
- ¼ teaspoon black pepper
- 1 tablespoon all-purpose flour
- ¾ cup half-and-half
- ¾ cup (3 ounces) shredded Gruyère cheese
- ¼ cup dry white wine
- 1 teaspoon Dijon mustard
- Sliced French bread

1 Melt 2 tablespoons butter in medium saucepan over medium heat. Add shrimp, seafood seasoning, ground red pepper and black pepper; cook and stir 3 minutes or until shrimp are pink and opaque. Remove to medium bowl.

2 Melt remaining 1 tablespoon butter in same saucepan over medium heat. Add flour; cook and stir 2 minutes. Gradually stir in half-and-half; cook and stir until mixture comes to a boil and thickens. Add cheese; cook and stir until cheese is melted. Stir in wine, mustard and cooked shrimp with any accumulated juices.

3 Coat inside of **CROCK-POT**® "No Dial" food warmer with nonstick cooking spray. Fill with warm dip. Serve with sliced French bread.

Scallops in Fresh Tomato and Herb Sauce

MAKES 4 SERVINGS

2 tablespoons vegetable oil
1 medium red onion, peeled and diced
1 clove garlic, minced
3½ cups fresh tomatoes, peeled*
1 can (12 ounces) tomato pureé
1 can (6 ounces) tomato paste
¼ cup dry red wine
2 tablespoons chopped fresh Italian parsley

1 tablespoon chopped fresh oregano
¼ teaspoon black pepper
1½ pounds fresh scallops, cleaned and drained
   Hot cooked pasta or rice (optional)

To peel tomatoes, place one at a time in simmering water about 10 seconds. (Add 30 seconds if tomatoes are not fully ripened.) Immediately plunge into a bowl of cold water for another 10 seconds. Peel skin with a knife.

1 Heat oil in medium skillet over medium heat. Add onion and garlic; cook and stir 7 to 8 minutes or until onion is soft and translucent. Remove to **CROCK-POT**® slow cooker.

2 Add tomatoes, tomato purée, tomato paste, wine, parsley, oregano and pepper. Cover; cook on LOW 6 to 8 hours.

3 Turn **CROCK-POT**® slow cooker to HIGH. Add scallops. Cover; cook on HIGH 15 minutes or until scallops are cooked through. Serve over pasta, if desired.

Lemon and Garlic Shrimp

MAKES 6 SERVINGS

1 pound large raw shrimp, peeled and deveined (with tails on)

½ cup (1 stick) unsalted butter, cubed

3 cloves garlic, crushed

2 tablespoons lemon juice

½ teaspoon paprika

Salt and black pepper

2 tablespoons finely chopped fresh Italian parsley

1 medium lemon, cut into 6 wedges

1 Coat inside of **CROCK-POT®** slow cooker with nonstick cooking spray. Add shrimp, butter and garlic; mix well. Cover; cook on HIGH 1¼ hours.

2 Turn off heat. Stir in lemon juice, paprika, salt and pepper. Spoon shrimp and liquid into serving bowls. Sprinkle with parsley. Serve with lemon wedges and crusty bread for dipping, if desired.

Miso-Poached Salmon

MAKES 6 SERVINGS

1½ cups water

2 green onions, cut into 2-inch long pieces, plus additional for garnish

¼ cup yellow miso paste

¼ cup soy sauce

2 tablespoons sake

2 tablespoons mirin

1½ teaspoons grated fresh ginger

1 teaspoon minced garlic

6 salmon fillets (4 ounces *each*)

Hot cooked rice

1 Combine water, 2 green onions, miso paste, soy sauce, sake, mirin, ginger and garlic in **CROCK-POT®** slow cooker; stir to blend. Cover; cook on HIGH 30 minutes.

2 Turn **CROCK-POT®** slow cooker to LOW. Add salmon, skin side down. Cover; cook on LOW 30 to 60 minutes or until salmon turns opaque and flakes easily with fork. Serve over rice with cooking liquid as desired. Garnish with additional green onions.

Shrimp Creole

MAKES 8 TO 10 SERVINGS

¼ cup (½ stick) butter
1 onion, chopped
¼ cup biscuit baking mix
3 cups water
2 cans (6 ounces *each*) tomato paste
1 cup chopped celery
1 cup chopped green bell pepper

2 teaspoons salt
½ teaspoon sugar
2 whole bay leaves
Black pepper
4 pounds large raw shrimp, peeled and deveined
Hot cooked rice

1 Heat medium skillet over medium heat. Add butter and onion; cook and stir 3 to 5 minutes or until onion is tender. Stir in biscuit mix. Place mixture in **CROCK-POT**® slow cooker.

2 Add water, tomato paste, celery, bell pepper, salt, sugar, bay leaves and black pepper. Cover; cook on LOW 6 to 8 hours.

3 Turn **CROCK-POT**® slow cooker to HIGH. Add shrimp. Cover; cook on HIGH 45 minutes to 1 hour or until shrimp are pink and opaque. Remove and discard bay leaves. Serve over rice.

Tuna Casserole

MAKES 6 SERVINGS

- 2 cans (10¾ ounces *each*) cream of celery soup
- 2 cans (5 ounces *each*) tuna in water, drained and flaked
- 1 cup water
- 2 carrots, chopped
- 1 small red onion, chopped
- ¼ teaspoon black pepper
- 1 raw egg, uncracked
- 8 ounces hot cooked egg noodles
  Plain dry bread crumbs
- 2 tablespoons chopped fresh Italian parsley

1 Stir soup, tuna, water, carrots, onion and pepper into **CROCK-POT®** slow cooker. Place whole unpeeled egg on top. Cover; cook on LOW 4 to 5 hours or on HIGH 1½ to 3 hours.

2 Remove egg; stir in pasta. Cover; cook on HIGH 30 to 60 minutes or until pasta is tender. Meanwhile, peel egg and mash in small bowl. Stir in bread crumbs and parsley. Top casserole with bread crumb mixture.

Note

This casserole calls for a raw egg. The egg will hard-cook in its shell in the **CROCK-POT®** slow cooker.

Seafood Stew

MAKES 6 SERVINGS

1 can (28 ounces) fire-roasted diced
   tomatoes

1 can (about 15 ounces) tomato sauce

1 pound calamari rings

1 package (8 ounces) uncooked yellow
   rice

2 cans (about 6 ounces *each*) clams,
   liquid drained and reserved

4 cloves garlic, minced

2 tablespoons fennel seeds

1 pound medium raw shrimp, peeled,
   deveined and cut in half (with tails
   on)

1 teaspoon grated lemon peel

½ teaspoon black pepper

1 Stir tomatoes, tomato sauce, calamari, rice, reserved clam juice, garlic and fennel seeds into **CROCK-POT®** slow cooker. Cover; cook on LOW 5 to 6 hours or on HIGH 2½ to 3 hours or until calamari are tender.

2 Stir clams, shrimp, lemon peel and pepper into **CROCK-POT®** slow cooker. Cover; cook on HIGH 5 minutes or until shrimp are pink and opaque.

Spaghetti Squash with Shrimp and Veggies

MAKES 4 SERVINGS

1 spaghetti squash (3 pounds)

4 cups fresh baby spinach

1 orange or red bell pepper, cut into 1-inch squares

½ cup julienned sun-dried tomatoes (not packed in oil)

3 tablespoons prepared pesto

2 tablespoons olive oil

1 teaspoon salt

½ pound peeled cooked medium shrimp (with tails on)

¼ cup grated Parmesan cheese (optional)

1 Pierce squash evenly 10 times with knife. Place squash in **CROCK-POT®** slow cooker; add 1 inch water. Cover; cook on HIGH 2½ hours. Remove squash to large cutting board; let stand until cool enough to handle.

2 Meanwhile, pour off all but 2 tablespoons of water from **CROCK-POT®** slow cooker. Add spinach, bell pepper, tomatoes, pesto, oil and salt; stir to blend. Cover; cook on HIGH 5 minutes.

3 Cut squash in half lengthwise. Remove and discard seeds and fibers. Scoop pulp into shreds; return to **CROCK-POT®** slow cooker. Toss well with spinach mixture; place shrimp on top. Cover; cook on HIGH 15 to 20 minutes or until shrimp are pink and opaque. Top each serving with cheese, if desired.

Shrimp Jambalaya

MAKES 8 SERVINGS

1 (8-ounce) box New Orleans style
  jambalaya mix

2½ cups water

1 can (about 14 ounces) diced tomatoes
  with green pepper, celery and onion

8 ounces andouille sausage, cut into
  ¼-inch-thick slices

1 teaspoon hot pepper sauce, plus
  additional for serving

1½ pounds large raw shrimp, peeled and
  deveined (with tails on)

1 Coat inside of **CROCK-POT**® slow cooker with nonstick cooking spray. Add jambalaya mix, water, tomatoes, sausage and 1 teaspoon hot pepper sauce; stir to blend. Cover; cook on LOW 2½ to 3 hours or until rice is cooked through.

2 Stir in shrimp. Cover; cook on LOW 30 minutes or until shrimp are cooked through. Serve with additional hot pepper sauce.

Bacon-Wrapped Scallops

MAKES 12 SERVINGS

24 sea scallops, side muscle removed

½ cup Belgian white ale

3 tablespoons chopped fresh cilantro

2 tablespoons honey

¼ teaspoon chipotle chili powder

12 slices bacon, halved

1 Pour ½ inch of water in bottom of **CROCK-POT**® slow cooker. Combine scallops, ale, cilantro, honey and chipotle chili powder in medium bowl; toss to coat. Refrigerate 30 minutes.

2 Place 1 scallop on end of 1 bacon half. Roll up jelly-roll style and secure with toothpick. Remove to large baking sheet. Repeat with remaining bacon and scallops. Brush tops of scallops with ale mixture.

3 Heat large skillet over medium heat. Add wrapped scallops; cook 5 to 7 minutes or until bacon is just beginning to brown. Remove to **CROCK-POT**® slow cooker. Cover; cook on LOW 1 hour.

Cajun Pork Sausage and Shrimp Stew

MAKES 6 SERVINGS

- 1 can (28 ounces) diced tomatoes
- 1 package (16 ounces) frozen mixed vegetables (potatoes, carrots, celery and onions)
- 1 package (14 to 16 ounces) kielbasa or smoked sausage, cut diagonally into ¾-inch-thick slices
- 2 teaspoons Cajun seasoning
- ¾ pound large raw shrimp, peeled and deveined (with tails on)
- 2 cups (8 ounces) frozen sliced okra, thawed
- Hot cooked rice or grits

1 Coat inside of **CROCK-POT**® slow cooker with nonstick cooking spray. Combine tomatoes, vegetables, sausage and Cajun seasoning in **CROCK-POT**® slow cooker; stir to blend. Cover; cook on LOW 5 to 6 hours or on HIGH 2 to 2½ hours.

2 Stir shrimp and okra into **CROCK-POT**® slow cooker. Cover; cook on HIGH 30 to 35 minutes or until shrimp are opaque. Serve over rice.

Pleasing Pork

Saucy Pork Loin and Potatoes

MAKES 6 SERVINGS

- 1 tablespoon olive oil
- 1 pork tenderloin (2 pounds)
- ½ cup chicken broth
- 3 tablespoons cornstarch
- ½ cup packed brown sugar
- ⅓ cup soy sauce
- ¼ cup lemon juice

- ¼ cup dry white wine
- 2 cloves garlic, minced
- 1 tablespoon ground mustard
- 1 tablespoon Worcestershire sauce
- 3 cups potatoes, cut into wedges
- Chopped fresh Italian parsley (optional)

1 Heat oil in large skillet over medium-high heat. Brown pork tenderloin 4 to 6 minutes on each side. Stir broth into cornstarch in small bowl until smooth. Place pork, broth mixture, brown sugar, soy sauce, lemon juice, wine, garlic, ground mustard and Worcestershire sauce in **CROCK-POT®** slow cooker. Cover; cook on LOW 4 hours.

2 Stir potatoes into **CROCK-POT®** slow cooker; turn tenderloin. Cover; cook on LOW 2 hours. Garnish with parsley.

Andouille and Cabbage

MAKES 8 SERVINGS

1 pound andouille sausage, cut evenly into 3- to 4-inch pieces

1 small head cabbage, cut evenly into 8 wedges

1 medium onion, cut into ½-inch wedges

3 medium carrots, quartered lengthwise and cut into 3-inch pieces

8 new potatoes, cut in half

1 can (about 14 ounces) chicken broth

½ cup apple juice

1 Coat inside of **CROCK-POT®** slow cooker with nonstick cooking spray. Heat large skillet over medium-high heat. Add sausage; cook and stir 6 to 8 minutes or until browned. Remove from heat.

2 Add cabbage, onion, carrots, potatoes, broth and apple juice to **CROCK-POT®** slow cooker; top with sausage. Cover; cook on HIGH 4 hours. Remove with slotted spoon to large serving bowl.

Tip

Andouille is a spicy, smoked pork sausage. Feel free to substitute your favorite smoked sausage or kielbasa.

Maple-Dry Rubbed Ribs

MAKES 4 SERVINGS

2 teaspoons chili powder, divided
1 teaspoon ground coriander
1 teaspoon garlic powder, divided
½ teaspoon salt
¼ teaspoon black pepper
3 to 3½ pounds pork baby back ribs,
   trimmed and cut in half

3 tablespoons maple syrup, divided
1 can (about 8 ounces) tomato sauce
¼ teaspoon ground cinnamon
¼ teaspoon ground ginger

1 Coat inside of **CROCK-POT**® slow cooker with nonstick cooking spray. Combine 1 teaspoon chili powder, coriander, ½ teaspoon garlic powder, salt and pepper in small bowl; stir to blend. Brush ribs with 1 tablespoon maple syrup; sprinkle with spice mixture. Remove ribs to **CROCK-POT**® slow cooker.

2 Combine tomato sauce, remaining 1 teaspoon chili powder, ½ teaspoon garlic powder, 2 tablespoons maple syrup, cinnamon and ginger in medium bowl; stir to blend. Pour tomato sauce mixture over ribs in **CROCK-POT**® slow cooker. Cover; cook on LOW 8 to 9 hours.

3 Remove ribs to large serving platter; cover with foil to keep warm. Turn **CROCK-POT**® slow cooker to HIGH. Cover; cook on HIGH 10 to 15 minutes or until sauce is thickened. Brush ribs with sauce and serve any remaining sauce on the side.

Peppered Pork Cutlets with Onion Gravy

MAKES 4 SERVINGS

½ teaspoon paprika
¼ teaspoon ground cumin
¼ teaspoon black pepper
⅛ teaspoon ground red pepper
   (optional)
4 boneless pork cutlets (4 ounces *each*)

2 cups thinly sliced onions
2 tablespoons all-purpose flour, divided
¾ cup water
1½ teaspoons chicken bouillon granules
2 tablespoons milk, divided
¼ teaspoon salt

1 Combine paprika, cumin, black pepper and ground red pepper, if desired, in small bowl; blend well. Sprinkle spice mixture evenly over one side of each cutlet, pressing down gently to adhere. If time allows, let stand 15 minutes to absorb flavors.

2 Spray large skillet with nonstick cooking spray; heat skillet over medium heat. Add pork, seasoned side down; cook 3 minutes or until browned. Remove to **CROCK-POT**® slow cooker.

3 Increase heat to medium-high; spray skillet with additional cooking spray. Add onions to skillet; cook and stir 4 minutes or until browned. Sprinkle with 1½ tablespoons flour; toss to coat. Add water and bouillon; stir to blend and bring to a boil. Add onions and any accumulated juices to **CROCK-POT**® slow cooker, spooning some of the sauce over pork. Cover; cook on LOW 4 to 5 hours.

4 Place pork on warm serving platter; set aside. Turn **CROCK-POT**® slow cooker to HIGH. Stir 1 tablespoon milk into onion mixture in **CROCK-POT**® slow cooker. (If a thicker consistency is desired, stir remaining 1 tablespoon milk into remaining ½ tablespoon flour in small bowl and add to onion mixture.) Add salt. Cover; cook on HIGH 10 minutes or until thickened. Spoon sauce over pork.

Sauerkraut Pork Ribs

MAKES 12 SERVINGS

1 tablespoon vegetable oil	¼ to ½ teaspoon black pepper
3 to 4 pounds pork country-style ribs	¾ cup water
1 large onion, thinly sliced	2 jars (about 28 ounces *each*) sauerkraut
1 teaspoon caraway seeds	12 medium red potatoes, quartered
½ teaspoon garlic powder	

1 Heat oil in large skillet over medium-low heat. Brown ribs on all sides. Remove to **CROCK-POT®** slow cooker. Drain fat.

2 Add onion to skillet; cook until tender. Add caraway seeds, garlic powder and pepper; cook 15 minutes. Remove onion mixture to **CROCK-POT®** slow cooker.

3 Add water to skillet, stirring to scrape up any brown bits from bottom of skillet. Pour pan juices into **CROCK-POT®** slow cooker. Partially drain sauerkraut, leaving some liquid; pour over meat. Top with potatoes. Cover; cook on LOW 6 to 8 hours or until potatoes are tender, stirring once during cooking.

Root Beer BBQ Pulled Pork

MAKES 8 SERVINGS

1 can (12 ounces) root beer
1 bottle (18 ounces) sweet barbecue sauce, divided
1 package (about 1 ounce) dry onion soup mix

1 boneless pork shoulder roast (6 to 8 pounds)
Salt and black pepper
Hamburger buns

1 Coat inside of **CROCK-POT®** slow cooker with nonstick cooking spray. Combine root beer and ½ bottle barbecue sauce in medium bowl. Rub dry soup mix on pork roast. Place barbecue mixture and roast in **CROCK-POT®** slow cooker. Cover; cook on LOW 8 to 10 hours.

2 Remove pork to large cutting board; shred with two forks. Reserve 1 cup barbecue mixture in **CROCK-POT®** slow cooker; discard remaining mixture. Turn **CROCK-POT®** slow cooker to HIGH. Stir shredded pork, remaining ½ bottle barbecue sauce, salt and pepper into **CROCK-POT®** slow cooker. Cover; cook on HIGH 20 minutes or until heated through. Serve on buns.

Mu Shu Pork Wraps

MAKES 4 SERVINGS

1 pound pork tenderloin, cut into ½-inch cubes
1 small zucchini, cut into strips
1 small summer squash, cut into strips
1 red bell pepper, cut into short thin strips
3 cloves garlic, minced

1 tablespoon dark sesame oil
2 cups prepared coleslaw mix or shredded cabbage
2 tablespoons hoisin sauce
¼ cup plum sauce
4 (10-inch) whole wheat wraps, warmed

1 Combine pork, zucchini, squash, bell pepper, garlic and sesame oil in **CROCK-POT®** slow cooker; stir to blend. Cover; cook on LOW 3 to 4 hours or on HIGH 1½ to 2 hours.

2 Turn off heat. Stir in coleslaw mix and hoisin sauce. Spread plum sauce down centers of wraps; top evenly with pork mixture. Roll up tightly.

Apple Stuffed Pork Loin Roast

MAKES 14 TO 16 SERVINGS

1 tablespoon butter

2 large tart apples, peeled and thinly sliced (about 2 cups)

1 medium onion, cut into thin strips (about 1 cup)

2 tablespoons packed brown sugar

1 teaspoon Dijon mustard

2 cloves garlic, minced

1 teaspoon coarse salt

1 teaspoon dried rosemary

½ teaspoon dried thyme

½ teaspoon black pepper

1 boneless center cut pork loin roast (4 to 5 pounds)

1 cup apple cider or apple juice

Hot cooked Brussels sprouts (optional)

1 Melt butter in large skillet over medium-high heat. Add apples and onion; cook and stir 5 minutes or until soft. Stir in brown sugar and mustard. Set aside.

2 Combine garlic, salt, rosemary, thyme and pepper in small bowl. Cut pork roast lengthwise down but not through bottom. Open like a book. Rub half of garlic mixture onto cut sides of pork.

3 Spread apple mixture evenly onto one cut side of roast. Close halves; tie roast with kitchen string at 2-inch intervals.

4 Coat inside of **CROCK-POT**® slow cooker with nonstick cooking spray. Place roast in **CROCK-POT**® slow cooker. Pour apple cider over roast. Rub outside of roast with remaining garlic mixture. Cover; cook on LOW 5 to 6 hours or on HIGH 2 to 3 hours.

5 Remove roast to large cutting board. Cover loosely with foil; let stand 10 to 15 minutes. Slice roast just before serving. Serve with Brussels sprouts, if desired.

Serving Suggestions

Serve with buttered noodles tossed with grated Parmesan and/or a tomato and cucumber salad.

Gingered Sherry Pork Roast

MAKES 4 SERVINGS

2 tablespoons extra virgin olive oil	1 cup dry sherry
1 clove garlic, chopped	3 tablespoons hoisin sauce
1 boneless pork loin roast (about 2½ pounds)	1 tablespoon soy sauce
12 baby red potatoes	2 teaspoons grated fresh ginger
12 baby carrots	¼ teaspoon black pepper
6 pearl onions	2 tablespoons chopped fresh chives (optional)

1 Heat oil in large skillet over medium-high heat. Add garlic; cook and stir 30 seconds. Remove garlic with slotted spoon. Add pork roast; brown about 3 to 4 minutes per side. Remove roast; set aside.

2 Place potatoes, carrots and onions in **CROCK-POT®** slow cooker. Place roast on top of vegetables. Combine sherry, hoisin sauce, soy sauce, ginger and pepper in small bowl. Pour over roast in **CROCK-POT®** slow cooker. Cover; cook on LOW 6 to 8 hours or on HIGH 4 to 5 hours. Baste occasionally with sherry sauce.

3 Remove roast to large cutting board. Cover loosely with foil; let stand 10 to 15 minutes. Slice and return roast to **CROCK-POT®** slow cooker. Serve pork with vegetables and sauce. Garnish with chives.

Pulled Pork with Honey-Chipotle Barbecue Sauce

MAKES 8 SERVINGS

1 tablespoon chili powder, divided	1 teaspoon salt
1 teaspoon chipotle chili powder, divided	1 bone-in pork shoulder (3½ pounds), trimmed
1 teaspoon ground cumin, divided	1 can (15 ounces) tomato sauce
1 teaspoon garlic powder, divided	5 tablespoons honey, divided

1 Coat inside of **CROCK-POT**® slow cooker with nonstick cooking spray. Combine 1 teaspoon chili powder, ½ teaspoon chipotle chili powder, ½ teaspoon cumin, ½ teaspoon garlic powder and salt in small bowl. Rub pork with chili powder mixture. Place pork in **CROCK-POT**® slow cooker.

2 Combine tomato sauce, 4 tablespoons honey, remaining 2 teaspoons chili powder, ½ teaspoon chipotle chili powder, ½ teaspoon cumin and ½ teaspoon garlic powder in large bowl. Pour tomato mixture over pork in **CROCK-POT**® slow cooker. Cover; cook on LOW 8 hours.

3 Remove pork to large bowl; cover loosely with foil. Turn **CROCK-POT**® slow cooker to HIGH. Cover; cook on HIGH 30 minutes or until sauce is thickened. Stir in remaining 1 tablespoon honey. Turn off heat.

4 Remove bone from pork and discard. Shred pork using two forks. Stir shredded pork back into **CROCK-POT**® slow cooker to coat well with sauce.

Pork Loin with Sherry and Red Onions

MAKES 8 SERVINGS

2½ pounds boneless pork loin, tied
½ teaspoon salt
½ teaspoon black pepper
2 tablespoons unsalted butter
3 large red onions, thinly sliced
1 cup pearl onions, blanched and peeled

½ cup dry sherry
2 tablespoons chopped fresh Italian parsley
2 tablespoons water
1½ tablespoons cornstarch

1 Rub pork with salt and pepper. Place pork in **CROCK-POT**® slow cooker. Melt butter in medium skillet over medium heat. Add red and pearl onions; cook and stir 5 to 7 minutes or until softened.

2 Add onion mixture, sherry and parsley to **CROCK-POT**® slow cooker over pork. Cover; cook on LOW 8 to 10 hours or on HIGH 4 to 5 hours.

3 Remove pork to large cutting board; cover loosely with foil. Let stand 10 to 15 minutes before slicing.

4 Stir water into cornstarch in small bowl until smooth; whisk into cooking liquid. Cover; cook on HIGH 15 minutes or until thickened. Serve pork with onions and sherry sauce.

Tip

Double all ingredients except for the sherry, water and cornstarch if using a 5-, 6- or 7-quart **CROCK-POT**® slow cooker.

Best Asian-Style Ribs

MAKES 6 TO 8 SERVINGS

6 ounces hoisin sauce

½ cup maraschino cherries, drained

½ cup rice wine vinegar

2 tablespoons minced fresh ginger

2 full racks pork baby back ribs, split into 3 sections *each*

Green onions (optional)

1 Combine hoisin sauce, cherries, vinegar and ginger in **CROCK-POT**® slow cooker; stir to blend. Add ribs; turn to coat.

2 Cover; cook on LOW 6 to 7 hours or on HIGH 3 to 3½ hours. Serve with green onions, if desired.

Simple Shredded Pork Tacos

MAKES 6 SERVINGS

1 boneless pork loin roast (2 pounds)

1 cup salsa

1 can (4 ounces) chopped mild green chiles

½ teaspoon garlic salt

½ teaspoon black pepper

Flour or corn tortillas

Optional toppings: salsa, sour cream, diced tomatoes, shredded cheese and/or shredded lettuce

1 Place roast, 1 cup salsa, chiles, garlic salt and pepper in **CROCK-POT**® slow cooker. Cover; cook on LOW 8 hours.

2 Remove pork to large cutting board; shred with two forks. Serve on tortillas with sauce and desired toppings.

Easy Mu Shu Pork

MAKES 6 SERVINGS

1 package (14 ounces) coleslaw mix, divided

1 package (10 ounces) shredded carrots, divided

1 package (6 ounces) shiitake mushrooms, sliced

3 cloves garlic, minced

¾ cup hoisin sauce, divided

3 tablespoons soy sauce

¾ pound boneless pork loin roast

12 (6-inch) flour tortillas

1 bunch green onions, chopped (optional)

2 tablespoons sesame oil (optional)

1 Place half each of coleslaw mix and carrots in **CROCK-POT®** slow cooker. Add mushrooms; toss to combine. Stir in garlic. Add ½ cup hoisin sauce and soy sauce; stir to combine. Place pork on top of vegetables. Cover; cook on LOW 4 to 5 hours.

2 Remove pork to large cutting board; shred with two forks. Stir shredded pork, remaining half each of coleslaw mix and carrots, and remaining ¼ cup hoisin sauce into **CROCK-POT®** slow cooker.

3 Warm tortillas according to package directions. Divide pork mixture among tortillas. Top with green onions and sesame oil, if desired.

Pecan and Apple Stuffed Pork Chops with Apple Brandy

MAKES 4 SERVINGS

- 4 thick-cut, bone-in pork loin chops (about 4 ounces *each*)
- 1 teaspoon salt, divided
- ½ teaspoon black pepper, divided
- 2 tablespoons vegetable oil
- ½ cup diced green apple
- ½ small onion, minced
- ¼ teaspoon dried thyme
- ½ cup apple brandy or brandy
- ⅔ cup cubed white bread
- 2 tablespoons chopped pecans
- 1 cup apple juice cocktail
- Sprigs fresh thyme (optional)
- Hot cooked baby carrots (optional)

1 Coat inside of **CROCK-POT®** slow cooker with nonstick cooking spray. Rinse pork chops and pat dry. Season with ½ teaspoon salt and ¼ teaspoon pepper. Heat oil in large skillet over medium-high heat. Add pork chops in batches; cook 3 to 5 minutes or until browned. Remove to large plate; set aside.

2 Heat same skillet over medium heat. Add apple, onion, dried thyme, remaining ½ teaspoon salt and remaining ¼ teaspoon pepper; cook and stir 3 minutes or until onion is translucent. Remove from heat. Pour in brandy. Return to medium heat; simmer until most liquid is absorbed. Stir in bread and pecans; cook 1 minute.

3 Cut each pork chop horizontally with sharp knife to form pocket. Divide stuffing among pork chops. Arrange pork chops in **CROCK-POT®** slow cooker, pocket side up.

4 Pour apple juice around pork chops. Cover; cook on HIGH 1½ to 1¾ hours. Garnish with fresh thyme. Serve with carrots, if desired.

Tip

Consider using your **CROCK-POT®** slow cooker as an extra "burner" that doesn't need watching. For example, you can cook this main dish in the **CROCK-POT®** slow cooker while you prepare the sides.

Ancho Chile and Lime Pork Tacos

MAKES 10 TO 12 SERVINGS

2 large plantain leaves
1 (4- to 6-pound) pork shoulder roast*
Juice of 4 to 5 medium limes
1 package (about 1 ounce) ancho chile paste
Salt
1 large onion, sliced
Pickled Red Onions (recipe follows)

Flour tortillas, warmed
Optional toppings: salsa, sour cream, guacamole, shredded cheese, lime slices and/or hot pepper sauce

Unless you have a 5-, 6- or 7-quart CROCK-POT® slow cooker, cut any roast larger than 2½ pounds in half so it cooks completely.

1 Line **CROCK-POT®** slow cooker with plantain leaves; top with pork roast. Combine lime juice, chile paste and salt in medium bowl; stir until well blended. Add paste mixture and onion to **CROCK-POT®** slow cooker; wrap leaves over pork. Cover; cook on LOW 8 to 10 hours.

2 Meanwhile, prepare Pickled Red Onions.

3 Serve with Pickled Red Onions and tortillas; top as desired.

Pickled Red Onions

Combine 1 cup sliced red onion and juice from 1 to 2 limes in small bowl; set aside until juice is absorbed. Makes 1 cup.

Apple-Cherry Glazed Pork Chops

MAKES 4 SERVINGS

½ to 1 teaspoon dried thyme
¼ teaspoon salt
¼ teaspoon black pepper
4 boneless pork loin chops
    (3 ounces *each*), trimmed
1⅓ cups unsweetened apple juice

1 small apple, unpeeled and sliced
¼ cup sliced green onions
¼ cup dried tart cherries
2 tablespoons water
2 teaspoons cornstarch

1 Combine thyme, salt and pepper in small bowl. Rub onto both sides of pork chops. Spray large skillet with nonstick cooking spray; heat over medium-high heat. Add pork in batches; cook 3 to 5 minutes or until browned on both sides. Remove to **CROCK-POT**® slow cooker.

2 Add apple juice, apple slices, green onions and cherries to same skillet. Simmer, uncovered, 2 to 3 minutes or until apple and onions are tender. Stir water into cornstarch in small bowl until smooth; whisk into skillet. Bring to a boil; cook and stir until thickened. Spoon over pork chops.

3 Cover; cook on LOW 3½ to 4 hours or until pork chops are tender. To serve, spoon fruit and cooking liquid over pork chops.

Mango Ginger Pork Roast

MAKES 4 TO 6 SERVINGS

1 boneless pork shoulder roast
   (about 4 pounds)*
½ to 1 teaspoon ground ginger
   Salt and black pepper
2 cups mango salsa
2 tablespoons honey

¼ cup apricot preserves
   Hot cooked rice (optional)

*Unless you have a 5-, 6- or 7-quart
CROCK-POT® slow cooker, cut any roast
larger than 2½ pounds in half so it cooks
completely.*

1 Season roast with ginger, salt and pepper. Add to
CROCK-POT® slow cooker.

2 Combine salsa, honey and preserves in medium bowl;
stir to blend. Pour over roast. Cover; cook on LOW 6 to
8 hours.

3 Turn **CROCK-POT®** slow cooker to HIGH. Cover; cook on
HIGH 3 to 4 hours. Serve with rice, if desired.

Barbecue Ribs

MAKES 6 SERVINGS

1 tablespoon olive oil
2 small red onions, finely chopped
3 to 4 cloves garlic, minced
1 cup packed brown sugar
1 cup ketchup
½ cup cider vinegar

Juice of 1 lemon
2 tablespoons Worcestershire sauce
1 tablespoon hot pepper sauce
½ teaspoon chili powder
2 racks pork baby back ribs, cut into
   3- to 4-rib sections

1 Heat oil in large skillet over medium heat. Add onions and
garlic; cook and stir 3 to 5 minutes or until softened. Stir in
brown sugar, ketchup, vinegar, lemon juice, Worcestershire
sauce, hot pepper sauce and chili powder; cook and stir
5 minutes. Remove half of sauce to **CROCK-POT®** slow
cooker. Reserve remaining sauce in skillet.

2 Add ribs to **CROCK-POT®** slow cooker; turn to coat.
Cover; cook on LOW 7 to 9 hours or on HIGH 4 to
6 hours. Serve ribs with reserved sauce.

Rosemary Pork with Red Wine Risotto

MAKES 4 TO 6 SERVINGS

1 boneless pork loin roast
 (about 3 pounds)*
1 teaspoon salt
1 teaspoon black pepper
2 tablespoons olive oil
6 sprigs fresh rosemary, divided
2 cups chicken broth, divided
½ cup minced onion

2 tablespoons butter, divided
3 cloves garlic, minced
1 cup uncooked Arborio rice
1 cup dry red wine
¾ cup grated Parmesan cheese

*Unless you have a 5-, 6- or 7-quart
CROCK-POT® slow cooker, cut any roast
larger than 2½ pounds in half so it cooks
completely.*

1 Season pork with salt and pepper. Heat oil in large skillet over medium-high heat. Add 3 sprigs rosemary; place pork roast on top. Brown pork roast 5 to 7 minutes on all sides. Remove roast and rosemary to **CROCK-POT®** slow cooker.

2 Add ¼ cup broth to skillet, stirring to scrape up browned bits from bottom of skillet. Add onion, 1 tablespoon butter and garlic; cook and stir 5 to 7 minutes or until onion is translucent.

3 Add rice to skillet; cook and stir 2 minutes or until rice just begins to brown. Stir in wine and remaining 1¾ cups broth. Pour mixture around roast. Cover; cook on HIGH 3 to 4 hours.

4 Remove and discard rosemary. Remove roast to large cutting board. Cover loosely with foil; let stand 10 to 15 minutes before slicing. Stir remaining 1 tablespoon butter and cheese into rice. Serve risotto with roast and garnish with remaining rosemary.

Fall-Apart Pork Roast with Mole

MAKES 6 SERVINGS

⅔ cup whole almonds

⅔ cup raisins

3 tablespoons vegetable oil, divided

½ cup chopped onion

4 cloves garlic, chopped

1 boneless pork shoulder roast (2¾ pounds), well trimmed*

1 can (about 14 ounces) fire-roasted diced tomatoes

1 cup cubed bread, any variety

½ cup chicken broth

2 ounces Mexican chocolate, chopped

2 tablespoons canned chipotle peppers in adobo sauce, chopped

1 teaspoon salt

Sprigs fresh cilantro (optional)

Unless you have a 5-, 6- or 7-quart CROCK-POT® slow cooker, cut any roast larger than 2½ pounds in half so it cooks completely.

1 Heat large skillet over medium-high heat. Add almonds; cook and stir 3 to 4 minutes or until fragrant. Add raisins; cook and stir 1 to 2 minutes or until raisins begin to plump. Place half of almond mixture in large bowl. Reserve remaining half for garnish.

2 Heat 1 tablespoon oil in same skillet. Add onion and garlic; cook and stir 2 minutes or until softened. Add to almond mixture; set aside.

3 Heat remaining 2 tablespoons oil in same skillet. Add pork; cook 5 to 7 minutes or until browned on all sides. Remove to **CROCK-POT®** slow cooker.

4 Add tomatoes, bread, broth, chocolate, chipotle peppers and salt to almond mixture. Add tomato mixture in batches to food processor or blender; process until smooth. Pour purée mixture over pork in **CROCK-POT®** slow cooker. Cover; cook on LOW 7 to 8 hours or on HIGH 3 to 4 hours.

5 Remove pork to large serving platter. Whisk sauce until smooth before spooning over pork. Garnish with reserved almond mixture and cilantro.

Orange Teriyaki Pork

MAKES 4 SERVINGS

1 pound cubed pork stew meat

1 package (16 ounces) frozen bell pepper blend for stir-fry

4 ounces sliced water chestnuts

½ cup orange juice

2 tablespoons quick-cooking tapioca

2 tablespoons packed brown sugar

2 tablespoons teriyaki sauce

½ teaspoon ground ginger

½ teaspoon ground mustard

1⅓ cups hot cooked rice

1 Spray large skillet with nonstick cooking spray; heat skillet over medium heat. Add pork; cook 5 to 7 minutes or until browned on all sides. Remove from heat; set aside.

2 Place bell peppers and water chestnuts in **CROCK-POT**® slow cooker. Top with pork. Mix orange juice, tapioca, brown sugar, teriyaki sauce, ginger and ground mustard in large bowl. Pour juice mixture over pork in **CROCK-POT**® slow cooker. Cover; cook on LOW 3 to 4 hours. Serve with rice.

Asian Noodles with Pork and Vegetables

MAKES 6 SERVINGS

¾ cup soy sauce

¾ cup honey

4 cloves garlic, chopped

1 tablespoon ground ginger

1 boneless pork shoulder roast (2½ pounds), trimmed

¾ cup Asian sweet chili sauce

¼ cup water

3 tablespoons cornstarch

2 packages (16 ounces *each*) frozen mixed Asian vegetables

1 tablespoon toasted sesame oil

Hot cooked soba noodles, rice or spaghetti

1 Mix soy sauce, honey, garlic and ginger in **CROCK-POT®** slow cooker. Add pork. Cover; cook on LOW 8 to 10 hours or on HIGH 5 to 6 hours. Remove pork to large cutting board.

2 Stir chili sauce into **CROCK-POT®** slow cooker; bring to a boil. Stir water into cornstarch in small bowl until smooth. Whisk cornstarch mixture into **CROCK-POT®** slow cooker until thickened. Shred pork with two forks.

3 Add vegetables and shredded pork to **CROCK-POT®** slow cooker. Cover; cook on HIGH 10 to 20 minutes. Stir in oil. Serve over soba noodles.

Shredded Apricot Pork Sandwiches

MAKES 10 TO 12 SANDWICHES

2 onions, thinly sliced	¼ cup water
1 cup apricot preserves	2 tablespoons cornstarch
½ cup packed dark brown sugar	1 tablespoon grated fresh ginger
½ cup barbecue sauce	1 teaspoon salt
¼ cup cider vinegar	1 teaspoon black pepper
2 tablespoons Worcestershire sauce	10 to 12 sesame or onion rolls, toasted
½ teaspoon red pepper flakes	
1 boneless pork top loin roast (4 pounds)*	

Unless you have a 5-, 6-, or 7-quart CROCK-POT® slow cooker, cut any roast larger than 2½ pounds in half so it cooks completely.

1 Combine onions, preserves, brown sugar, barbecue sauce, vinegar, Worcestershire sauce and red pepper flakes in large bowl; stir to blend. Place pork in **CROCK-POT®** slow cooker. Pour apricot mixture over top. Cover; cook on LOW 8 to 9 hours.

2 Remove pork to large cutting board; shred with two forks. Skim fat from sauce in **CROCK-POT®** slow cooker.

3 Stir water into cornstarch in small bowl until smooth. Stir in ginger, salt and black pepper. Whisk cornstarch mixture into sauce. Turn **CROCK-POT®** slow cooker to HIGH. Cook, uncovered, on HIGH 15 to 30 minutes or until thickened. Return pork to **CROCK-POT®** slow cooker; mix well. Serve on rolls.

Boneless Pork Roast with Garlic

MAKES 4 TO 6 SERVINGS

1 boneless pork rib roast
  (2 to 2½ pounds)
  Salt and black pepper
3 tablespoons olive oil, divided
4 cloves garlic, minced

¼ cup chopped fresh rosemary
½ lemon, cut into ⅛- to ¼-inch slices
½ cup chicken broth
¼ cup dry white wine

1 Season pork with salt and pepper. Combine 2 tablespoons oil, garlic and rosemary in small bowl. Rub over pork. Roll and tie pork with kitchen string. Tuck lemon slices under string and into ends of roast.

2 Heat remaining 1 tablespoon oil in skillet over medium heat. Add pork; cook 6 to 8 minutes or until browned on all sides. Remove to **CROCK-POT**® slow cooker.

3 Return skillet to heat. Add broth and wine, scraping up any browned bits from bottom of skillet. Pour over pork in **CROCK-POT**® slow cooker. Cover; cook on LOW 8 to 9 hours or on HIGH 4 to 4½ hours.

4 Remove roast to large cutting board. Cover loosely with foil; let stand 10 to 15 minutes before removing kitchen string and slicing. Pour pan juices over sliced pork to serve.

Peachy Pork

MAKES 6 TO 8 SERVINGS

2 cans (about 15 ounces *each*) sliced
   peaches in heavy syrup, undrained

6 to 8 boneless pork blade or top loin
   chops (about 2 pounds)

1 onion, thinly sliced

½ cup golden raisins

¼ cup packed light brown sugar

3 tablespoons cider vinegar

2 tablespoons tapioca

1 teaspoon salt

¾ teaspoon ground cinnamon

¼ teaspoon red pepper flakes

2 tablespoons water

2 tablespoons cornstarch

1 Cut peach slices in half. Place peaches with juice, pork chops, onion, raisins, brown sugar, vinegar, tapioca, salt, cinnamon and red pepper flakes in **CROCK-POT**® slow cooker. Cover; cook on LOW 7 to 8 hours.

2 Turn off heat. Remove pork to large serving platter; cover loosely with foil to keep warm. Let cooking liquid stand 5 minutes. Skim off and discard fat. Stir water into cornstarch in small bowl until smooth; whisk into peach mixture. Turn **CROCK-POT**® slow cooker to HIGH. Cover; cook on HIGH 15 minutes or until thickened.

Southern Smothered Pork Chops

MAKES 6 TO 8 SERVINGS

6 to 8 bone-in pork chops
   Salt and black pepper

2 tablespoons vegetable oil

3 cups water

1 can (10½ ounces) cream of mushroom
   soup

1 large onion, chopped

5 cloves garlic, chopped

2 tablespoons Italian seasoning

1 package (about ½ ounce) pork gravy
   mix

1 package (about 1 ounce) dry
   mushroom and onion soup mix

   Corn on the cob (optional)

1 Season pork with salt and pepper. Heat oil in large skillet over medium-high heat. Add pork; brown 3 to 4 minutes on each side.

2 Place pork, water, soup, onion, garlic, Italian seasoning, gravy mix and dry soup mix in **CROCK-POT**® slow cooker; stir to blend. Cover; cook on LOW 5 hours. Serve with corn, if desired.

Asian Pork with Noodles

MAKES 6 SERVINGS

2 cans (about 14 ounces *each*) chicken broth

¼ cup hoisin sauce

2 tablespoons honey

2 tablespoons unseasoned rice vinegar

2 tablespoons soy sauce

2 cloves garlic, minced

2 tablespoons chopped fresh ginger

1 pound pork tenderloin

1 pound baby bok choy, sliced

1 cup sliced shiitake mushrooms

8 ounces uncooked rice noodles

¼ cup chopped peanuts, divided

1 Combine broth, hoisin sauce, honey, vinegar, soy sauce, garlic and ginger in **CROCK-POT**® slow cooker; stir to blend. Add pork. Cover; cook on LOW 6 hours.

2 Remove pork to large cutting board. Turn **CROCK-POT**® slow cooker to HIGH. Add bok choy, mushrooms and noodles to **CROCK-POT**® slow cooker. Cover; cook on HIGH 20 to 30 minutes.

3 Shred pork with two forks. Stir pork back into **CROCK-POT**® slow cooker. Cover; cook on HIGH 5 to 10 minutes or until heated through. Ladle soup into bowls; top evenly with peanuts.

Sweet and Spicy Pork Picadillo

MAKES 4 SERVINGS

1 tablespoon olive oil

1 yellow onion, cut into ¼-inch pieces

2 cloves garlic, minced

1 pound boneless pork country-style ribs, trimmed and cut into 1-inch cubes

1 can (about 14 ounces) diced tomatoes

3 tablespoons cider vinegar

2 canned chipotle peppers in adobo sauce, chopped*

½ cup raisins

½ teaspoon ground cumin

½ teaspoon ground cinnamon

You may substitute dried chipotle peppers, soaked in warm water about 20 minutes to soften before chopping.

1 Heat oil in large skillet over medium-low heat. Add onion and garlic; cook and stir 4 minutes. Add pork; cook and stir 5 to 7 minutes or until browned. Remove to **CROCK-POT®** slow cooker.

2 Add tomatoes, vinegar, chipotle peppers, raisins, cumin and cinnamon to **CROCK-POT®** slow cooker; stir to blend. Cover; cook on LOW 5 hours or on HIGH 3 hours. Remove pork to large cutting board; shred with two forks. Return pork to **CROCK-POT®** slow cooker; stir to blend. Cover; cook on HIGH 30 minutes.

Lemon Pork Chops

MAKES 4 SERVINGS

1 tablespoon vegetable oil	1 green bell pepper, cut into strips
4 boneless pork chops	1 tablespoon lemon-pepper seasoning
3 cans (8 ounces *each*) tomato sauce	1 tablespoon Worcestershire sauce
1 large onion, quartered and sliced	1 lemon, quartered, plus additional for garnish

1 Heat oil in large skillet over medium-low heat. Add pork chops; cook 5 to 7 minutes or until browned on both sides. Drain fat. Remove to **CROCK-POT®** slow cooker.

2 Combine tomato sauce, onion, bell pepper, lemon-pepper seasoning and Worcestershire sauce in medium bowl; stir to blend. Add to **CROCK-POT®** slow cooker.

3 Squeeze juice from lemon quarters over mixture; drop squeezed lemons into **CROCK-POT®** slow cooker. Cover; cook on LOW 6 to 8 hours or until pork is tender. Remove squeezed lemons before serving. Serve with additional lemon quarters, if desired.

Tip

Browning pork before adding it to the **CROCK-POT®** slow cooker helps reduce the fat. Just remember to drain the fat from the skillet before transferring the pork to the **CROCK-POT®** slow cooker.

Rough-Cut Smoky Red Pork Roast

MAKES 8 SERVINGS

1 boneless pork shoulder roast
(about 4 pounds)*

1 can (about 14 ounces) stewed
tomatoes, drained

1 can (6 ounces) tomato paste with
basil, oregano and garlic

1 cup chopped red bell pepper

2 to 3 canned chipotle peppers in
adobo sauce, finely chopped and
mashed with fork**

1½ to 2 tablespoons sugar

1 teaspoon salt

*Unless you have a 5-, 6- or 7-quart
CROCK-POT® slow cooker, cut any roast
larger than 2½ pounds in half so it cooks
completely.

**For less heat, remove seeds from chipotle
peppers before mashing.

1 Coat inside of **CROCK-POT**® slow cooker with nonstick cooking spray. Place pork, fat
side up, in bottom. Combine tomatoes, tomato paste, bell pepper and chipotle peppers
in small bowl. Pour over pork. Cover; cook on HIGH 5 hours.

2 Scrape tomato mixture into cooking liquid. Remove pork to large cutting board; let
stand 15 minutes before slicing. Stir sugar and salt into cooking liquid. Cook, uncovered,
on HIGH 15 minutes or until sauce is thickened. Pour sauce over pork slices to serve.

Mexican Carnitas

MAKES 4 SERVINGS

1 boneless pork shoulder roast
   (2 pounds)
1 tablespoon garlic salt
1 tablespoon black pepper
1½ teaspoons adobo seasoning
1 medium onion, chopped
1 can (16 ounces) green salsa
½ cup water

¼ cup chopped fresh cilantro
   Juice of 2 medium limes
3 cloves garlic, minced
4 (6-inch) flour tortillas, warmed
   Optional toppings: chopped green
     bell pepper, tomatoes and red
     onion
   Lime wedges (optional)

1 Coat inside of **CROCK-POT**® slow cooker with nonstick cooking spray. Season pork with garlic salt, pepper and adobo seasoning.

2 Place pork, onion, salsa, water, cilantro, lime juice and garlic in **CROCK-POT**® slow cooker. Cover; cook on LOW 4 to 5 hours. Serve in tortillas with desired toppings. Garnish with lime wedges.

Asian Pork Tenderloin

MAKES 4 SERVINGS

½ cup bottled garlic ginger sauce
¼ cup sliced green onions
1 pork tenderloin (about 1 pound)
1 large red onion, cut into slices

1 medium red bell pepper, cut into
   1-inch pieces
1 medium zucchini, cut into ¼-inch
   slices
1 tablespoon olive oil

1 Combine sauce and green onions in large resealable food storage bag. Add pork. Seal bag; turn to coat. Place bag on large baking sheet; refrigerate 30 minutes or overnight.

2 Combine red onion, bell pepper, zucchini and oil in large bowl; toss to coat. Place vegetables in **CROCK-POT**® slow cooker. Remove pork from bag; place on top of vegetables. Discard marinade. Cover; cook on LOW 6 to 7 hours or on HIGH 4 to 5 hours.

3 Remove pork to large cutting board. Cover loosely with foil; let stand 10 to 15 minutes before slicing. Serve pork with vegetables.

Vegetable-Stuffed Pork Chops

MAKES 4 SERVINGS

4 bone-in pork chops	1 small onion, chopped
Salt and black pepper	½ cup uncooked converted long grain rice
1 cup frozen corn	1 can (8 ounces) tomato sauce
1 medium green bell pepper, chopped	
½ cup Italian-style seasoned dry bread crumbs	

1 Cut pocket into each pork chop, cutting from edge to bone. Lightly season pockets with salt and black pepper. Combine corn, bell pepper, bread crumbs, onion and rice in large bowl; stir to blend. Stuff pork chops with rice mixture. Secure open side with toothpicks.

2 Place any remaining rice mixture in **CROCK-POT**® slow cooker. Add stuffed pork chops to **CROCK-POT**® slow cooker. Pour tomato sauce over pork chops. Cover; cook on LOW 8 to 10 hours.

3 Remove pork chops to large serving platter. Remove and discard toothpicks. Serve with extra rice mixture.

Tip

Your butcher can cut a pocket in the pork chops to save you time and to ensure even cooking.

Vegetables and Grains

Slow Cooker Green Beans

MAKES 6 TO 8 SERVINGS

1 tablespoon olive oil

1 pound fresh green beans, trimmed and cut in half

1 teaspoon fresh garlic slivers

1 can (10½ ounces) French Onion soup

¾ cup water

¼ teaspoon black pepper

¼ cup (about 2 ounces) chopped pimientos

¼ cup sliced almonds, toasted*

To toast almonds, spread in single layer in heavy skillet. Cook and stir over medium heat 1 to 2 minutes or until nuts are lightly browned.

1 Heat oil in large skillet over high heat. Add beans; cook and stir 5 minutes or until beans begin to char and blister. Add garlic; cook 1 minute. Remove bean mixture to **CROCK-POT®** slow cooker.

2 Add soup, water, pepper and pimientos to **CROCK-POT®** slow cooker; stir to blend. Cover; cook on LOW 4 hours or on HIGH 2 hours. Sprinkle almonds over beans just before serving.

Colcannon

MAKES 8 SERVINGS

6 tablespoons butter, cut into small pieces

3 pounds russet potatoes, peeled and cut into 1-inch pieces

2 medium leeks (white and light green parts only), thinly sliced

½ cup water

2½ teaspoons kosher salt

¼ teaspoon black pepper

1 cup milk

½ small head (about 1 pound) savoy cabbage, cored and thinly sliced

4 slices bacon, crisp-cooked and crumbled

1 Sprinkle butter on bottom of **CROCK-POT**® slow cooker. Layer half of potatoes, leeks, remaining potatoes, water, salt and pepper. Cover; cook on HIGH 5 hours or until potatoes are tender, stirring halfway through cooking time.

2 Mash potatoes in **CROCK-POT**® slow cooker until smooth. Stir in milk and cabbage. Cover; cook on HIGH 30 to 40 minutes or until cabbage is crisp-tender. Stir bacon into potato mixture.

Asparagus and Cheese

MAKES 4 TO 6 SERVINGS

1½ pounds fresh asparagus, trimmed	⅔ cup slivered almonds
2 cups crushed saltine crackers	4 ounces American cheese, cubed
1 can (10¾ ounces) condensed cream of asparagus soup, undiluted	1 egg
1 can (10¾ ounces) condensed cream of chicken or cream of celery soup, undiluted	

Combine asparagus, crackers, soups, almonds, cheese and egg in **CROCK-POT®** slow cooker; toss to coat. Cover; cook on HIGH 3 to 3½ hours.

Tip

Cooking times are guidelines. **CROCK-POT®** slow cookers, just like ovens, cook differently depending on a variety of factors. For example, cooking times will be longer at higher altitudes. You may need to slightly adjust cooking times.

Buttery Vegetable Gratin

MAKES 12 SERVINGS

3 leeks, halved lengthwise and cut into
   1-inch pieces

1 red bell pepper, cut into ½-inch pieces

5 tablespoons unsalted butter, divided

4 tablespoons grated Parmesan cheese,
   divided

1 teaspoon fresh thyme, divided

¾ teaspoon salt, divided

¼ plus ⅛ teaspoon black pepper, divided

2 zucchini (about 1½ pounds *total*), cut
   into ¾-inch-thick slices

2 yellow squash (about 1½ pounds
   total), cut into ¾-inch-thick slices

1½ cups fresh bread crumbs

1 Coat inside of **CROCK-POT®** slow cooker with nonstick cooking spray. Place leeks and bell pepper in bottom of **CROCK-POT®** slow cooker. Dot with 1 tablespoon butter, 1 tablespoon cheese, ½ teaspoon thyme, ¼ teaspoon salt and ⅛ teaspoon black pepper.

2 Arrange zucchini in single layer over leeks, overlapping as necessary. Dot with 1 tablespoon butter, 1 tablespoon cheese, remaining ½ teaspoon thyme, ¼ teaspoon salt and ⅛ teaspoon black pepper.

3 Arrange yellow squash in single layer over zucchini, overlapping as necessary. Dot with 1 tablespoon butter, remaining 2 tablespoons cheese, ¼ teaspoon salt and ⅛ teaspoon black pepper. Cover; cook on LOW 4 to 5 hours or until vegetables are soft.

4 Meanwhile, melt remaining 2 tablespoons butter in large skillet over medium-high heat. Add bread crumbs; cook and stir 6 minutes or until crisp and golden brown. Remove to medium bowl; set aside to cool. Sprinkle over vegetable mixture just before serving.

Cheesy Cauliflower

MAKES 8 TO 10 SERVINGS

3 pounds cauliflower florets	¼ teaspoon ground mustard
¼ cup water	2 cups milk
5 tablespoons unsalted butter	2 cups (8 ounces) shredded sharp
1 cup finely chopped onion	Cheddar cheese
6 tablespoons all-purpose flour	Salt and black pepper

1 Coat inside of **CROCK-POT**® slow cooker with nonstick cooking spray. Add cauliflower and water.

2 Melt butter in medium saucepan over medium-high heat. Add onion; cook 4 to 5 minutes or until slightly softened. Add flour and ground mustard; cook and stir 3 minutes or until well combined. Whisk in milk until smooth. Bring to a boil; cook 1 to 2 minutes or until thickened. Stir in cheese, salt and pepper; cook and stir until cheese is melted. Pour cheese mixture over top of cauliflower in **CROCK-POT**® slow cooker. Cover; cook on LOW 4 to 4½ hours.

Baked Beans

MAKES 6 TO 8 SERVINGS

2 cans (about 15 ounces *each*)
   baked beans
1 cup ketchup
½ cup barbecue sauce
½ cup packed brown sugar

5 slices bacon, chopped
½ green bell pepper, chopped
½ onion, chopped
1½ teaspoons prepared mustard
   Sprigs fresh Italian parsley (optional)

Place all ingredients except parsley in **CROCK-POT®** slow cooker; stir to blend. Cover; cook on LOW 8 to 12 hours or on HIGH 4 to 5 hours. Garnish with parsley.

Golden Barley with Cashews

MAKES 4 SERVINGS

2 tablespoons olive oil
1 cup hulled barley, sorted
3 cups vegetable broth
1 cup chopped celery
1 medium green bell pepper, chopped

1 medium yellow onion, chopped
1 clove garlic, minced
¼ teaspoon black pepper
   Chopped cashew nuts

1 Heat large skillet over medium heat. Add oil and barley; cook and stir 10 minutes or until barley is slightly browned. Remove to **CROCK-POT®** slow cooker.

2 Add broth, celery, bell pepper, onion, garlic and black pepper; stir to blend. Cover; cook on LOW 4 to 5 hours or on HIGH 2 to 3 hours or until liquid is absorbed. Top with cashews.

Barley Risotto with Fennel

MAKES 6 SERVINGS

1 medium bulb fennel, cored and finely diced (about ½ cup)
1 cup uncooked pearl barley
1 carrot, finely chopped
1 shallot, finely chopped
2 teaspoons ground fennel seed
1 clove garlic, minced

1 container (32 ounces) chicken broth
1 cup water
1½ cups frozen cut green beans
½ cup grated Parmesan cheese
1 tablespoon grated lemon peel
1 teaspoon black pepper

1 Coat inside of **CROCK-POT®** slow cooker with nonstick cooking spray. Combine diced fennel, barley, carrot, shallot, ground fennel and garlic in **CROCK-POT®** slow cooker; stir to blend. Pour in broth and water. Cover; cook on HIGH 3 hours or until barley is thick and creamy.

2 Turn off heat. Stir green beans, cheese, lemon peel and pepper into risotto. (If risotto appears dry, stir in a few tablespoons of additional water.)

Gratin Potatoes with Asiago Cheese

MAKES 4 TO 6 SERVINGS

6 slices bacon, cut into 1-inch pieces
6 medium baking potatoes, peeled
   and thinly sliced

½ cup grated Asiago cheese
Salt and black pepper
1½ cups whipping cream

1 Heat large skillet over medium heat. Add bacon; cook and stir until crisp. Remove to paper towel-lined plate using slotted spoon.

2 Pour bacon drippings into **CROCK-POT**® slow cooker. Layer one fourth of potatoes on bottom of **CROCK-POT**® slow cooker. Sprinkle one fourth of bacon over potatoes and top with one fourth of cheese. Season with salt and pepper.

3 Repeat layers three times. Pour cream over all. Cover; cook on LOW 7 to 9 hours or on HIGH 5 to 6 hours.

Frijoles Borrachos (Drunken Beans)

MAKES 8 SERVINGS

6 slices bacon, chopped

1 medium yellow onion, chopped

1 tablespoon minced garlic

3 jalapeño peppers, seeded and finely diced*

1 tablespoon dried oregano

1 can (12 ounces) beer

6 cups water

1 pound dried pinto beans, rinsed and sorted

1 can (about 14 ounces) diced tomatoes

1 tablespoon salt

¼ cup chopped fresh cilantro

Jalapeño peppers can sting and irritate the skin, so wear rubber gloves when handling peppers and do not touch your eyes.

1 Heat large skillet over medium-high heat. Add bacon; cook 5 minutes or until mostly browned and crisp. Remove to **CROCK-POT**® slow cooker. Discard all but 3 tablespoons of drippings.

2 Heat same skillet over medium heat. Add onion; cook 6 minutes or until softened and lightly browned. Add garlic, jalapeño peppers and oregano; cook 30 seconds or until fragrant. *Increase heat to medium-high.* Add beer; bring to a simmer. Cook 2 minutes, stirring to scrape up any brown bits from bottom of skillet. Remove mixture to **CROCK-POT**® slow cooker.

3 Add water, beans, tomatoes and salt to **CROCK-POT**® slow cooker. Cover; cook on LOW 7 hours or on HIGH 3 to 4 hours. Mash beans slightly until broth is thickened and creamy. Top with cilantro.

Balsamic-Honey Glazed Root Vegetables

MAKES 6 SERVINGS

4 medium carrots, cut into ½-inch pieces

2 medium parsnips, cut into ¾-inch pieces

1½ pounds sweet potatoes, peeled and cut into 1-inch pieces

2 medium red onions, each cut through root end into 6 wedges

¼ cup honey

3 tablespoons unsalted butter, melted

1 tablespoon balsamic vinegar

1 teaspoon salt

¼ teaspoon black pepper

1 Combine carrots, parsnips, sweet potatoes, onions, honey, butter, vinegar, salt and pepper in **CROCK-POT**® slow cooker; toss to coat vegetables. Cover; cook on LOW 4 to 5 hours.

2 Remove vegetables to large bowl using slotted spoon. Turn **CROCK-POT**® slow cooker to HIGH. Cover; cook on HIGH 15 minutes or until sauce is thickened. Return vegetables to **CROCK-POT**® slow cooker; toss to coat.

Blue Cheese Potatoes

MAKES 5 SERVINGS

2 pounds red potatoes, peeled and cut into ½-inch pieces

1¼ cups chopped green onions, divided

2 tablespoons olive oil, divided

1 teaspoon dried basil

½ teaspoon salt

¼ teaspoon black pepper

½ cup crumbled blue cheese

1 Layer potatoes, 1 cup green onions, 1 tablespoon oil, basil, salt and pepper in **CROCK-POT®** slow cooker. Cover; cook on LOW 7 hours or on HIGH 4 hours.

2 Gently stir in cheese and remaining 1 tablespoon oil. Cover; cook on HIGH 5 minutes. Remove potatoes to large serving platter; top with remaining ¼ cup green onions.

Cheesy Corn and Peppers

MAKES 8 SERVINGS

2 pounds frozen corn

2 poblano peppers, chopped

2 tablespoons butter, cubed

1 teaspoon salt

½ teaspoon ground cumin

¼ teaspoon black pepper

3 ounces cream cheese, cubed

1 cup (4 ounces) shredded sharp Cheddar cheese

1 Coat inside of **CROCK-POT®** slow cooker with nonstick cooking spray. Combine corn, poblano peppers, butter, salt, cumin and black pepper in **CROCK-POT®** slow cooker. Cover; cook on HIGH 2 hours.

2 Stir in cheeses. Cover; cook on HIGH 15 minutes or until cheeses are melted.

Cauliflower Mash

MAKES 6 SERVINGS

2 heads cauliflower (8 cups florets)	Salt
1 tablespoon butter	Sprigs fresh Italian parsley (optional)
1 tablespoon milk	

1 Arrange cauliflower in **CROCK-POT®** slow cooker. Add enough water to fill **CROCK-POT®** slow cooker by about 2 inches. Cover; cook on LOW 5 to 6 hours. Drain well.

2 Place cooked cauliflower in food processor or blender; process until almost smooth. Add butter; process until smooth. Add milk as needed to reach desired consistency. Season with salt. Garnish with parsley.

Lemon-Mint Red Potatoes

MAKES 4 SERVINGS

2 pounds new red potatoes

3 tablespoons extra virgin olive oil

1 teaspoon salt

½ teaspoon Greek seasoning or dried oregano

¼ teaspoon garlic powder

¼ teaspoon black pepper

4 tablespoons chopped fresh mint, divided

2 tablespoons butter

2 tablespoons lemon juice

1 teaspoon grated lemon peel

1 Coat inside of **CROCK-POT**® slow cooker with nonstick cooking spray. Add potatoes and oil, stirring gently to coat. Sprinkle with salt, Greek seasoning, garlic powder and pepper. Cover; cook on LOW 7 hours or on HIGH 4 hours.

2 Stir in 2 tablespoons mint, butter, lemon juice and lemon peel until butter is completely melted. Cover; cook on HIGH 15 minutes. Sprinkle with remaining 2 tablespoons mint.

Slow-Cooked Succotash

MAKES 8 SERVINGS

 2 teaspoons olive oil
 1 cup diced onion
 1 cup diced green bell pepper
 1 cup diced celery
 1 teaspoon paprika
1½ cups frozen corn

1½ cups frozen lima beans
 1 cup canned diced tomatoes
 1 tablespoon minced fresh Italian parsley
 Salt and black pepper

1 Heat oil in large skillet over medium heat. Add onion, bell pepper and celery; cook and stir 5 minutes or until vegetables are crisp-tender. Stir in paprika.

2 Stir onion mixture, corn, beans, tomatoes, parsley, salt and black pepper into **CROCK-POT**® slow cooker. Cover; cook on LOW 6 to 8 hours or on HIGH 3 to 4 hours.

Chunky Ranch Potatoes

MAKES 8 SERVINGS

3 pounds unpeeled red potatoes, quartered

1 cup water

½ cup ranch dressing

½ cup grated Parmesan or Cheddar cheese

¼ cup minced fresh chives

1 Place potatoes in **CROCK-POT®** slow cooker. Add water. Cover; cook on LOW 7 to 9 hours or on HIGH 4 to 6 hours.

2 Stir in ranch dressing, cheese and chives. Break up potatoes into large pieces.

Creamy Curried Spinach

MAKES 6 TO 8 SERVINGS

3 packages (10 ounces *each*) frozen
  spinach
1 onion, chopped
4 teaspoons minced garlic
2 tablespoons curry powder

2 tablespoons butter, melted
¼ cup chicken broth
¼ cup whipping cream
1 teaspoon lemon juice

Combine spinach, onion, garlic, curry powder,
butter and broth in **CROCK-POT**® slow cooker.
Cover; cook on LOW 3 to 4 hours or on HIGH
2 hours. Stir in cream and lemon juice during last
30 minutes of cooking.

Corn on the Cob with Garlic Herb Butter

MAKES 4 TO 5 SERVINGS

4 to 5 ears of corn, husked
½ cup (1 stick) unsalted butter, softened
3 to 4 cloves garlic, minced

2 tablespoons finely minced fresh
  Italian parsley
Salt and black pepper

1 Place each ear of corn on piece of foil. Combine butter, garlic and parsley in small bowl;
spread onto corn. Season with salt and pepper; tightly seal foil.

2 Place ears in **CROCK-POT**® slow cooker, overlapping
if necessary. Add enough water to come one fourth
of the way up each ear. Cover; cook on LOW 4 to
5 hours or on HIGH 2 to 2½ hours.

Braised Cabbage

MAKES 6 SERVINGS

3 slices bacon
1 head (about 3 pounds) green
    cabbage, cut into 1-inch-thick
    wedges

1 medium red onion, thinly sliced
3 cups chicken broth
2 tablespoons butter, cubed

1 Heat medium skillet over medium heat. Add bacon; cook and stir until crisp. Remove to paper towel-lined plate using slotted spoon; crumble. Set aside. Pour off all but 2 tablespoons drippings from skillet. Coat inside of **CROCK-POT** slow cooker with bacon drippings.

2 Layer cabbage and onion in **CROCK-POT** slow cooker. Pour in broth; top with butter. Cover; cook on LOW 6 to 7 hours or on HIGH 3 to 4 hours. Sprinkle cabbage with crumbled bacon just before serving.

White Beans and Tomatoes

MAKES 8 TO 10 SERVINGS

¼ cup olive oil

2 medium onions, chopped

1 tablespoon minced garlic

4 cups water

2 cans (about 14 ounces *each*) cannellini beans, rinsed and drained

1 can (about 28 ounces) crushed tomatoes

4 teaspoons dried oregano

2 teaspoons kosher salt

Black pepper (optional)

Sprigs fresh oregano (optional)

1 Heat oil in large skillet over medium heat. Add onions; cook 15 minutes or until tender and translucent, stirring occasionally. Add garlic; cook 1 minute.

2 Remove mixture to **CROCK-POT**® slow cooker. Add water, beans, tomatoes, dried oregano and salt. Cover; cook on LOW 8 hours or on HIGH 4 hours. Stir in pepper, if desired. Garnish with fresh oregano.

Garlicky Mustard Greens

MAKES 4 SERVINGS

2 pounds mustard greens	¾ cup chopped red bell pepper
1 teaspoon olive oil	½ cup vegetable broth
1 cup chopped onion	1 tablespoon cider vinegar
2 cloves garlic, minced	1 teaspoon sugar

1 Remove stems and any wilted leaves from greens. Stack several leaves; roll up. Cut crosswise into 1-inch slices. Repeat with remaining greens.

2 Heat oil in large saucepan over medium heat. Add onion and garlic; cook and stir 5 minutes or until onion is tender. Combine greens, onion mixture, bell pepper and broth in **CROCK-POT®** slow cooker; stir to blend. Cover; cook on LOW 3 to 4 hours or on HIGH 2 hours.

3 Combine vinegar and sugar in small bowl; stir until sugar is dissolved. Stir into cooked greens; serve immediately.

Cheesy Polenta

MAKES 6 SERVINGS

6 cups vegetable broth	4 tablespoons (½ stick) unsalted butter, cubed
1½ cups uncooked medium-grind instant polenta	
½ cup grated Parmesan cheese, plus additional for serving	Fried sage leaves (optional)

1 Coat inside of **CROCK-POT**® slow cooker with nonstick cooking spray. Heat broth in large saucepan over high heat. Remove to **CROCK-POT**® slow cooker; whisk in polenta.

2 Cover; cook on LOW 2 to 2½ hours or until polenta is tender and creamy. Stir in ½ cup cheese and butter. Serve with additional cheese. Garnish with sage.

Curried Cauliflower and Potatoes

MAKES 6 SERVINGS

3 tablespoons vegetable oil

1 medium onion, chopped

1 tablespoon minced garlic

1 tablespoon curry powder

1½ teaspoons salt

1½ teaspoons grated fresh ginger

1 teaspoon ground turmeric

1 teaspoon yellow or brown mustard seeds

¼ teaspoon red pepper flakes

1 medium head cauliflower, cut into 1-inch pieces

2 pounds fingerling potatoes, cut into halves

½ cup water

1 Heat oil in medium skillet over medium heat. Add onion; cook 8 minutes or until softened. Add garlic, curry powder, salt, ginger, turmeric, mustard seeds and red pepper flakes; cook and stir 1 minute. Remove onion mixture to **CROCK-POT**® slow cooker.

2 Stir in cauliflower, potatoes and water. Cover; cook on HIGH 4 hours.

Beets in Spicy Mustard Sauce

MAKES 4 SERVINGS

3 pounds beets, peeled, halved and cut into ½-inch slices

¼ cup sour cream

2 tablespoons spicy brown mustard

2 teaspoons lemon juice

2 cloves garlic, minced

¼ teaspoon black pepper

⅛ teaspoon dried thyme

Lemon wedges (optional)

Sprigs fresh thyme (optional)

1 Place beets in **CROCK-POT**® slow cooker. Add enough water to cover by 1 inch. Cover; cook on LOW 7 to 8 hours.

2 Combine sour cream, mustard, lemon juice, garlic, pepper and dried thyme in small bowl; stir to blend. Spoon over beets; toss to coat. Cover; cook on LOW 15 minutes. Serve with lemon wedges, if desired. Garnish with thyme sprigs.

Candied Sweet Potatoes

MAKES 4 SERVINGS

3 medium sweet potatoes (1½ to 2 pounds), sliced into ½-inch rounds

½ cup water

¼ cup (½ stick) butter, cut into small pieces

3 tablespoons sugar

1 tablespoon vanilla

1 teaspoon ground nutmeg

Combine potatoes, water, butter, sugar, vanilla and nutmeg in **CROCK-POT**® slow cooker; stir to blend. Cover; cook on LOW 7 hours or on HIGH 4 hours.

Barley Salad

MAKES 16 SERVINGS

2 onions, chopped
2 sweet potatoes, diced
1 cup uncooked pearl barley
1 teaspoon salt
½ teaspoon ground cinnamon
¼ teaspoon ground red pepper (optional)

1½ cups water
2 apples, peeled and chopped
1 cup dried cranberries
1 cup chopped pecans

1 Spread onions and potatoes on bottom of **CROCK-POT®** slow cooker. Add barley, salt, cinnamon and ground red pepper, if desired. Pour in water; cook on LOW 4 hours or on HIGH 2 hours.

2 Stir in apples, cranberries and pecans. Serve warm or at room temperature.

Artichoke and Tomato Paella

MAKES 8 SERVINGS

4 cups vegetable broth
2 cups uncooked converted rice
½ (10-ounce) package frozen chopped spinach, thawed and drained
1 green bell pepper, chopped
1 medium tomato, sliced into wedges
1 medium yellow onion, chopped
1 medium carrot, diced

3 cloves garlic, minced
1 tablespoon minced fresh Italian parsley
Salt and black pepper
1 can (13¾ ounces) artichoke hearts, quartered, rinsed and well drained
½ cup frozen peas, thawed

Combine broth, rice, spinach, bell pepper, tomato, onion, carrot, garlic, parsley, salt and black pepper in **CROCK-POT®** slow cooker; mix well. Cover; cook on LOW 4 hours or on HIGH 2 hours. Stir in artichoke hearts and peas. Cover; cook on HIGH 15 minutes.

BBQ Baked Beans

MAKES 12 SERVINGS

3 cans (about 15 ounces *each*) white
  beans, drained
4 slices bacon, chopped

¾ cup prepared barbecue sauce
½ cup maple syrup
1½ teaspoons ground mustard

Coat inside of **CROCK-POT®** slow cooker with nonstick cooking spray. Add beans, bacon, barbecue sauce, maple syrup and mustard; stir to blend. Cover; cook on LOW 4 hours, stirring halfway through cooking time.

Lemon Cauliflower

MAKES 6 SERVINGS

1 tablespoon butter	½ teaspoon grated lemon peel
3 cloves garlic, minced	6 cups (about 1½ pounds) cauliflower florets
2 tablespoons lemon juice	¼ cup grated Parmesan cheese
½ cup water	Lemon wedges (optional)
4 tablespoons chopped fresh Italian parsley, divided	

1 Heat butter in small saucepan over medium heat. Add garlic; cook and stir 2 to 3 minutes or until soft. Stir in lemon juice and water.

2 Combine garlic mixture, 1 tablespoon parsley, lemon peel and cauliflower in **CROCK-POT**® slow cooker; stir to blend. Cover; cook on LOW 4 hours.

3 Sprinkle with remaining 3 tablespoons parsley and cheese before serving. Garnish with lemon wedges.

Harvard Beets

MAKES 6 SERVINGS

2 pounds fresh beets, peeled and cut into 1-inch cubes	¼ cup water
⅔ cup sugar	1 teaspoon salt
½ cup cider vinegar	1 tablespoon cornstarch
	2 tablespoons butter

1 Place beets in **CROCK-POT®** slow cooker. Add sugar, vinegar, water and salt; stir to blend. Cover; cook on HIGH 3 hours or until beets are just tender.

2 Remove 2 tablespoons juice from **CROCK-POT®** slow cooker to small bowl. Stir cornstarch into juice until smooth; whisk into **CROCK-POT®** slow cooker. Stir in butter. Cover; cook on HIGH 30 minutes.

Mashed Rutabagas and Potatoes

MAKES 8 SERVINGS

2 pounds rutabagas, peeled and cut into ½-inch pieces

1 pound potatoes, peeled and cut into ½-inch pieces

½ cup milk

½ teaspoon ground nutmeg

2 tablespoons chopped fresh Italian parsley

Sprigs fresh Italian parsley (optional)

1 Place rutabagas and potatoes in **CROCK-POT®** slow cooker; add enough water to cover vegetables. Cover; cook on LOW 6 hours or on HIGH 3 hours. Remove vegetables to large bowl using slotted spoon. Discard cooking liquid.

2 Mash vegetables with potato masher. Add milk, nutmeg and chopped parsley; stir until smooth. Garnish with parsley sprigs.

Collard Greens

MAKES 12 SERVINGS

1 tablespoon olive oil	2 cloves garlic, minced
3 turkey necks	1 tablespoon apple cider vinegar
5 bunches collard greens, stemmed and chopped	1 teaspoon sugar
5 cups chicken broth	Salt and black pepper
1 small onion, chopped	Red pepper flakes (optional)

1 Heat oil in large skillet over medium-high heat. Add turkey necks; cook and stir 3 to 5 minutes or until brown.

2 Combine turkey necks, collard greens, broth, onion and garlic in **CROCK-POT**® slow cooker; stir to blend. Cover; cook on LOW 5 to 6 hours. Remove and discard turkey necks. Stir in vinegar, sugar, salt, black pepper and red pepper flakes, if desired.

Brussels Sprouts with Bacon, Thyme and Raisins

MAKES 8 SERVINGS

2 pounds Brussels sprouts, ends
   trimmed and cut in half lengthwise

1 cup chicken broth

⅔ cup golden raisins

2 thick slices applewood smoked bacon,
   chopped

2 tablespoons chopped fresh thyme

Combine sprouts, broth, raisins, bacon and thyme in **CROCK-POT®** slow cooker; stir to blend. Cover; cook on LOW 3 to 4 hours.

Cheesy Mashed Potato Casserole

MAKES 10 TO 12 SERVINGS

4 pounds Yukon Gold potatoes, peeled
   and cut into 1-inch pieces

2 cups vegetable broth

3 tablespoons unsalted butter, cubed

½ cup milk, heated

⅓ cup sour cream

2 cups (8 ounces) shredded sharp
   Cheddar cheese, plus additional
   for garnish

½ teaspoon salt

¼ teaspoon black pepper

   Chopped fresh Italian parsley (optional)

1 Coat inside of **CROCK-POT®** slow cooker with nonstick cooking spray. Add potatoes and broth; dot with butter. Cover; cook on LOW 4½ to 5 hours.

2 Mash potatoes with potato masher; stir in milk, sour cream, 2 cups cheese, salt and pepper until cheese is melted. Garnish with additional cheese and parsley.

Dazzling Desserts

Vanilla Sour Cream Cheesecake

MAKES 6 TO 8 SERVINGS

¾ cup graham cracker crumbs
¼ cup plus 3 tablespoons sugar, divided
¼ teaspoon ground nutmeg
2 tablespoons unsalted butter, melted
1 package (8 ounces) cream cheese, softened

2 eggs
¼ cup sour cream
1½ teaspoons vanilla
1½ tablespoons all-purpose flour
Fresh strawberries, sliced (optional)
Sprigs fresh mint (optional)

1 Combine graham cracker crumbs, 1 tablespoon sugar and nutmeg in medium bowl; stir to blend. Stir in butter until well blended. Press mixture into bottom and 1 inch up sides of 7-inch springform pan.

2 Beat cream cheese in large bowl with electric mixer at high speed 3 to 4 minutes or until smooth. Add remaining ¼ cup plus 2 tablespoons sugar; beat 1 to 2 minutes. Beat in eggs, sour cream and vanilla until blended. Stir in flour. Pour batter into crust.

3 Fill 6-quart **CROCK-POT**® slow cooker with ½-inch water and set small wire rack in bottom. Set springform pan on rack. Cover top of stoneware with clean kitchen towel. Cover; cook on HIGH 2 hours.

4 Turn off heat and let stand 1 hour without opening lid. Remove lid; remove cheesecake to wire rack. Cool completely. Cover with plastic wrap; refrigerate 4 to 5 hours or until well chilled.

5 To serve, run tip of knife around edge of cheesecake and remove springform mold. Top with strawberries, if desired. Garnish with mint. Cut into wedges to serve.

Bananas Foster

MAKES 12 SERVINGS

12 bananas, cut into quarters
 1 cup flaked coconut
 1 cup dark corn syrup
⅔ cup butter, melted
¼ cup lemon juice
 2 teaspoons grated lemon peel

 2 teaspoons rum
 1 teaspoon ground cinnamon
½ teaspoon salt
12 slices prepared pound cake
 1 quart vanilla ice cream

1 Combine bananas and coconut in **CROCK-POT®** slow cooker. Combine corn syrup, butter, lemon juice, lemon peel, rum, cinnamon and salt in medium bowl; stir to blend. Pour over bananas.

2 Cover; cook on LOW 1 to 2 hours. To serve, arrange bananas on pound cake slices. Top with ice cream and warm sauce.

Fudge and Cream Pudding Cake

MAKES 8 TO 10 SERVINGS

1 cup all-purpose flour	1 cup whipping cream
½ cup packed light brown sugar	1 tablespoon vegetable oil
5 tablespoons unsweetened cocoa powder, divided	1 teaspoon vanilla
2 teaspoons baking powder	1½ cups hot water
½ teaspoon ground cinnamon	½ cup packed dark brown sugar
⅛ teaspoon salt	Whipped cream (optional)

1 Prepare foil handles by tearing off three 18×2-inch strips heavy foil (or use regular foil folded to double thickness). Crisscross foil strips in spoke design; place in **CROCK-POT®** slow cooker. Coat inside of 5-quart **CROCK-POT®** slow cooker and foil handles with nonstick cooking spray.

2 Combine flour, light brown sugar, 3 tablespoons cocoa, baking powder, cinnamon and salt in medium bowl. Add whipping cream, oil and vanilla; stir to blend. Pour batter into **CROCK-POT®** slow cooker.

3 Combine hot water, dark brown sugar and remaining 2 tablespoons cocoa in medium bowl; stir to blend. Pour sauce over cake batter. *Do not stir.* Cover; cook on HIGH 2 hours. Turn off heat. Let stand 10 minutes.

4 Remove to large plate using foil handles. Discard foil. Cut into wedges to serve and serve with whipped cream, if desired.

Chai Tea Cherries 'n' Cream

MAKES 8 SERVINGS

2 cans (15½ ounces *each*) pitted cherries in pear juice
2 cups water
½ cup orange juice
1 cup sugar
4 cardamom pods
2 whole cinnamon sticks, broken in half
1 teaspoon grated orange peel

¼ ounce coarsely chopped candied ginger
4 whole cloves
2 whole black peppercorns
4 green tea bags
1 container (6 ounces) black cherry yogurt
1 quart vanilla ice cream
Sprigs fresh mint (optional)

1 Drain cherries, reserving juice. Combine reserved pear juice, water and orange juice in **CROCK-POT®** slow cooker. Stir in sugar, cardamom pods, cinnamon sticks, orange peel, ginger, cloves and peppercorns. Cover; cook on HIGH 1½ hours.

2 Remove spices with slotted spoon; discard. Stir in tea bags and reserved cherries. Cover; cook on HIGH 30 minutes.

3 Turn off heat. Remove and discard tea bags. Remove cherries from liquid; set aside. Let liquid cool until just warm. Whisk in yogurt until smooth.

4 To serve, divide warm cherries and yogurt sauce among wine or cocktail glasses. Top each serving with ice cream; swirl lightly. Garnish with mint.

Pineapple Rice Pudding

MAKES 8 SERVINGS

1 can (20 ounces) crushed pineapple in juice, undrained

1 can (13½ ounces) unsweetened coconut milk

1 can (12 ounces) evaporated milk

¾ cup uncooked Arborio rice

2 eggs, lightly beaten

¼ cup granulated sugar

¼ cup packed brown sugar

½ teaspoon ground cinnamon

¼ teaspoon salt

¼ teaspoon ground nutmeg

Toasted coconut and pineapple slices (optional)*

To toast coconut, spread in single layer in small heavy-bottomed skillet. Cook and stir over medium heat 1 to 2 minutes or until lightly browned. Remove from skillet immediately.

1 Combine crushed pineapple with juice, coconut milk, evaporated milk, rice, eggs, granulated sugar, brown sugar, cinnamon, salt and nutmeg in **CROCK-POT**® slow cooker; stir to blend. Cover; cook on HIGH 3 to 4 hours or until thickened and rice is tender.

2 Stir to blend. Serve warm or chilled. Garnish with toasted coconut and pineapple slices.

Figs Poached in Red Wine

MAKES 4 SERVINGS

2	cups dry red wine	2	(3-inch) whole cinnamon sticks
1	cup packed brown sugar	1	teaspoon finely grated orange peel
12	dried Calimyrna or Mediterranean figs (about 6 ounces)	4	tablespoons whipping cream (optional)

1 Combine wine, brown sugar, figs, cinnamon sticks and orange peel in **CROCK-POT®** slow cooker. Cover; cook on LOW 5 to 6 hours or on HIGH 4 to 5 hours.

2 Remove and discard cinnamon sticks before serving. Top figs with syrup and cream, if desired.

Cherry Delight

MAKES 8 TO 10 SERVINGS

1	can (21 ounces) cherry pie filling	½	cup (1 stick) butter, melted
1	package (about 18 ounces) yellow cake mix	⅓	cup chopped walnuts

Coat inside of **CROCK-POT®** slow cooker with nonstick cooking spray. Place pie filling in **CROCK-POT®** slow cooker. Combine cake mix and butter in medium bowl. Spread evenly over pie filling. Sprinkle with walnuts. Cover; cook on LOW 3 to 4 hours or on HIGH 1½ to 2 hours.

Brioche and Amber Rum Custard

MAKES 4 TO 6 SERVINGS

2 tablespoons unsalted butter, melted
3½ cups whipping cream
4 eggs
½ cup packed dark brown sugar
⅓ cup amber or light rum
2 teaspoons vanilla

1 loaf (20 to 22 ounces) brioche bread, torn into pieces *or* 5 large brioche, cut into thirds*
½ cup coarsely chopped pecans
Caramel or butterscotch topping (optional)

If desired, trim and discard heels.

1 Butter inside of **CROCK-POT®** slow cooker with melted butter. Combine cream, eggs, brown sugar, rum and vanilla in large bowl; stir to blend.

2 Mound one fourth of brioche pieces in bottom of **CROCK-POT®** slow cooker. Ladle one fourth of cream mixture over brioche. Sprinkle with one third of pecans. Repeat layers with remaining brioche, cream mixture and pecans until all ingredients are used.

3 Cover; cook on LOW 3 to 3½ hours or on HIGH 1½ to 2 hours or until custard is set and toothpick inserted into center comes out clean. Drizzle with caramel topping, if desired. Serve warm.

Coconut Rice Pudding

MAKES 6 SERVINGS

2 cups water
1 cup uncooked converted long grain rice
1 tablespoon unsalted butter
 Pinch salt
2¼ cups evaporated milk
1 can (14 ounces) cream of coconut
½ cup golden raisins

3 egg yolks, beaten
 Grated peel of 2 limes
1 teaspoon vanilla
 Shredded coconut, toasted (optional)*

To toast coconut, spread in single layer in heavy-bottomed skillet. Cook and stir over medium heat 1 to 2 minutes. Remove from heat.

1 Place water, rice, butter and salt in medium saucepan. Bring to a boil over high heat, stirring frequently. Reduce heat to low. Cover; cook 10 to 12 minutes. Remove from heat. Let stand, covered, 5 minutes.

2 Coat inside of **CROCK-POT®** slow cooker with nonstick cooking spray. Add rice mixture, evaporated milk, cream of coconut, raisins, egg yolks, lime peel and vanilla; stir to blend.

3 Cover; cook on LOW 4 hours or on HIGH 2 hours. Stir every 30 minutes, if possible. Pudding will thicken as it cools. Garnish each serving with toasted coconut.

Pumpkin Bread Pudding

MAKES 8 SERVINGS

2 cups whole milk	2 teaspoons vanilla
½ cup (1 stick) plus 2 tablespoons butter, divided	½ teaspoon ground nutmeg
1 cup packed brown sugar, divided	¼ teaspoon salt
1 cup canned solid-pack pumpkin	16 slices cinnamon raisin bread, torn into small pieces (8 cups *total*)
3 eggs	½ cup whipping cream
1 tablespoon ground cinnamon	2 tablespoons bourbon (optional)

1 Coat inside of **CROCK-POT**® slow cooker with nonstick cooking spray. Combine milk and 2 tablespoons butter in medium microwavable bowl. Microwave on HIGH 2½ to 3 minutes or until very warm.

2 Whisk ½ cup brown sugar, pumpkin, eggs, cinnamon, vanilla, nutmeg and salt in large bowl until well blended. Whisk in milk mixture until blended. Add bread cubes; toss to coat. Remove bread mixture to **CROCK-POT**® slow cooker.

3 Cover; cook on HIGH 2 hours or until knife inserted into center comes out clean. Turn off heat. Uncover; let stand 15 minutes.

4 Combine remaining ½ cup butter, remaining ½ cup brown sugar and cream in small saucepan; bring to a boil over high heat, stirring frequently. Remove from heat. Stir in bourbon, if desired. Spoon bread pudding into individual bowls; top with sauce.

Mixed Berry Cobbler

MAKES 8 SERVINGS

1 package (16 ounces) frozen mixed berries
¾ cup granulated sugar
2 tablespoons quick-cooking tapioca
2 teaspoons grated lemon peel
1½ cups all-purpose flour
½ cup packed brown sugar

2¼ teaspoons baking powder
¼ teaspoon ground nutmeg
¾ cup milk
2 tablespoons unsalted butter, melted
Vanilla ice cream or whipped cream (optional)

1 Coat inside of **CROCK-POT**® slow cooker with nonstick cooking spray. Combine berries, granulated sugar, tapioca and lemon peel in medium bowl. Remove to **CROCK-POT**® slow cooker.

2 Combine flour, brown sugar, baking powder and nutmeg in medium bowl. Add milk and butter; stir just until blended. Drop spoonfuls of dough on top of berry mixture. Cover; cook on LOW 4 hours. Turn off heat. Uncover; let stand 30 minutes. Serve with ice cream, if desired.

Tip

Cobblers are year-round favorites. Experiment with seasonal fresh fruits, such as pears, plums, peaches, rhubarb, blueberries, raspberries, strawberries, blackberries or gooseberries. Also try different apple varieties such as Granny Smith, Fuji, Gala or a mix of your favorites.

Chocolate Orange Fondue

MAKES 1½ CUPS

½ cup whipping cream
1½ tablespoons butter
6 ounces 60% to 70% bittersweet chocolate, coarsely chopped

⅓ cup orange liqueur
¾ teaspoon vanilla
Marshmallows, strawberries and/or cubes pound cake

1 Bring cream and butter to a boil in medium saucepan over medium heat. Remove from heat. Stir in chocolate, liqueur and vanilla until chocolate is melted. Place over medium-low heat; cook and stir 2 minutes until smooth.

2 Coat inside of **CROCK-POT**® "No Dial" food warmer with nonstick cooking spray. Fill with warm fondue. Serve with marshmallows, strawberries and pound cake.

Cinnamon-Ginger Poached Pears

MAKES 6 SERVINGS

3 cups water
1 cup sugar
10 slices fresh ginger
2 whole cinnamon sticks

1 tablespoon chopped candied ginger (optional)
6 Bosc or Anjou pears, peeled and cored

1 Combine water, sugar, ginger, cinnamon and candied ginger, if desired, in **CROCK-POT**® slow cooker. Add pears. Cover; cook on LOW 4 to 6 hours or on HIGH 1½ to 2 hours.

2 Remove pears to serving plate using slotted spoon. Cook syrup, uncovered, on HIGH 30 minutes or until thickened. Remove and discard cinnamon sticks before serving.

English Bread Pudding

MAKES 6 TO 8 SERVINGS

16 slices day-old, firm-textured white
    bread (1 small loaf)
1¾ cups milk
 1 package (8 ounces) mixed dried fruit,
    cut into small pieces
 1 medium apple, chopped
½ cup chopped peanuts

⅓ cup packed brown sugar
¼ cup (½ stick) butter, melted
 1 egg, lightly beaten
 1 teaspoon ground cinnamon
¼ teaspoon ground nutmeg
¼ teaspoon ground cloves
   Whipped cream (optional)

1 Tear bread, with crusts, into 1- to 2-inch pieces; place in **CROCK-POT**® slow cooker. Pour milk over bread; let soak 30 minutes. Stir in dried fruit, apple and nuts.

2 Combine brown sugar, butter, egg, cinnamon, nutmeg and cloves in medium bowl; stir to blend. Pour brown sugar mixture over bread mixture; stir to blend. Cover; cook on LOW 3½ to 4 hours or until toothpick inserted into center of pudding comes out clean. Garnish with whipped cream.

Poached Autumn Fruits with Vanilla-Citrus Broth

MAKES 4 TO 6 SERVINGS

2 Granny Smith apples, peeled, cored and halved (reserve cores)

2 Bartlett pears, peeled, cored and halved (reserve cores)

1 orange, peeled and halved

½ cup dried cranberries

⅓ cup sugar

5 tablespoons honey

1 vanilla bean, split and seeded (reserve seeds)

1 whole cinnamon stick

Vanilla ice cream (optional)

1 Place apple and pear cores in **CROCK-POT**® slow cooker. Squeeze juice from orange halves into **CROCK-POT**® slow cooker. Add orange halves, cranberries, sugar, honey, vanilla bean and seeds and cinnamon stick. Add apples and pears. Pour in enough water to cover fruit; stir gently to combine. Cover; cook on HIGH 2 hours or until fruit is tender.

2 Remove apple and pear halves; set aside. Strain cooking liquid and discard solids. Simmer gently over low heat until liquid is reduced by half and thickened. Dice apple and pear halves. To serve, spoon fruit with sauce into bowls. Top with vanilla ice cream, if desired.

Rocky Road Brownie Bottoms

MAKES 6 SERVINGS

½ cup packed brown sugar

½ cup water

2 tablespoons unsweetened cocoa powder

2½ cups packaged brownie mix

1 package (about 4 ounces) instant chocolate pudding mix

½ cup milk chocolate chips

2 eggs, beaten

3 tablespoons butter, melted

2 cups mini marshmallows

1 cup chopped pecans or walnuts, toasted*

½ cup chocolate syrup

To toast pecans, spread in single layer in heavy skillet. Cook and stir over medium heat 1 to 2 minutes or until nuts are lightly browned.

1 Prepare foil handles by tearing off three 18×2-inch strips heavy foil (or use regular foil folded to double thickness). Crisscross foil strips in spoke design; place in **CROCK-POT**® slow cooker. Coat inside of **CROCK-POT**® slow cooker with nonstick cooking spray.

2 Combine brown sugar, water and cocoa in small saucepan over medium heat; bring to a boil over medium-high heat. Meanwhile, combine brownie mix, pudding mix, chocolate chips, eggs and butter in medium bowl; stir until well blended. Spread batter in **CROCK-POT**® slow cooker; pour boiling sugar mixture over batter.

3 Cover; cook on HIGH 1½ hours. Turn off heat. Top brownies with marshmallows, pecans and chocolate syrup. Let stand 15 minutes. Use foil handles to lift brownie to large serving platter.

Note

Recipe can be doubled for a 5-, 6- or 7-quart **CROCK-POT**® slow cooker.

Spicy Fruit Dessert

MAKES 4 TO 6 SERVINGS

2 cups canned pears, drained and diced

2 cups carambola (star fruit), sliced and seeds removed

1 can (6 ounces) frozen orange juice concentrate

¼ cup orange marmalade

¼ teaspoon pumpkin pie spice

Pound cake or ice cream

Whipped cream (optional)

Combine pears, carambola, orange juice concentrate, marmalade and pumpkin pie spice in **CROCK-POT**® slow cooker. Cover; cook on LOW 4 to 6 hours or on HIGH 2 to 3 hours or until cooked through. Serve warm over pound cake with whipped cream, if desired.

Minted Hot Cocoa

MAKES 6 TO 8 SERVINGS

6 cups milk	½ teaspoon mint extract
¾ cup semisweet chocolate pieces	10 sprigs fresh mint, tied together with kitchen string, plus additional for garnish
½ cup sugar	
½ cup unsweetened cocoa powder	
1 teaspoon vanilla	Whipped cream (optional)

1 Combine milk, chocolate, sugar, cocoa, vanilla and mint extract in **CROCK-POT**® slow cooker; stir to blend. Add 10 mint sprigs. Cover; cook on LOW 3 to 4 hours.

2 Uncover; remove and discard mint sprigs. Whisk cocoa mixture well; cover until ready to serve. Garnish each serving with whipped cream and additional mint sprigs.

Warm Peanut-Caramel Dip

MAKES 1¾ CUPS

¾ cup peanut butter	⅓ cup milk
¾ cup caramel topping	Sliced apples

1 Combine peanut butter, caramel topping and milk in medium saucepan; cook over medium heat until smooth and creamy, stirring occasionally.

2 Coat inside of **CROCK-POT**® "No Dial" food warmer with nonstick cooking spray. Fill with warm dip. Serve with apples.

Peach Cobbler

MAKES 4 TO 6 SERVINGS

2 packages (16 ounces *each*) frozen
  peaches, thawed and drained
½ cup plus 1 tablespoon sugar, divided
2 teaspoons ground cinnamon, divided

½ teaspoon ground nutmeg
¾ cup all-purpose flour
6 tablespoons butter, cubed

1 Combine peaches, ½ cup sugar, 1½ teaspoons cinnamon and nutmeg in **CROCK-POT**®
slow cooker; stir to blend.

2 Combine flour, remaining 1 tablespoon sugar and remaining ½ teaspoon cinnamon in
small bowl. Cut in butter with pastry blender or two knives until mixture resembles
coarse crumbs. Sprinkle over peach mixture. Cover; cook on HIGH 2 hours.

Tip

To make cleanup easier when cooking sticky or sugary foods, spray the inside of the
CROCK-POT® slow cooker with nonstick cooking spray before adding ingredients.

Fresh Berry Compote

MAKES 4 SERVINGS

2 cups fresh blueberries	4 slices (1½×½ inches) lemon peel with no white pith
4 cups fresh sliced strawberries	
2 tablespoons orange juice	1 whole cinnamon stick *or* ½ teaspoon ground cinnamon
½ to ¾ cup sugar	

1 Place blueberries in **CROCK-POT**® slow cooker. Cover; cook on HIGH 45 minutes or until blueberries begin to soften.

2 Add strawberries, orange juice, ½ cup sugar, lemon peel and cinnamon stick; stir to blend. Cover; cook on HIGH 1 to 1½ hours or until strawberries soften and sugar is dissolved. Check for sweetness and add more sugar if necessary, cooking until added sugar is dissolved.

3 Remove stoneware from **CROCK-POT**® slow cooker to heatproof surface and let cool. Serve compote warm or chilled.

Tip

To turn this compote into a fresh fruit topping for cake, ice cream, waffles or pancakes, carefully spoon out fruit, leaving cooking liquid in **CROCK-POT**® slow cooker. Stir ¼ cup cold water into 1 to 2 tablespoons cornstarch in small bowl until smooth; whisk into cooking liquid. Cover; cook on HIGH 10 to 15 minutes or until thickened. Return fruit to sauce; stir to blend.

Fresh Bosc Pear Granita

MAKES 6 SERVINGS

1 pound fresh Bosc pears, peeled, cored and cubed

1¼ cups water

¼ cup sugar

½ teaspoon ground cinnamon

1 tablespoon lemon juice

Fresh raspberries (optional)

Lemon slices (optional)

Fresh mint leaves (optional)

1 Place pears, water, sugar and cinnamon in **CROCK-POT**® slow cooker. Cover; cook on HIGH 2½ to 3½ hours or until pears are very soft and tender. Stir in lemon juice.

2 Remove pears and syrup to blender or food processor; blend until smooth. Strain mixture, discarding any pulp. Pour liquid into 13×9-inch baking pan. Cover tightly with plastic wrap. Place pan in freezer.

3 Stir every hour, tossing granita with fork. Crush any lumps in mixture as it freezes. Freeze 3 to 4 hours or until firm. You may keep granita in freezer up to 2 days before serving; toss granita every 6 to 12 hours. Garnish with raspberries, lemon slices and mint.

Dulce de Leche

MAKES ABOUT 1½ CUPS

    1 can (14 ounces) sweetened condensed milk

1 Pour milk into 9×5-inch loaf pan. Cover tightly with foil. Place loaf pan in **CROCK-POT**® slow cooker. Pour enough water to reach halfway up sides of loaf pan. Cover; cook on LOW 5 to 6 hours or until golden and thickened.

2 Coat inside of **CROCK-POT**® "No Dial" food warmer or fondue pot with nonstick cooking spray. Fill with warm dip.

Serving Suggestion

Try this Dulce de Leche as a fondue with bananas, apples, shortbread, chocolate wafers, pretzels and/or waffle cookies.

Bittersweet Chocolate-Espresso Crème Brûlée

MAKES 5 SERVINGS

½ cup chopped bittersweet chocolate
5 egg yolks
1½ cups whipping cream

½ cup granulated sugar
¼ cup espresso
¼ cup Demerara or raw sugar

1 Arrange five 6-ounce ramekins or custard cups inside of **CROCK-POT**® slow cooker. Pour enough water to come halfway up sides of ramekins (taking care to keep water out of ramekins). Divide chocolate among ramekins.

2 Whisk egg yolks in small bowl; set aside. Heat small saucepan over medium heat. Add cream, granulated sugar and espresso; cook and stir until mixture begins to boil. Pour hot cream in thin, steady stream into egg yolks, whisking constantly. Pour through fine-mesh strainer into clean bowl.

3 Ladle into prepared ramekins over chocolate. Cover; cook on HIGH 1 to 2 hours or until custard is set around edges but still soft in centers. Carefully remove ramekins; cool to room temperature. Cover; refrigerate until serving.

4 Spread tops of custards with Demerara sugar just before serving. Serve immediately.

Cherry Rice Pudding

MAKES 6 SERVINGS

1½ cups milk
1 cup hot cooked rice
3 eggs, beaten
½ cup sugar
¼ cup dried cherries or cranberries

½ teaspoon almond extract
¼ teaspoon salt
Butter
1 cup water
Ground nutmeg (optional)

1 Combine milk, rice, eggs, sugar, cherries, almond extract and salt in large bowl; stir to blend. Pour into greased 1½-quart casserole dish. Cover dish with buttered foil, butter side down.

2 Place rack in **CROCK-POT**® slow cooker; pour in water. Place casserole on rack. Cover; cook on LOW 4 to 5 hours.

3 Remove casserole from **CROCK-POT**® slow cooker. Let stand 15 minutes before serving. Garnish with nutmeg.

5-Ingredient Kheer

MAKES 6 TO 8 SERVINGS

4 cups whole milk	½ cup golden raisins
¾ cup sugar	3 whole green cardamom pods *or* ¼ teaspoon ground cardamom
1 cup uncooked white basmati rice, rinsed and drained	

1 Coat inside of **CROCK-POT®** slow cooker with nonstick cooking spray. Add milk and sugar; stir until sugar is dissolved. Add rice, raisins and cardamom.

2 Cover; cook on HIGH 1 hour. Stir. Cover; cook on HIGH 1½ to 2 hours or until milk is absorbed.

Hot Toddies

MAKES 10 SERVINGS

8 cups water	1 (1-inch) piece fresh ginger, peeled and cut into 4 slices
2 cups bourbon	1 whole cinnamon stick
¾ cup honey	Lemon slices (optional)
⅔ cup lemon juice	

1 Combine water, bourbon, honey, lemon juice, ginger and cinnamon stick in **CROCK-POT®** slow cooker; stir to blend. Cover; cook on HIGH 2 hours. Turn **CROCK-POT®** slow cooker to WARM.

2 Remove and discard cinnamon stick and ginger pieces. Ladle into individual mugs; garnish with lemon slices.

Apple Crumble Pot

MAKES 6 TO 8 SERVINGS

4 Granny Smith apples (about 2 pounds), cored and *each* cut into 8 wedges

1 cup packed dark brown sugar, divided

½ cup dried cranberries

1 cup plus 2 tablespoons biscuit baking mix, divided

2 tablespoons butter, cubed

1½ teaspoons ground cinnamon, plus additional for topping

1 teaspoon vanilla

¼ teaspoon ground allspice

½ cup rolled oats

3 tablespoons cold butter, cubed

½ cup chopped pecans

Whipped cream (optional)

1 Coat inside of **CROCK-POT**® slow cooker with nonstick cooking spray. Combine apples, ⅔ cup brown sugar, cranberries, 2 tablespoons baking mix, 2 tablespoons butter, 1½ teaspoons cinnamon, vanilla and allspice in **CROCK-POT**® slow cooker; toss gently to coat.

2 Combine remaining 1 cup baking mix, oats and remaining ⅓ cup brown sugar in large bowl. Cut in 3 tablespoons cold butter with pastry blender or two knives until mixture resembles coarse crumbs. Sprinkle evenly over filling in **CROCK-POT**® slow cooker. Top with pecans. Cover; cook on HIGH 2 to 2½ hours or until apples are tender. *Do not overcook.*

3 Turn off heat. Let stand, uncovered, 15 to 30 minutes before serving. Top with whipped cream sprinkled with additional cinnamon, if desired.

Tequila-Poached Pears

MAKES 4 SERVINGS

4 Anjou pears, peeled	½ cup sugar
2 cups water	Grated peel and juice of 1 lime
1 can (11½ ounces) pear nectar	Vanilla ice cream (optional)
1 cup tequila	

1 Place pears in **CROCK-POT**® slow cooker. Combine water, nectar, tequila, sugar, lime peel and lime juice in medium saucepan. Bring to a boil over medium-high heat, stirring frequently. Boil 1 minute; pour over pears.

2 Cover; cook on LOW 4 to 6 hours or on HIGH 2 to 3 hours or until pears are tender. Serve warm with poaching liquid and vanilla ice cream, if desired.

Tip

Poaching fruit in a sugar, juice or alcohol syrup helps the fruit retain its shape and become more flavorful.

Fruit and Nut Baked Apples

MAKES 4 SERVINGS

4 large baking apples, such as Rome Beauty or Jonathan
1 tablespoon lemon juice
⅓ cup chopped dried apricots
⅓ cup chopped walnuts or pecans

3 tablespoons packed brown sugar
½ teaspoon ground cinnamon
2 tablespoons unsalted butter, melted
½ cup water
  Caramel topping (optional)

1 Scoop out center of each apple, leaving 1½-inch-wide cavity about ½ inch from bottom. Peel top of apple down about 1 inch. Brush peeled edges evenly with lemon juice. Combine apricots, walnuts, brown sugar and cinnamon in small bowl; stir to blend. Add butter; mix well. Spoon mixture evenly into apple cavities.

2 Pour water in bottom of **CROCK-POT**® slow cooker. Place 2 apples in bottom of **CROCK-POT**® slow cooker. Arrange remaining 2 apples above but not directly on top of bottom apples. Cover; cook on LOW 3 to 4 hours or until apples are tender. Serve warm or at room temperature with caramel topping, if desired.

Tip

Ever wonder why you need to brush lemon juice around the top of an apple? Citrus fruits, like lemons, contain an acid that keeps apples, potatoes and other white vegetables from discoloring once they are cut or peeled.

Mocha Supreme

MAKES 8 SERVINGS

2 quarts strong brewed coffee
½ cup instant hot chocolate beverage mix
1 whole cinnamon stick, broken in half

1 cup whipping cream
1 tablespoon powdered sugar

1 Place coffee, hot chocolate mix and cinnamon stick halves in **CROCK-POT®** slow cooker; stir. Cover; cook on HIGH 2 to 2½ hours or until heated through. Remove and discard cinnamon stick halves.

2 Beat cream in medium bowl with electric mixer on high speed until soft peaks form. Add powdered sugar; beat until stiff peaks form. Ladle mocha mixture into mugs; top with whipped cream.

Tip

To whip cream more quickly, chill the beaters and bowl in the freezer 15 minutes.

"Peachy Keen" Dessert Treat

MAKES 8 TO 12 SERVINGS

1⅓ cups old-fashioned oats	2 teaspoons ground cinnamon
1 cup sugar	½ teaspoon ground nutmeg
1 cup packed light brown sugar	2 pounds fresh peaches (about 8 medium), sliced
⅔ cup buttermilk baking mix	

Combine oats, sugars, baking mix, cinnamon and nutmeg in large bowl. Stir in peaches until well blended. Pour mixture into **CROCK-POT®** slow cooker. Cover; cook on LOW 4 to 6 hours.

Spiced Vanilla Applesauce

MAKES 6 CUPS

5 pounds (about 10 medium) sweet apples (such as Fuji or Gala), peeled and cut into 1-inch pieces	2 teaspoons vanilla
	1 teaspoon ground cinnamon
½ cup water	¼ teaspoon ground nutmeg
	¼ teaspoon ground cloves

1 Combine apples, water, vanilla, cinnamon, nutmeg and cloves in **CROCK-POT®** slow cooker; stir to blend. Cover; cook on HIGH 3 to 4 hours or until apples are very tender.

2 Turn off heat. Mash mixture with potato masher to smooth out any large lumps. Let cool completely before serving.

Triple White Chocolate Fantasy

MAKES 36 PIECES

2 pounds white almond bark, broken into pieces

1 bar (4 ounces) white chocolate, broken into pieces*

1 package (12 ounces) white chocolate chips

3 cups candy-coated chocolate pieces or colored sprinkles

Use your favorite high-quality chocolate candy bar.

1 Place almond bark, chocolate bar and chocolate chips in **CROCK-POT**® slow cooker. Cover; cook on HIGH 1 hour. *Do not stir.*

2 Turn **CROCK-POT**® slow cooker to LOW. Cover; cook on LOW 1 hour, stirring every 15 minutes. Stir in chocolate pieces.

3 Spread mixture onto large baking sheet covered with waxed paper; cool completely. Break into pieces. Store in tightly covered container.

Variations

Here are a few ideas for other imaginative items to add in along with or instead of the candy-coated chocolate pieces: raisins, crushed peppermint candy, crushed toffee, peanuts or pistachio nuts, chopped gum drops, chopped dried fruit or candied cherries.

Metric Conversion Chart

VOLUME MEASUREMENTS (dry)

$^1/_8$ teaspoon = 0.5 mL
$^1/_4$ teaspoon = 1 mL
$^1/_2$ teaspoon = 2 mL
$^3/_4$ teaspoon = 4 mL
1 teaspoon = 5 mL
1 tablespoon = 15 mL
2 tablespoons = 30 mL
$^1/_4$ cup = 60 mL
$^1/_3$ cup = 75 mL
$^1/_2$ cup = 125 mL
$^2/_3$ cup = 150 mL
$^3/_4$ cup = 175 mL
1 cup = 250 mL
2 cups = 1 pint = 500 mL
3 cups = 750 mL
4 cups = 1 quart = 1 L

VOLUME MEASUREMENTS (fluid)

1 fluid ounce (2 tablespoons) = 30 mL
4 fluid ounces ($^1/_2$ cup) = 125 mL
8 fluid ounces (1 cup) = 250 mL
12 fluid ounces (1$^1/_2$ cups) = 375 mL
16 fluid ounces (2 cups) = 500 mL

WEIGHTS (mass)

$^1/_2$ ounce = 15 g
1 ounce = 30 g
3 ounces = 90 g
4 ounces = 120 g
8 ounces = 225 g
10 ounces = 285 g
12 ounces = 360 g
16 ounces = 1 pound = 450 g

DIMENSIONS

$^1/_{16}$ inch = 2 mm
$^1/_8$ inch = 3 mm
$^1/_4$ inch = 6 mm
$^1/_2$ inch = 1.5 cm
$^3/_4$ inch = 2 cm
1 inch = 2.5 cm

OVEN TEMPERATURES

250°F = 120°C
275°F = 140°C
300°F = 150°C
325°F = 160°C
350°F = 180°C
375°F = 190°C
400°F = 200°C
425°F = 220°C
450°F = 230°C

BAKING PAN SIZES

Utensil	Size in Inches/Quarts	Metric Volume	Size in Centimeters
Baking or	8×8×2	2 L	20×20×5
Cake Pan	9×9×2	2.5 L	23×23×5
(square or	12×8×2	3 L	30×20×5
rectangular)	13×9×2	3.5 L	33×23×5
Loaf Pan	8×4×3	1.5 L	20×10×7
	9×5×3	2 L	23×13×7
Round Layer	8×1½	1.2 L	20×4
Cake Pan	9×1½	1.5 L	23×4
Pie Plate	8×1¼	750 mL	20×3
	9×1¼	1 L	23×3
Baking Dish	1 quart	1 L	—
or Casserole	1½ quart	1.5 L	—
	2 quart	2 L	—